P9-DML-296

THE PAOLANTONIO REPORT

Also by Sal Paolantonio

Rizzo: The Last Big Man in Big City America

THE PAOLANTONIO REPORT

The Most Overrated and Underrated Players, Teams, Coaches, and Moments in NFL History

Sal Paolantonio
with Reuben Frank

Library of Congress Cataloging-in-Publication Data
Paolantonio, Sal, 1956–
The Paolantonio report : the most overrated and underrated players, teams, coaches, and moments in NFL history / Sal Paolantonio with Reuben Frank.
p. cm.
ISBN-13: 978-1-60078-025-7
ISBN-10: 1-60078-025-3
1. National Football League—History. 2. National Football League—Anecdotes. 3. Football—United States—History. 4. Football—United States—Anecdotes. I. Frank, Reuben, 1959– II. Title.
GV955.5.N35P36 2007
796.332—dc22 2007019649

This book is available in quantity at special discounts for your group or organization. For further information, contact:

Triumph Books
542 South Dearborn Street, Suite 750
Chicago, Illinois 60605
(312) 939-3330 | Fax (312) 663-3557

Printed in U.S.A.
ISBN: 978-1-60078-025-7
Design by Patricia Frey
Editorial and page production by Prologue Publishing Services, LLC.
All photos courtesy of AP/Wide World Photos unless otherwise indicated.

This book is dedicated to the hundreds and hundreds of former NFL players who built a great American game but now struggle with debilitating injuries and struggle to make ends meet.

Contents

Introduction

It is the middle of July, usually a Monday morning, the first day of Philadelphia Eagles training camp, the first day when the players are wearing full pads, the day when hitting is to begin.

I like to arrive just after the summer sun begins to bake the South Mountain of Lehigh University, before most of the other reporters are on the scene, so that I can watch the players come onto the field, usually in packs of two or three, adjusting their gear, getting ready for full contact.

And then it hits me—that distinct, pungent aroma of grass and dew. It smells like a horse farm in the morning, an odor so strong it's intoxicating. So is the scene. This large gathering of humanity begins the rituals of the day—stretching, running, tackling, pile-driving different pieces of equipment and each other, while coaches bark like crazed dogs.

You can't look away for a second. The urgent commands, the choreographed movement, the powerful collisions, the spectacular quickness—and that distinct smell, now made more powerful by the sweat and heat of five dozen professional football players all trying to survive and advance, stick for another day with the team and the rest of the guys—all while trying to prevent the other guy from accomplishing the same primitive goal. Survive and advance, stay one more day. It is life played out in a pressure cooker—each practice, each day a distinct struggle to hang on to your livelihood.

This is the stuff I like about the National Football League: the passion, the struggle, the anger, the brotherhood, the teamwork. It is humanity's last stop before being domesticated, a place where excuses, personal history, private ghosts, and public agendas are left at the door. Except, of course, if you're Terrell Owens.

Unlike baseball, a game, really, of numbers, what makes pro football great is nearly impossible to measure. As former NFL running back Merrill Hoge, my colleague on the *State Farm NFL Matchup Show* on ESPN, says all the time, "Don't talk to me about stats. I don't care about stats. It's the matchups."

Yes, the matchups. And the schemes, and philosophies, and heart, and toughness, and a lot of other incalculable elements make up the essence of professional football. And by incalculable, I don't mean you *can't* figure out whether a player has it—or not. But assigning a number, quantifying it—that can be fool's gold. Someone once said, "If you torture the numbers long enough, you can get them to say anything."

So that's what made writing this book so difficult. That and the fact that we all live on *SportsCenter*. I don't say that because I make my living on *SportsCenter*. This is not a shameless plug for my network. No, I mean so much of what we think we know about players, teams, coaches, and the history of the NFL comes from TV. No other sport has been so thoroughly told through the lens of television. NFL Films—what I like to call Hollywood East—has done a spectacular job for 40 years, setting down the history of the league, providing indelible images of our favorite professional sport.

Those, then, are the challenges for this book. Take on the conventional images and story lines. Take a wider view. Go beyond what the camera lens has shown us. Step back and explain the accepted history in a different light.

Call it Monday Morning Quarterbacking, extreme edition.

For instance? The Catch—Joe Montana to Dwight Clark in the NFC Championship game in 1982—overhyped. At the very least, misnamed. Its historical significance? Way overrated.

Joe Namath—the eternal poster child for the NFL—is one of numerous players throughout the history of the league whose reputation doesn't live up to what he actually accomplished as a player.

Why did one of the NFL's all-time interception leaders never make a single Pro Bowl team? How did one of the game's leading rushers actually perform in the biggest games of his career? Why doesn't one of the most productive wide receivers in NFL history get Hall of Fame consideration?

So *don't* put this book back on the shelf, you fantasy-football freaks. There is plenty of statistical analysis in these pages to keep you engaged and, hopefully, outraged.

But because the NFL—more than any other pro sports league in human history—has been cinematic and because there have been some new books published chronicling the official history of the league, this book will attempt to go beyond both.

There are pivotal moments in the league that have been underrated and underreported. For example, how in the world did the New York Giants—playing in the shadow of the greatest sports franchise of its generation, the Yankees—allow the genius of Vince Lombardi to leave town in 1959? That ushered in a long era of darkness in pro football in New York—briefly interrupted by the supernova of Namath. What event ignited a pro football renaissance on Broadway? How about an interception return for a touchdown?

Jim Mora, the former head coach of the Indianapolis Colts, was once widely ridiculed for staring down at some football writers and exclaiming, "You don't know what you don't know. And you'll never know."

He was so right. Unless you study film of a game like the coaches do, or unless you dig deep into the trends and numbers and examine the real meaning of events, you can get caught up in the NFL's hype machine—or worse, you have to rely on what coaches tell you. And we all learned the hard way, Coach Mora, that coaches want you to know very little.

So think of this book as getting you to training camp practice really early, giving you a view of events, players, coaches, and teams you've never had before.

But be careful.

Sometimes your long-held beliefs are going to be challenged by a second look, a wider perspective, a different set of numbers. And sometimes, like in the opening chapter, you're going to be down on the field at old Foxboro Stadium where I was, seeing and feeling the events come right at you.

—Sal Paolantonio

Moorestown, New Jersey, 2007

CHAPTER 1

Moments

The Most Underrated Moment in NFL History

JANUARY 19, 2002: ADAM VINATIERI'S 45-YARD FIELD GOAL IN THE AFC DIVISIONAL PLAYOFFS

It had been snowing since noon, for nine hours at least. The kind of heavy, blinding snow you remember as a kid, not this global warming stuff that arrives suddenly, then quickly evaporates. This was a real New England storm on the night of the last game at Foxboro Stadium.

And the sun had long ago disappeared behind the western foothills of Massachusetts, so the temperature had dropped below 20 degrees. The wind had picked up, whipping through the old stadium like a runaway truck, howling through the stands, where every fan was standing, steam rising from his or her head. Behind the stadium, the trees were swaying, bending to nature, and you would half expect that through the forest and the gray, steamy fog and the snow the Headless Horseman himself would appear like a ghost, riding through the New England night to slay the Oakland Raiders and save the Patriots' season.

Instead it was little Adam Vinatieri who came to save the day. The Patriots place-kicker, who is generously listed at 6′ in the team media guide, trotted onto the field on a night when nobody had any business doing anything but looking for shelter, a blanket, and an old movie by the fireplace. The last thing

When Adam Vinatieri connected on this kick to win the AFC divisional playoff game against the Oakland Raiders in January 2002, it changed the fortunes of many and helped spawn the Patriots' dynasty.

anybody expected was for Vinatieri to kick a 45-yard field goal in the most dramatic moment in the team's history.

But that is exactly what Patriots head coach Bill Belichick asked Vinatieri to do.

The score: Raiders 13, Patriots 10. On the clock: just 27 seconds left in the fourth quarter. Just 27 seconds before Tom Brady would become just another first-year quarterback with an uncertain future, before Belichick would be just another head coach looking for his first trip to the conference title game, before Foxboro Stadium would become extinct.

The ball rested on the Raiders' 28-yard line. Belichick turned to special-teams coach Brad Seely and asked him if Vinatieri could make it. Seely looked at Belichick as if to say, "Make it? We are in the middle of a blizzard. Who the hell knows?" But Seely did what special-teams coaches do in this kind of once-in-a-lifetime circumstance. He nodded that it was a go.

"We wanted to get it closer," said Vinatieri. "But we had no choice. So, let's try it."

Vinatieri, who has adventure in his blood (his great-great-grandfather Felix was in General George Armstrong Custer's military band), walked out onto the field with the confidence of an astronaut.

Patriots long snapper Lonie Paxton fired a strike to holder Ken Walter. The season, the stadium, both sidelines froze. Vinatieri approached the ball. His plant foot, the left foot, slipped. And he hit the ball a little high. It barely cleared the Raiders rush and hugged low to the ground, disappearing in the snow.

"A line drive," Vinatieri said.

Yes, a line drive, as if a missile launched from a ship, skimming along the top of whitecaps in the open ocean, trying to find its target against a mother lode of obstacles made by nature and man.

And then the Foxboro faithful let loose a roar, and Vinatieri knew the game was tied.

"When I hit it, I knew it was straight enough," Vinatieri said. "I just didn't know if it would get there. I was like 'C'mon, baby. C'mon, baby.'"

After the game, Vinatieri's kick was nearly forgotten in a torrent of other memorable moments that long day into night. Vinatieri would make another kick, a 23-yarder in overtime to win the game. And Paxton would sprint into the end zone and do snow angels, an indelible image for a game that seemed to require divine intervention. And, of course, the biggest controversy to linger from the Patriots' win was the tuck rule call on Brady's nonfumble, which kept the Patriots in the game and sent the Raiders' coach, Jon Gruden, into a classic Chuckie tirade, which later landed him in Tampa, where he would finally win the Super Bowl.

But clearly Vinatieri's 45-yarder into the snow was the pivotal moment, the seminal play.

"That's the biggest kick I've ever seen," said Patriots linebacker Tedy Bruschi.

Bill Parcells, who signed Vinatieri out of South Dakota State in 1996, went further, saying, "Greatest football play I ever saw."

Here's what you're thinking: "A kicker? You picked a *kicker* to start this book?"

Even though it is not even mentioned in Michael MacCambridge's critically acclaimed *America's Game*, and it was left out of David Halberstam's brilliant *The Education of a Coach*, an appreciation of all things Belichick, Vinatieri's kick set off a chain reaction of events that allowed the Patriots to become the 21st century's first NFL dynasty. It changed the way all NFL teams approach place-kicking, which has become a profoundly dominant force in the current game. Precisely because it was left out of those books by those prestigious authors and because it had such profound impact, that kick is the most underrated moment in NFL history.

So listen up: here's what Vinatieri's kick set in motion.

The Patriots beat the Raiders in that divisional playoff game 16–13, creating the early legend of Tom Brady, who went on to defeat the heavily favored Pittsburgh Steelers at Heinz Field in the AFC Championship game on January 27, 2002.

The following Sunday, Brady led the Patriots on the game-winning drive in one of the greatest upsets in Super Bowl history, a 20–17 win over the St. Louis Rams in the Superdome in New Orleans. The game-winning 48-yard field goal with no time left on the clock was kicked by Vinatieri.

Two years later, the dynasty was hatched. In Houston, in Super Bowl XXXVIII, Brady collected his second Super Bowl MVP trophy after the Patriots came back to defeat the Carolina Panthers 32–29. The game-winning 41-yard field goal with seconds remaining was kicked by Vinatieri.

The following year the Patriots cemented their place in history with their third Super Bowl victory in four years—a feat no other team had accomplished. In Jacksonville, in Super Bowl XXXIX, New England beat the Philadelphia Eagles, again by three points, 24–21. The margin of victory: a fourth-quarter, 22-yard field goal by Vinatieri.

The Patriots established a dynasty at a time when the rest of the league had struggled to achieve continuity. Tempted by the quick payoff of free agency or struggling with the vagaries of the NFL's first salary cap, the other 31 teams had yet to find the right combination of player selection and draft intelligence to come close to what the Patriots had accomplished. Vinatieri's kick allowed the Patriots' brain trust—owner Robert Kraft, vice president for player personnel Scott Pioli, and Belichick—to go forward knowing they were doing things the right way—picking players and making moves (like taking Brady in the sixth round of the draft and not overpaying for aging players such as Lawyer Milloy and Ty Law) that would pay big dividends.

Yet, inexplicably, in the spring of 2006 the Patriots allowed Vinatieri—the Bobby Orr, the Larry Bird of pro football in New England—to walk away. He was signed by the Indianapolis Colts.

If Adam Vinatieri hadn't kicked that game-tying, 45-yard field goal in a snowstorm, Brady might not be posing for ads for the Gap and Movado and dating supermodels. Well, maybe he'd still be dating supermodels. But Bill Belichick might not be prowling the sideline in his trademark hoodie like a Sith lord from the *Star Wars* saga, spawning a legion of followers now patrolling the sidelines as head coaches in Cleveland (Romeo Crennel), New York (Eric Mangini), and Notre Dame (Charlie Weis).

Without that kick, New England Patriots owner Kraft may not have made his new crown jewel, Gillette Stadium, into a palace with a license to print money and thus become a potent force in NFL circles as a leader in finances and broadcasting.

Without that kick, there would have been no league-wide trend to find more accurate kickers. Vinatieri, who would go on to become the most prolific place-kicker in NFL postseason history, became the prototype.

Each year, kickers are getting more and more accurate, breaking the record every season for field-goal accuracy, which in 2006 was an all-time high of 81.4 percent, which is slightly worse than Vinatieri's career average going into the 2006 season.

The Vinatieri factor has led the NFL to try different methods to stop the overreliance on field goals. Take the K-balls, those fresh-from-the-box footballs that were actually introduced in 1999 but enforced more closely since 2004. But that, of course, hasn't worked. And no one has ever accused Vinatieri of doctoring the balls he has kicked for game-winners in big games time and again. Certainly, any doctoring that may have occurred in the Snow Bowl on January 19, 2002, would certainly have been erased by the arctic conditions.

Jan Stenerud is the only full-time place-kicker in the Pro Football Hall of Fame. He made just 66.8 percent of his field goals, which today would hardly qualify him to be Vinatieri's holder.

Especially in a snowstorm.

Postscript: In Miami for Super Bowl XLI, Adam Vinatieri, now wearing a Colts uniform, remembered his Snow Bowl kick.

"It's still the best moment of my career," he said. "Best kick ever. But if you gave me 100 shots at that field goal, I probably make it just 10 times."

Really?

"Yeah, we always laugh at it," he said. "I'm still laughing at it. Every time I see a film clip of it. 'Forty-five yards into a blinding snowstorm? C'mon. That's not possible.'"

On February 4, 2007, in Miami, Vinatieri won his fourth Super Bowl ring, kicking three field goals to help beat the Chicago Bears 29–17.

But Vinatieri was the victim of a bad hold on an extra point and actually missed—wide left!—on a 36-yard field goal at the end of the first half. It was his first postseason miss—ever.

Excuse: it was raining.

The Rest of the Most Underrated

2. THE DAY VINCE LOMBARDI LEFT NEW YORK

Wellington Mara screwed up. He let Vince Lombardi out of his contract.

It was a winter of discontent in New York. The Giants had just lost back-to-back NFL Championship games to the Baltimore Colts: the thriller in 1958, considered the NFL's greatest game, then a blowout in 1959. For all the money they spent, all the heartache they'd gone through, the Mara family, owners of the New York Giants since Calvin Coolidge was president, had exactly four NFL titles to show for their effort: 1927, 1934, 1938, and 1956.

Lombardi, coaching the Giants offense alongside Tom Landry, who coached the defense, had helped to restore that championship attitude in New

York, which was dominated by the Duke, the Mick, Joltin' Joe, and the Say Hey Kid. In 1956, the year Mickey Mantle won the Triple Crown, Lombardi helped to put football back on the map in the Five Boroughs. The Maras were grateful to have their first title since before World War II.

A year earlier, CBS-TV had signed the first-ever national broadcast contract with the NFL. *Sports Illustrated*, the country's first but still-fledgling magazine dedicated only to sports, decided to have full-time coverage of the league.

The Giants moved from the old, rundown Polo Grounds to the sparkling House That Ruth Built in the Bronx. The Giants at Yankee Stadium were on national TV with a boy-wonder star running back named Frank Gifford. It was all aligned for New York to become the mecca of football.

But then Johnny Unitas spoiled the party. In the NFL title game the Baltimore Colts beat the Giants the following two seasons, and the Maras were left wondering what was next. Wellington Mara was not about to fire head coach Jim Lee Howell. Mara was loyal—perhaps to a fault. But he was sitting on a gold mine, two assistant coaches who were in high demand: Lombardi and Landry.

Mara and Lombardi shared something in common—a Jesuit heritage forged at Fordham University. Mara also liked the fact that Lombardi had his coaching roots at St. Cecilia High School in Englewood, New Jersey, where his star player was a guy named Mickey Corcoran. (Remember that name.)

Twice Mara had almost lost Lombardi, but both times he stopped Lombardi from leaving. In 1955 the Giants owner persuaded Lombardi not to return to West Point as an assistant coach. And in 1958 Mara talked Lombardi out of taking a low-ball offer to become the head coach of the Philadelphia Eagles.

But now the Green Bay Packers, which had not tasted a championship since 1944 (by beating the Giants that year 14–7 in the NFL title game), needed a head coach. Lombardi, who had two years remaining on his Giants contract as offensive coordinator, flew to Wisconsin to meet with a group of civic leaders that ran the team—even though his wife Marie tried to talk him out of it. They were Jersey kids, Vince and Marie. They had moved to a nice, modest brick colonial in Fair Haven, New Jersey, not far from where Marie grew up in Red Bank.

At the same time, commissioner Bert Bell, realizing the power of a national TV audience, needed the game to be reseeded at its roots, in the heartland, in the Midwest. But he also needed a strong team in the country's top media markets to milk the networks out of more and more cash.

Mara understood this. There is not a single shred of evidence to suggest that the NFL and Mara conspired to undermine the Giants' future by allowing Lombardi to go to Green Bay, but it's a nice idea. It's merely an accident of history. Mara was loyal to Howell. He thought Lombardi's incendiary personality was too volatile for the head job, that Lombardi was not ready for prime time in New York. Obviously, it was one of the greatest blunders in professional sports history.

On February 2, 1959, Vince and Marie Lombardi flew to Green Bay. And, as John Facenda, the late, great voice of NFL Films, once said, "Lombardi—a certain magic still lingers in the very name."

Had Lombardi stayed in New York, would Pete Rozelle's vision of a national game on national TV—with teams in small markets and big markets on the same financial playing field—have survived and flourished? Probably not.

Had Lombardi not gone to Green Bay, would there have been an insatiable desire for a successful AFL franchise in New York? Probably not. Which means there would have been no Broadway Joe Namath. And maybe the AFL would have taken many more years to challenge the NFL's hegemony. And you do the calculations for what that would have meant for TV contracts, the future of the Super Bowl as an unparalleled national extravaganza, and the extraordinary growth of the league.

Now, had Lombardi stayed in New York, had Mara hired him to become head coach of the Giants, would the legendary coach had enough control over the personnel to put his unique stamp on the team and win all those championships? Maybe not.

But one thing is for sure: the pilot light went out on Giants football for three decades.

And how's this for the ultimate ironic footnote to this story? The guy Mara hired to restore Giants pride in 1983 was that guy named Parcells. You want to know the name of his high school basketball coach? Mickey Corcoran, who played for Lombardi at St. Cecilia's.

Postscript: Inexplicably, Mara repeated his gaffe of not hiring Lombardi by passing on Tom Landry, who went on to Dallas and his own history-making career.

Jim Lee Howell lasted just one more season. In 1961 Mara hired Allie Sherman, and the Giants entered the dark territory of mediocrity that lasted a generation.

3. THE DALLAS COWBOYS' DECISION TO DRAFT BOB HAYES

Let's be clear about this: you cannot write a history of the NFL without including a chapter about Bob Hayes. Therefore, Hayes should be in the Pro Football Hall of Fame. That he died in 2002 just shy of his 60th birthday without that honor is just a sin.

Hayes revolutionized the NFL. To be more exact, the guy who recruited him and convinced the Dallas Cowboys to draft Hayes in the seventh round in 1964—*that* guy revolutionized the game of pro football. *That* guy's name is Gil Brandt, the Cowboys' longtime personnel guru. Before Brandt introduced Hayes to the NFL, track stars were shunned by NFL scouts. Too many of them had flunked the training camp test—the rigors of the two-a-days in the sweltering summer heat, the repetition of practice, the memorization of plays, and then the ability to catch the ball in traffic while somebody was trying to take away your manhood.

As Jim Brown once said, "If you had a little rabbit in you, this game is not for you."

This is why Hayes lasted until the seventh round of the draft—even though at the time he was one of three most-accomplished athletes in the world.

At the Olympics in Tokyo in the summer of 1964, Hayes not only won the gold medal in the 100 meters in a world-record 10.05 seconds, he anchored the American 400-meter relay team, which also took home the gold. His 100-meter split in that race was an electrifying 8.6 seconds, another world record. So, Bullet Bob had another nickname: the World's Fastest Human.

It was Brandt who saw how Hayes's speed could change the NFL game. Brandt convinced then-Cowboys head coach Landry to draft him, but Landry remained unconvinced until Hayes tore it up in Cowboys camp.

"Then when we got to the regular season, he did the same thing," said Brandt.

Hayes's rookie season: 12 touchdowns, averaging a league-high 21.8 yards per catch. When Dallas won Super Bowl VI on January 16, 1972, beating the Miami Dolphins 24–3, Hayes became the only athlete to win an Olympic gold medal and a Super Bowl ring.

Still is.

For defensive coordinators, Hayes was a nightmare. He occupied cornerbacks, who quickly found being physical with Hayes first meant you had to get on him, which wasn't easy. Hayes also helped to create the concept of umbrella-zone defensive schemes—on every down, not just third-and-long, or Hail Mary passes.

Then, on the other side of the ball, what Hayes did forced offensive coordinators to find ways to open up the secondary like he did. He forced coordinators to find ways to keep the safeties from creeping down to the line of scrimmage and blowing up the running game. Everybody wanted to stop Hayes or imitate what he did with his speed. But there was no one like him.

As for cornerback play, Hayes forced the issue again. The concept of bump-and-run coverage was basically invented to stop Hayes and his imitators. Without Hayes, the whole idea of a coveted cover corner may not have existed—and then been handsomely compensated once free agency came around decades later. So next time you cash a big check, Deion Sanders, give thanks to Bob Hayes.

Hayes's numbers are Hall of Fame–worthy: three Pro Bowls, averaging 20 yards per catch, and 71 touchdown passes. But more than that, Hayes was a trailblazer. His impact on the game lasted decades. He forced the league to think of speed as an essential element of the pro game, forced teams to look for speed—on both sides of the ball—instead of stigmatizing it.

Postscript: Hayes not only made his living off speed, he had a need for it. Years after football, he developed a drug and alcohol dependency, serving 10 months in prison after pleading guilty to delivering narcotics to an undercover police officer.

Apparently, that incident kept him out of the Hall of Fame—even if similar circumstances did not prevent Lawrence Taylor and Michael Irvin from getting in.

Put Hayes in the Hall.

4. DOUG WILLIAMS'S MVP PERFORMANCE IN SUPER BOWL XXII IN 1988

Doug Williams was determined to make history. But first he had to go to the dentist.

It was Saturday, January 30, 1988, the day before Super Bowl XXII, and Williams was in pain. He was about to take on the Denver Broncos and the legendary John Elway, but his lower right molar was throbbing like one of those red beating hearts you see pulsating in the cartoons. He could not eat, could hardly speak. What if it got worse and he couldn't call the signals in the game? What if it got swollen and he couldn't buckle his chin strap? What if a toothache kept him from being the first black quarterback to start a Super Bowl game? Cue the conspiracy theorists, baby.

So on the day before the biggest game of his life, Williams had root canal surgery.

The next day he had one of the biggest games a quarterback has ever had on Super Bowl Sunday. The Washington Redskins won 42–10. And Williams almost didn't make it through the first quarter. He was knocked out of the game on the first series with a hyperextended knee. At that point, his old coach, Eddie Robinson of Grambling State, was sitting in the stands, challenging God. "I know you didn't bring me out here for this," Robinson was quoted as saying after the game.

Backup quarterback Jay Schroeder lasted just two plays. From that point on to the halftime show, Williams led the Redskins to five touchdowns for 35 points. That onslaught was the most points scored in a half in a Super Bowl, a record that still stands.

It buried Elway and the Broncos. But, more importantly, that performance—in one single half of championship football—erased a stereotype that had permeated the NFL since the time of leather helmets: that a black quarterback couldn't get it done, didn't have what it took to lead his team to a world championship.

For some reason, Williams's accomplishment has not received its due. Perhaps it's because Williams wasn't the first black quarterback. Indeed, there was George Taliaferro, Willie Thrower, Marlin Briscoe, Joe Gilliam, and James Harris. And so Williams didn't break the color barrier at his position, true enough. But Williams, by winning the biggest game on the biggest stage,

Doug Williams's performance in Super Bowl XXII, particularly in the first half, led to a big win for the Washington Redskins—and aspiring black quarterbacks everywhere.

proving he had heart and toughness—and the guile and brilliance to pick apart a very good Denver defense—inspired a generation of young black quarterbacks.

Warren Moon, Steve McNair, Randall Cunningham, Donovan McNabb, Vince Young—all of them have talked about the inspiration that Williams provided. What Williams did was eliminate a long-held belief—whether it was stated or not—that a black man would never be a championship quarterback in the NFL.

Postscript: The title of Doug Williams's autobiography says it all: Quarterblack.

5. GEORGE MARTIN'S 78-YARD INTERCEPTION FOR A TOUCHDOWN IN 1986

Obscure, yes. But, in the case of George Martin, not all that unusual. The Giants' defensive end had scored six touchdowns in his 12-year career—at the time, the most of any defensive lineman in NFL history.

This one, however, would help change history, the history of football in New York and league history. It would be historically important in many, many ways for years and years to come.

Let's go big picture first. In the 1980s the NFL was in small-market purgatory and had labor unrest. The league had big stars, but the teams that dominated were from San Francisco, Cincinnati, Denver, and Buffalo. The Los Angeles teams—the Rams and Raiders—made some noise, but the pro football fires in Southern California were slowly burning out. The Chicago Bears had their fling in 1985 but didn't do much else.

Then there were strikes—57 days in 1982 and another month-long strike in 1987.

The NFL, headquartered on Park Avenue and molded on Madison Avenue, needed an end to the long run through dark territory in New York.

Bill Parcells was supposed to be the savior. But his first three years at the Giants helm produced less-than-spectacular results—a fifth-place finish and two second-place finishes in the NFC East.

Fast-forward to week 12 of the 1986 season. The Giants were battling with the Washington Redskins, under Coach Joe Gibbs, for supremacy in the division. The Denver Broncos, who would win the AFC Championship under quarterback John Elway that season, were at the Meadowlands, leading the Giants 6–3 in a typical Parcells game—a stifling defense and quarterback Phil Simms playing conservatively, if ineffectually.

The Broncos had the ball, first down on the Giants' 13-yard line. With a touchdown, Denver would send the Giants into the halftime locker room reeling, with two big road games coming up—at Western Division–leading San Francisco and division archrival Washington—back-to-back.

For some inexplicable reason, the Broncos called a pass play. Their right tackle, Ken Lanier, tried to cut block left defensive end George Martin. Martin, all 255 pounds of him, leapt over Lanier's block, got his big right paw in the air, tipped Elway's pass into the flat, and then gathered it in.

Then it was 78 yards, and Martin was off to the races with just Elway standing in the way of the go-ahead touchdown. At around the Denver 30-yard line, Lawrence Taylor—leading the posse of Giants defenders down the field, started begging for the football. Martin thought about giving it up, but he had a record to maintain. So he faked a lateral and continued chugging along, landing like a huge bear in the end zone. *The New York Times* timed his run: 13 seconds.

Thirteen seconds. That's all it took to catapult the Giants to victory that day. Later Parcells would call that play the single-greatest motivating force for the rest of the Giants' season. They went to San Francisco and beat the 'Niners. Then they went to Washington and beat the Redskins.

That year the Giants won their first NFC East title, then faced the Broncos in Super Bowl XXI. This time they plastered Denver 39–20, turning on the spotlights on pro football in New York.

There are many who believe that had the Giants not won the NFL title in 1986, the league would have suffered a repeat of the debilitating strike of 1982. In 1987 the players walked off the job again. But many coaches—Parcells was the leader—refused to play along with the league's mandate to aggressively pursue replacement players. A mockery was made. But through Parcells's attitude and words, the players were told this was no way to achieve their goals. They were being ridiculed as pampered millionaires. With the spotlight of labor unrest focused squarely on the nation's media mecca, the players relented and returned to work in just 24 days.

But they were also emboldened. The National Football League Players Association filed an antitrust suit against the league in federal court in Minnesota—the case that would eventually bring about free agency.

If Martin hadn't intercepted that pass and launched the Giants toward the NFL title, and if Parcells hadn't finally been vindicated, and pro football hadn't been restored to glory in New York, who knows what would have happened in 1987?

But we do know how it turned out. Forced by the federal courts, the league saw the light, achieved labor peace, and then gained spectacular prosperity, becoming the most powerful and wealthy professional sports empire the world has ever seen.

Postscript: George Martin's record for touchdowns by a defensive end has stood for 20 years. In 2006 Miami Dolphins defensive end Jason Taylor, the NFL Defensive Player of the Year, returned an interception 51 yards for a touchdown, giving him seven for his career, tying Martin's record.

The Most Overrated Moment in NFL History

THE CATCH

It's funny how one word—*the*—can brand a person, an idea, or a moment. We have The Donald. The Drive. The Last Supper. (Yes, that last reference is a little over the top, but this is a sports book, so relax. Besides, this chapter is about to denigrate a holy moment in NFL history, so you might want to preserve your outrage.)

You know where this is going. The Catch—it's been overrated and overhyped for years. It's even a misnomer. It should be called The Pass. But we'll get to that in a second.

For those of you who have been Sherpas in the Himalayan Mountains for the past 25 years, let me first explain what the catch was and how it became The Catch.

It was January 10, 1982, at Candlestick Park in San Francisco, and the 49ers had third-and-three from the 6-yard line of the Dallas Cowboys, trailing 27–21 in the NFC Championship game.

'Niners head coach Bill Walsh called a play now commonly known as sprint-right option. Quarterback Joe Montana rolled to his right and had two options on the play, to pass the ball to wide receiver Freddie Solomon or to Dwight Clark. In the first quarter Solomon had caught an eight-yard touchdown pass on the exact same play call.

This time Solomon was not open. Montana kept rolling and rolling right, waiting for Clark to work his way free in the back of the end zone, out from behind Cowboys defensive back Everson Walls, whose coverage was almost perfect.

It was a nice catch by Clark, no doubt about that. It made the cover of *Sports Illustrated*, which called it the Super Catch. *Super* was quickly dropped, however, because in cases like these, the word *the* suffices as the proper adjective.

But the throw—that was a thing of absolute beauty. Montana never gets credit for The Throw. He was running out of real estate along the sideline. He had three Cowboys ready to climb down his throat.

Later, humble to the end, Montana would describe his pass "like throwing paper into a trash can. You have no idea of whether you can make it." It's just like Montana, who was very close to Clark, to play down his role. But Montana threw that football under significant duress to the only spot where Clark, who was 6′4″, could catch it—at the top of his leap in the back of the end zone.

The Catch got all the credit, but The Throw was the thing. It had the right trajectory, the right touch, the right height. In short, it was the kind of pass that Montana would execute for the rest of his career. The kind that would send him to eight Pro Bowls, the kind of pass that would collect all those Lombardi trophies, the kind of pass that would put him, and others, in Canton. After the year of The Catch, Clark would not make another Pro Bowl, and he would catch just one more touchdown pass in eight more postseason games with the 'Niners.

And The Catch got credit not just for being the signature moment of that game but also for a rivalry decided and a dynasty delivered. Upon further review, that's overrated, too.

First of all, the 'Niners should have easily won that game. San Francisco had 393 total yards to the Cowboys' 250. But the 49ers committed six turnovers in the game. They seemed determined to give it away. And as for The Catch providing the signature moment of the 'Niners finally bulldozing the Cowboys out of their way—not so. The Cowboys were just not good enough. In fact, that game was one of a long line of postseason games that the Cowboys found ways to lose in that era.

From 1978 to 1983, the Cowboys had five successive years in which they underperformed in the postseason. They lost Super Bowl XIII to the Steelers in the 1978 season. The following season they lost to the 9–7 Los Angeles Rams 21–19 in the divisional playoffs. In 1980 Dallas went down hard in Philadelphia, losing 20–7 to Ron Jaworski's Eagles, a team that was embarrassed by the Raiders in Super Bowl XV. After the loss to the 'Niners in 1981, the Cowboys lost their third-straight NFC Championship game in 1982, this time to the eventual Super Bowl–champion Redskins.

So, despite the claims that The (so-called) Catch ushered in the demise of the Cowboys, that's simply wrong. At that point, Dallas was already in a slow crawl toward the heart of darkness. The loss to the 'Niners was symptomatic, not catalytic of what Dallas was doing to itself.

While Dwight Clark leapt high to make a pretty grab in the NFC Championship game against the Cowboys in 1982, the throw from Joe Montana might have been even more impressive. (Photo courtesy Getty Images)

Postscript: So, why did the Catch take on a pop culture life of its own? Blame that Sports Illustrated *cover. And ESPN.*

ESPN's Chris Berman, the most influential sports broadcaster of his generation, was at that game, standing five feet from Clark's shoe bottoms. He did more to create the legend than anybody else.

From that moment on, Berman became a sports broadcasting icon, and his rise dovetailed nicely with the 49ers' dynasty of the 1980s.

"At that moment," Berman said years later, "I'm not sure any of us knew what we were seeing. But this was history. This was the Ice Bowl, Alan Ameche, the Immaculate Reception, all of that. I've easily shown that highlight 500 times. Who doesn't know it?"

But with all due respect to my esteemed colleague at ESPN, perhaps now we have a better understanding of what that day meant.

The Rest of the Most Overrated

2. "WIDE RIGHT" SCOTT NORWOOD'S MISS IN SUPER BOWL XXV

Marv Levy put his kicker in an impossible situation. He had to know that.

Scott Norwood did not lose Super Bowl XXV for the Buffalo Bills. The simple fact of the matter is that Parcells and Belichick outcoached Levy.

Let's look at the two teams and then at the game itself.

Going into the Super Bowl, the New York Giants were inferior in nearly every respect to the Bills. In the 1990 season Buffalo went 13–3. They scored 53 touchdowns to their opponents' 30 in the regular season. In two playoff games, the Bills outscored the opposition 95–37.

Quarterback Jim Kelly was in a season-long groove. He had a passer rating of 101.2. In the history of the NFL's biggest game, that rating was second by just two-tenths of a point to Kurt Warner's 101.4 rating in 2001. How ironic that the head coach of the team that beat Warner in Super Bowl XXXVI that year, Belichick, was the defensive coordinator who beat Kelly in Super Bowl XXV.

Just about everybody who has looked at this Super Bowl has focused on Parcells's ability to play keep-away from the Bills. The time of possession set a Super Bowl record: the Giants held on to the football a whopping 40 minutes and 33 seconds. Everybody knows that. But let's flip the script.

Belichick, Parcells's alter ego and defensive coordinator, had a strategy that was just as integral to slowing down Kelly. It was as simple as it was unorthodox. He called upon the Giants defensive players to do something that was against their core beliefs and counterintuitive to something that Belichick had preached to them all year. Belichick wanted them to allow Bills running back Thurman Thomas to have moderate success running the football.

Belichick wanted Carl Banks and Harry Carson and Pepper Johnson and Lawrence Taylor to play rope-a-dope, to create the illusion, at least, that the Bills could run the football at will and thus had no need to put the ball in the very hot hand of their future Hall of Fame quarterback.

During the season, Thomas averaged a highly respectable 4.8 yards per carry. In Super Bowl XXV Thomas would carry the ball 15 times for 135 yards. That's nine yards per carry, a number that would have embarrassed the Giants defense at any other time that season. In fact, that Giants defense had gone the entire year without giving up a 100-yard rusher until two days before Christmas in Phoenix. Johnny Johnson barely broke the barrier, coming in at 108 yards. And after the game Belichick was furious and the defensive players were so angry—even though the Giants won the game—that no one would ever contemplate that Belichick might actually tell his players to allow a runner to go more than 100 yards.

But in Super Bowl XXV that's exactly what Belichick wanted.

The result of this dual strategy is now the stuff of Super Bowl legend. The Giants had the Bills offense off balance and on the ropes all game. So, with four seconds remaining and the Giants winning 20–19, Levy sent Norwood out onto the field to kick a 47-yard field goal to claim the Lombardi Trophy.

If you look at this field-goal attempt through the larger lens of what transpired in Super Bowl XXV, you can easily come to the conclusion that it was a desperation attempt by a coach to save a failed strategy.

Now, let's take this a step further.

As Norwood lined up to try that kick in the Super Bowl, the Giants kicker, Matt Bahr, stood next to Parcells and reminded him that Norwood had made only one kick outdoors of that length all year.

Bahr was wrong. Norwood had made two. But Norwood had not made a field goal of that length—47 yards or longer—since week three of that 1990 season, during a 30–7 whipping of the Jets at the Meadowlands. It was a 48-yarder with the wind. That was September 24, four months before the Super Bowl. Four months!

In the week one home opener, Norwood connected on a 47-yarder. That was the second one.

In week four he missed a 48-yarder. That was the last attempt he made of that length that year. In all of that season, he was 6–10 in field-goal attempts from 40–49 yards. The longest he attempted in the postseason that yea was a 39-yarder in the divisional playoffs. He made it.

So here was Norwood, trying to make a 47-yarder—something he had not attempted in *four months*—to win the biggest game of his life on the biggest stage there is. Now, what are the odds that he makes that field goal? In retrospect, it's amazing he came as close as he did.

So the next time you see that NFL Films beauty shot of Norwood's ill-advised kick sailing wide right, don't blame him for losing that game. As NFL moments go, Norwood's miss is about as overrated as you can get. And considering all the blame that has been heaped on him unfairly, it's amazing, too, that he has showed this much courage in facing a lifetime of strange looks.

He was being asked to do what he had not done since the opening month of the season. If the kick had gone through, it would have been one of the most *underrated* moments in NFL history.

Postscript: ...and Bill Parcells might not be going to the Hall of Fame.

3. MICHAEL STRAHAN BREAKING THE SINGLE-SEASON SACK RECORD IN 2001

It was a stroll. A stumble. In the end, a sham. But it was not a sack. Not by anybody's definition of the word, and not by anybody's understanding of pro football's signature play. In no other sport do they attack the man with the ball with such reckless disregard for human dignity, with such rapacious, choreographed violence than the way the quarterback is assaulted when he goes back to pass.

When Randy Johnson is in his windup, when Roger Federer is about to deliver a blistering serve, when Tiger Woods is lining it up in the tee box, nobody is attempting to decapitate them or separate them from the ball.

Rushing the passer, sacking the quarterback—that's the urgency of pro football. You got three seconds, buddy, to get rid of that thing. You better have a clock in your head. Here comes Reggie White's bull rush. Here comes Dwight Freeney off his spin move. Here comes the marauding Deacon Jones, the rage of L.T., the fury of Mark Gastineau, who in 1984 set the single-season record of 22 sacks with the New York Jets.

In 1984 the Jets were in the exact predicament as the Giants faced in 2001. Both teams were about to finish 7–9, both about to finish third in their respective divisions. To keep things interesting in the Meadowlands, the Jets had Gastineau and Joe Klecko and the rest of the Sack Exchange, part of the Gang Green defense.

Gastineau was all hair and flourishes. It was his sack dance after getting to the quarterback that made sack dancing such an objectionable sidelight to the game. He became a caricature of himself. But he had speed and moves, arms flailing, with a tremendous heart. He could get to the passer. And that he did. Twenty-two sacks in 1984—now that kept the *J-E-T-S, Jets, Jets, Jets* fans happy.

Fast-forward to 2001, a lost football season in New York. The events of 9/11 extinguished all possible joy. Out of respect for the tragedy on that day, the league cancelled week two of the season. The Giants were just coming off an embarrassing loss in the Super Bowl, too. So, nobody was in a mood for anything fraudulent.

With a performance for the ages, Giants defensive end Michael Strahan kept the season alive, going on a one-man rampage. He was a reason to come to Giants Stadium to watch football.

It started with three sacks against the Saints in the last week of September. Two weeks later he wreaked havoc on the Rams in St. Louis with four sacks. Then, with two more in each of the following two weeks, something special was happening. The Giants weren't winning, but Strahan was putting on a show.

In the second-to-last week of the season, the Giants went down to Philly. A .500 season was still there for the taking. But the Eagles, on their way to the NFC Championship game that year, won 24–21, not before Strahan tortured right tackle Jon Runyan all day at Veterans Stadium, sacking Donovan McNabb three times.

So, on the last day of the season, at home at the Meadowlands, Strahan had 21.5 sacks, just a half sack shy of Gastineau's record. Brett Favre and the Green Bay Packers were in town.

It was January 6, 2002. Mark Gastineau was in attendance.

And all day the Pack's O-line, knowing Strahan wanted the record bad, stoned him. Strahan got three quarterback hurries. Twice he hit Favre. But no sacks.

Then, with two minutes and 46 seconds left, Favre called a running play to the left. He was supposed to hand the ball to running back Ahman Green. Instead, Favre kept it and ambled to his right. Tight end Bubba Franks, thinking it was a running play to the left, did not block Strahan, who walked right into Favre, who fell to the ground like a wounded bird. A sack it was not.

"What the heck was Favre thinking?" wrote Michael Freeman the next day in *The New York Times.*

After the game, Packers head coach Mike Sherman—as tough a New England Yankee as you'll encounter—was clearly not thrilled with No. 4's actions.

"Strahan can get sacks on his own," said Sherman. "We don't have to give it to him."

But give it to him they did. There it is in the NFL's official *Record & Fact Book*: Most Sacks, Season—22.5, Michael Strahan, New York Giants, 2001.

Postscript: Michael Freeman also wrote this in the Times *the next day: "This is not to blame Strahan. He simply took advantage of what Favre did. Strahan said that if Favre did throw him the high, slow curveball, "I was not in the huddle calling the plays. I can just react to what happened."*

4. CHUCK BEDNARIK'S KNOCKOUT OF FRANK GIFFORD IN 1960

Again, an image defined history.

It was November 20, 1960, at Yankee Stadium, a moment in NFL history captured by the collision of two Hall of Famers: Chuck "Concrete Charlie" Bednarik and Frank Gifford. It was a moment defined by Bednarik leveling Gifford, knocking him to the dusty stadium turf like a rag doll getting leveled by a Mack truck.

As Gifford went limp and hit the ground, the ball he was carrying came loose like a child's toy, ignored amidst the violence of it all. As Eagles defensive back Tom Brookshier would later tell Hall of Fame pro football writer Ray Didinger, Gifford "looked like a corpse."

Linebacker Chuck Weber recovered the fumble. Bednarik knew the game was in the bag. The Eagles were 6–1 at that point. The Giants were 5–1–1. So this was a big win, a game that would catapult Philadelphia to the NFL title for the first time in a generation.

But when *Sports Illustrated* snapped the now-famous photograph of that moment—Gifford lifeless, Bednarik appearing to celebrate his hit and Gifford's demise—that moment came to unfairly define Bednarik, his contribution to the Eagles' season, and his career.

Here's what Gifford told *New Yorker* magazine in January 2007: "They made more of it than it really was because Bednarik made a career of it. Still does. It was more of a situation where I was off balance when he hit me. And then I kind of semi-fell, snapped my head back, and I had a concussion."

In New York, where images and history are often defined and redefined for us, this one moment has been dissected and scrutinized, and it has overshadowed Bednarik's larger contributions and accomplishments.

First of all, consider this: Bednarik actually wasn't going to play in 1960. He had gotten his championship ring as a rookie in 1949, so at age 34, in 1959, he retired. The Eagles had a Concrete Charlie Day at Franklin Field. They gave him a nifty retirement gift: a color TV, with a bonus check thrown in for a whopping $1,000. But the following spring Bednarik's wife Emma gave birth to their fifth child. And since that going-away bonus wasn't going to cover a whole lot of expenses, Bednarik asked to play one more year. His salary: $15,000.

The Eagles got every penny's worth. Bednarik played center and linebacker. He was the last of a breed, the last of the two-way players. In the NFL Championship game against the Green Bay Packers—the only championship game Lombardi would lose as a head coach—Bednarik was on the field for 139 of the 142 plays in the box score.

What Bednarik should be remembered for was his last significant play in an Eagles uniform, tackling Packers running back Jim Taylor at the Philadelphia 9-yard line. As time expired, Bednarik not only stood as the last man between Taylor and the goal line, but he held Taylor down on the ground until time expired. The Eagles won 17–13—their last NFL title.

Postscript: For the best description of and insight into Concrete Charlie's career, read The Eagles Encyclopedia *by Ray Didinger and Robert S. Lyons. Said Didinger, "Chuck has a love-hate relationship with [his hit on Gifford]. Sometimes he'll tell the story with relish and delight. And sometimes he'll just blow it off, 'Aw, that's just one f*cking play.'"*

5. THE NEW ENGLAND PATRIOTS' THIRD SUPER BOWL VICTORY IN FOUR YEARS

This was the Super Bowl win that supposedly cemented the modern-day dynasty of Belichick's New England Patriots. As NFL moments go, they don't get more overrated. This was one ugly win against a Philadelphia Eagles team that should have walked away with the Lombardi Trophy.

The Eagles—more specifically, McNabb—played a C-minus football game and lost by only three points. If they had played an average game and pulled a grade of C, there would have been no Patriots dynasty.

For Philly, the game was oh-so-winnable. Indeed, looking back on it, the Patriots' reign—as it came to be known—should have ended in Jacksonville at Super Bowl XXXIX.

The Eagles opened the game with the following four possessions: punt, punt, interception, and fumble. Actually, there were two interceptions. The Eagles were driving for the opening score of the game. They had the ball on the New England 24-yard line, and McNabb made one of the worst throws of his checkered postseason history. Asante Samuel picked him off. But that pick was nullified by a penalty. On the very next play, Rodney Harrison intercepted McNabb in the Patriots' end zone. Drive dead.

While McNabb was inept, Brady was worse. The Patriots opened the game with four successive punts. Then, after Philadelphia took a 7–0 lead, Brady was sacked deep in Philadelphia territory, fumbled, and the Eagles recovered. The next series shows how pitiful Coach Andy Reid's game plan was. He called for a run to the left behind left tackle Tra Thomas, their weakest run blocker. Running right behind Runyan was the way to go.

Running back Brian Westbrook lost a yard. Two ill-advised pass plays later, the Eagles punted. The Patriots tied it 7–7 at halftime.

Unable to run left, which was their primary option for some reason, the Eagles were overly reliant on McNabb. He threw the ball 51 times and was clearly worn out late in the fourth quarter, when the Eagles were trying to mount a comeback.

Down 24–14, with the ball on their own 21-yard line, the Eagles squandered precious time on play after play, strolling to the line of scrimmage, seemingly oblivious to the fact that they needed two scores to win the game.

It was clearly the worst instance of fourth-quarter time management in a Super Bowl in the game's history.

In his book *The Education of a Coach*, Halberstam describes Belichick's disbelief on the sideline: "Have I got the score right?" Belichick said to his assistants Mangini and Crennel in his headset. According to Halberstam, both told Belichick that the score was right. "Then what the hell are they trying to do?" Belichick replied.

The Eagles did get one more touchdown, a 30-yard touchdown pass from McNabb to Greg Lewis. But three minutes and 45 seconds were gone. The Eagles tried an onside kick that failed. The Patriots punted, pinning the Eagles on their 4-yard line. Game over.

The Patriots walked off with their third Super Bowl title in four years—a first in league history. And don't be mistaken: during the season, this Patriots team was truly dominant, finishing 14–2, setting a record for consecutive wins with 18. New England should have pasted the Eagles in Super Bowl XXXIX.

Instead, they ambled through it. What we really witnessed was the final jog to the finish line of a long Patriots run. If the Eagles had eliminated just one or two easily avoidable mistakes, the Patriots would have been defeated in Jacksonville. As an exclamation point on a dynastic era, that Patriots win was hollow, very overrated.

Postscript: The following spring, Terrell Owens would utter the famous words about Donovan McNabb that would unravel their relationship and lead to Owens's dismissal from the team: "I wasn't the one who got tired in the Super Bowl."

The Most Underrated Moment in NFL History

THE CREATION OF THE FIRST DOWN IN 1882

It was rugby. And it was boring.

Here was this primitive Old World game brought over from England and played mostly by college boys at Harvard, Princeton, and Rutgers.

And here was a restless nation in the year 1876, the year of the Centennial, when the thirst for new territory, for westward expansion, seemed unquenchable.

So it didn't fit. Football, as it was being played by European rules in the New World, wasn't an attractive game. The rules of the London Football Association called for players from both teams to mass about the ball, all trying to kick it out to a teammate. In essence, soccer with a scrum.

The first intercollegiate contest occurred in 1869 between Princeton and Rutgers. But American players—and spectators—quickly grew tired of it. Nothing happened. There was no premium placed on advancing the ball. Territory and scoring points—the core of what America was becoming—was not a factor.

The boys at Harvard made the first move. They called it the Boston game, which allowed running with the football and tackling, a little more open and physical brand of rugby than was played in Wales and England. Said the *Harvard Advocate* in 1874, the Boston game was much better "than the somewhat sleepy game now played by our men."

In 1876, however, Princeton and Penn still competed under soccer rules, while Harvard and Yale competed under the modified Boston game. Something had to be done. The four schools held a convention to form the Intercollegiate Football Association in 1876. The Harvard boys convinced the group to adopt the Boston game. It was far more compelling. It simply asked the players to do more in more wide-open space.

For the next six years—while the nation was undergoing rapid change in every other walk of life, and while the best and the brightest from the top Eastern schools were being drawn to the wide-open opportunity of westward expansion—this new game proved too stodgy for the players and the fans. Indeed, there were too few of the latter.

So this new association kept tinkering with the rules, and this time, the changes were profound, changes that dovetailed nicely with a changing nation.

First thing to go: the scrum. It represented everything that was un-American: a mass of humanity moving in no particular direction with no particular purpose. Instead, one team was given possession of the ball and a line of scrimmage was created—a line on the field clearly delineating which team had the ball and which team did not.

"A scrimmage takes place when the holder of the ball, being in the field of play, puts it down on the ground in front of him and puts it in play with his foot," said amendment number one, which was adopted in 1880. "The man who first receives the ball from the snap-back shall be called the quarter-back, and shall not then rush forward with the ball under penalty of foul."

Of course, Michael Vick would balk at that last part of the rule. Yet, without that rule change, there would be no Michael Vick. By creating the position of "quarter-back," football's founders created a man on the field who would stand out among equals, a concept that needs no cultural interpretation or historical context.

But that rule also established possession, a particularly American notion. But to clearly translate the American geopolitical mindset of the time to a game on the field, there needed to be one more critical change in the game: the team possessing the ball needed to be able to advance it while holding on to the territory it had already captured. That was key: hold and advance.

Ah, manifest destiny! Now that's something American players and spectators could embrace.

And, in 1882, that is exactly what happened. That year, the year Thomas Edison switched on the first commercial electric lights in New York, the association members got together and created a great idea—the concept of the first down.

Here was the new rule they created: "If on three consecutive fairs and downs a team shall not have advanced the ball five yards or lost 10, they must give up the ball to the other side at the spot where the fourth down was made."

It was a convoluted way of saying that the team with possession must advance the ball five yards or give it up. But, more important, it meant that if the team with the ball advanced it five yards, it kept the ball and the territory it had earned and kept going—kept possession of the football.

Capture territory. Hold it. Advance. What is more American than that? Where's Horace Greeley when you need him? It was the mantra of a nation that was advancing across the Rocky Mountains, establishing the continent as its own, fighting acre by acre for land held for centuries by native peoples.

The nation needed a game that reflected that haughty attitude, that movement forward at all costs, that violence. America needed a game that not only reflected its immigrant roots but also the demands of a nation constantly looking for new ways to accomplish these lofty national goals.

The first down separated American football from its European ancestors' rugby and soccer, and its institution and impact on the modern game should not be underestimated. (Photo courtesy Getty Images)

(It is no wonder that the leaders of the Military Academy at West Point became the prime movers of the game, passing down the traditions of Army football from Douglas MacArthur to Red Blaik to Lombardi to Parcells. "This obsession with field position—with *territory*—is a legacy of my coaching days at West Point, where we'd get free advice from every major on campus," Parcells wrote in his autobiography in 1995.)

"The Rugby code was all right for Englishman who had been brought up upon traditions as old and as binding as the laws themselves," wrote Walter Camp, the father of modern football, in 1894. American football, wrote Camp, was evolving from "the nondescript running and kicking" to "a scientific contest."

Without that rule change in 1882, we would not have offense and defense. We would not have had innovations to advance the ball, the "quarter-back" running it and, of course, passing it. That rule change allowed for the institution of a vast statistical record of the game. Without it, there would be no specialization or, later, the need for substitutions.

That simple rule change—it later became 10 yards for a first down as advancing the ball became more innovative—created in a game the twin engines of what built a nation: the brute violence of expansion with the strategic organization of corporate power.

It also created a natural story line—just like the nation's movement west. Years later, before football games were broadcast, fans would gather on North Broad Street in North Philadelphia in front of *The Philadelphia Inquirer* building. The newspaper had a replica of a football field and gave minute-by-minute updates of Penn football games.

What kept their attention? Advancing the football across that fake field. The change of possession. The natural ebb and flow of the game created by a simple rule change in 1882. The first down.

Now this story line defines our sporting lives for six months a year, nearly every day of the week: movement across the field of territory, with a quick strike, real-time precision, rehearsed mayhem, a unique brand of controlled violence.

If that rule change had not been made in 1882, we'd still be watching rugby's slow-moving scrum.

Or worse, soccer.

CHAPTER 2

Super Bowl Teams

The Most Overrated Super Bowl Team in NFL History

THE 1985 BEARS

Know what you're thinking: no way is this real. Got to be some kind of joke. One of the most celebrated football teams in history—*overrated?* That has to be about as brash and obnoxious as, well, the 1985 Bears!

Well, yes, they were cocky and arrogant. They hated you, and they didn't care if you hated them. But they just didn't lose.

The 1985 Chicago Bears had the greatest defense ever assembled. One of the most prodigious running backs in NFL history. A head coach who became his own *Saturday Night Live* skit—who else in NFL history can make that claim? An innovative defensive coordinator worshipped by his players. A renegade quarterback who got his kicks laughing at authority.

And in 2006 the 1985 Bears were given their place in football history by a fabulous NFL Films series called *America's Game*. These one-hour, first-person narratives filled with rare locker room footage and those trademark, field-level, slow-motion views of the game told the story of the first 40 Super Bowl winners. Then a panel of pro football writers, players, coaches, and front-office executives chose the top 20 of all time. The Bears came in second, right behind the 1972 Miami Dolphins, who I'll deal with next. So don't touch that dial.

William "Refrigerator" Perry and the 1985 Bears only won one Super Bowl in an era when they undoubtedly had the team and talent to become a dynasty.

Back to the Bears. That 1985 team has been put on a pretty high pedestal. And why not? That's where they put themselves. Remember, this is a team that taped its own Super Bowl video *halfway* through the season.

The Bears, coached by surly former All-Pro tight end Mike Ditka, won their first 12 games and rolled to a 15–1 regular-season record, losing only to Dan Marino and the Dolphins on a Monday night in Miami. The Bears' 15 wins came by an average score of 29–11, none by fewer than six points.

That was nothing. The Bears made a mockery of the postseason, winning three games by a combined score of 91–10, the greatest postseason margin of victory during the Super Bowl era. Without breaking a sweat, they blanked the Giants and Rams by a combined 45–0 to reach the Super Bowl, and their domination over the Patriots in Super Bowl XX was so great that New England managed just seven yards on 11 runs—none of them longer than three yards—and benched quarterback Tony Eason before he completed a pass.

The final score was 46–10, at the time the most lopsided Super Bowl ever. What's more, the Bears mocked the shaken Patriots, using 400-pound defensive tackle William Perry to smash his way into the end zone during a 21-point third quarter.

But the Bears were more than an outstanding football team. They captivated the nation with their array of oddball characters and personalities. They had guys named Mongo and Fridge. They had the Grammy-nominated "Super Bowl Shuffle." They had quarterback Jim McMahon mooning a helicopter during Super Bowl week in New Orleans and infuriating Commissioner Rozelle with his taunting headbands.

The second greatest Super Bowl team ever? Well, for one season, they were right there. So what happened?

The Bears remained a very good team the next few years, but the magic vanished. The banquet circuit that winter softened them up. McMahon couldn't stay healthy. Legendary Payton turned 32 years old and ran out of steam. And although the Bears went 14–2 during the 1986 regular season and won their division, there was something missing. With Doug Flutie now at quarterback, the Bears got hammered—at home—by the Redskins in their playoff opener. The Redskins scored the game's last 20 points, and it wasn't Joe Theismann or Doug Williams doing the damage, it was Jay Schroeder, playing in just his second career postseason game. Final score: 27–13 Redskins. The Bears were one-and-done.

In 1987 the Bears again won the NFC Central, finishing 11–4. Again, they were one-and-done in the postseason, again losing to the 'Skins.

In 1988 Chicago was rescued by the fog in the first round of the playoffs, beating the Eagles in a Soldier Field game where players couldn't see their own fingers three feet in front of their noses, much less a football coming out of the shrouded atmosphere. The next week, the Bears were demolished by the San Francisco 49ers—a team assembling a true dynasty, true greatness—at, of all places, Soldier Field.

During their seven-year run, the Bears reached the conference championship game just twice, winning only once. And this is before the salary cap and free agency, when keeping elite squads intact was just a matter of will and wallet.

Now go back to 1986, when the Bears won a remarkable 14 games and went nowhere. In NFL history, 21 teams have won 14 games. Nineteen of those reached at least a conference championship game. Only the 1986 Bears and the 2005 Colts failed to get beyond the conference semifinal round. But a year later, the Colts finally won their Super Bowl. Not the Bears. They just gradually faded out of the NFC elite, never becoming the team they could have been.

After the Super Bowl in 1985, the Bears won just two more playoff games in seven more seasons under Ditka. It would be more than two decades before they finally got to another Super Bowl.

How can one of the most dominating Super Bowl champions be overrated? Dynasty was at their doorstep, and they turned it away. That team had three Hall of Famers—Walter Payton, Dan Hampton, and Mike Singletary. Yet they reached just one Super Bowl. They were a peerless champion. For one year. They should have been much more.

Postscript: Maybe the greatest NFL Films shot of all time is the camera focused on the ferocious eyes of Bears middle linebacker Mike Singletary, who is screaming at the opposing line of scrimmage: "Hey, baby, we gonna be here all day, baby. I like this kind of party. I like this kind of party, baby!" Hopefully Mr. Singletary didn't read this section.

The Rest of the Most Overrated

2. THE 1972 DOLPHINS

There's no sense backing into this. The popular mythology is that the 1972 Dolphins are the greatest football team ever. They're not.

Going 14–0 and winning the Super Bowl has gone down as the most remarkable achievement in football history, probably in sports history. And each year that goes by without another undefeated team only serves to magnify how hard it is to do. Every time a team opens up 10–0, 11–0, maybe 12–0, the old Dolphins start popping up on TV, waxing nostalgic, feeding the myth. As the years go by without another perfect season, the mightier the myth seems to be. And, don't forget, that NFL Films panel voted this team the best Super Bowl squad ever.

But when you examine exactly what went into their 14–0 record, the 1972 Dolphins don't look quite so mighty. One of the top 10 teams in NFL history? Probably. The best? No way. That's why they're overrated.

That Dolphins team was the beneficiary of a ridiculously easy schedule in a terribly weak AFC. Counting the division rivals—the Colts, Patriots, and Bills twice—Miami's 14 opponents had a combined record of 70–122–4, a .367 winning percentage—the worst ever for a Super Bowl champion. Oh, now you're beginning to wonder, too.

There's an old adage in sports: you can only beat who you play. Well, the 1972 Dolphins beat a bunch of nobodies. None of their opponents reached the playoffs, and only two of them—the Giants and Chiefs—finished over .500. And they were both 8–6. The 1972 Dolphins are the only Super Bowl winner since the merger that didn't face a playoff team and the only Super Bowl winner ever that didn't face a team that had won nine or more games.

When you think of the greatest team ever, you think of the 1979 Steelers or the 1989 49ers. Those teams just steamrolled their opponents. There's something to be said for a team that knows how to win close games, but the Dolphins weren't good enough to blow anybody out in 1972. They beat the 7–7 Vikings by two, the 4–9–1 Bills by one, and the 7–7 Jets by four. And then they sputtered in their first two postseason games, overcoming a 14–13 fourth-quarter deficit to beat the Cleveland Browns, whose quarterback was the one and only Mike Phipps. That year the Browns had scored the least amount of points of any playoff team. Phipps completed a lowly 47.2 percent of his passes during the 1972 season.

In the AFC Championship game, the Dolphins had to overcome a 10–7 third-quarter deficit to beat the Steelers.

In the Super Bowl, the Dolphins faced the Redskins. Washington's quarterback? Billy Kilmer, who was 2–4 in the playoffs in his career. George Allen's offense was pretty one-dimensional. Kilmer did go to the Pro Bowl that season, but the Redskins offense finished 17th in the league in passing the football. Kilmer couldn't beat them. The Dolphins played conservatively (ignoring, of course, Garo Yepremian's imitation of, well, Billy Kilmer) and won an efficient game 14–7.

In this case, efficient—even if it's perfect—doesn't translate into the greatest Super Bowl team ever. That's why the 1972 Dolphins so prominently make this list of overrated Super Bowl teams.

Postscript: Though the defense carried the Dolphins through the postseason in 1972, only one member of that defense made it to the Hall of Fame: middle linebacker Nick Buoniconti. Five members of that offense are in Canton.

3. THE 1996 GREEN BAY PACKERS

This team was built around one of the most prolific passers and dynamic leaders in the modern game, and the team was built to last. Indeed, it was built for multiple Super Bowl titles, but that didn't happen. The 1996 Green Bay Packers were one-and-done, and that's why they make this list.

The Pack finished the season 13–3—all three losses coming on the road—on their way to dominating the NFC playoffs, beating first the 'Niners by three touchdowns, then the Panthers by 17 points in the NFC Championship game. Indeed, with Hall of Famer Reggie White anchoring the defense, the 1996 Packers were one of only two post-merger Super Bowl participants to lead the league both in points scored (456) and points allowed (210).

General manager Ron Wolf and head coach Mike Holmgren had built a team reminiscent of the Lombardi days in Titletown except for one important difference: it all unraveled rather quickly. Signs of stress began during Super Bowl XXXI.

The Packers faced a New England Patriots team that couldn't compare on the talent level but had a few guys who could coach their butts off—the boss, Bill Parcells, and his consigliere, Bill Belichick, along with capos Maurice Carthon, Romeo Crennel, Dante Scarnecchia, Al Groh, Charlie Weis, and Mike Sweatman. In this game, Parcells and his fun bunch got brain lock. (Parcells was also publicly feuding with team owner Robert Kraft during Super Bowl week. That proved to be a big distraction.)

The Pats never challenged the Packers on the ground, the weakest point of the Packers' defense. And Sweatman, the special teams coach, continually had the ball kicked right at the explosive Desmond Howard, who that year had set the league record for punt-return yardage in a single season. In the Super Bowl, Howard returned four kickoffs for 154 yards, including a 99-yard dagger for a touchdown that put the game away. He also returned six punts for 90 yards, and he was the first special-teams player to be named Super Bowl MVP.

Favre got off to his typically nervous start. That put the Packers in an early 14–10 hole. It could have proven much more costly on that day and historically embarrassing, however. This Packers team losing to that Patriots team would have been, well, like the Bills losing to the Giants in Super Bowl XXV.

But in the end, Howard saved Wolf, Holmgren, and Favre. White, too, was too much for the Pats' O-line, and Drew Bledsoe gladly donated four interceptions to the cause. And the Packers brought the Lombardi Trophy home to Green Bay, where it belongs.

But the Packers' underwhelming Super Bowl performance foreshadowed things to come. The following year, in Super Bowl XXXII, Terrell Davis played John Elway's wingman, and Denver head coach Mike Shanahan learned from Parcells's mistake—he attacked the Packers weak run defense. Elway was not sacked, and the Broncos won their first Super Bowl title.

Soon Wolf and Holmgren began fighting over turf and organizational control. Holmgren left Green Bay, where they had named a street after him, and started cashing Paul Allen's big checks in Seattle. Wolf retired. And Favre has been left with one Lombardi Trophy in his cabinet, where there should be many more.

The NFL Films panel put the 1996 Packers in the top 20 Super Bowl teams of all time, ranking the team at number 16. No way. This team is number three on this list of overrated Super Bowl teams. They needed the best special-teams performance in Super Bowl history to beat a weaker, poorly coached Patriots team. And they squandered a shot at back-to-back titles and a chance at uttering the dynasty word.

Postscript: Let's go back to Desmond Howard's pivotal 99-yard kickoff return for a touchdown in Super Bowl XXXI. The third quarter was winding down. Patriots running back Curtis Martin had just scored. It was 27–21 Packers, but Green Bay was feeling the heat, and the Pats knew it.

Here's what Howard told NFL Films: "The best thing they could do on kick returns was to kick them high and not real short and not real deep. I think they were effective with that. The only mistake they made is when they started to come back. I think they got a little cocky. They got a little arrogant. That's the one they finally kicked deep."

4. THE 1999 TENNESSEE TITANS

This is certainly a different take, picking the *loser* of a Super Bowl as an overrated team. But here's what we remember about the 1999 Tennessee Titans: they came oh-so-close to beating the high-flying St. Louis Rams in Super Bowl XXXIV. If only Kevin Dyson's right arm was about half a foot longer. If only Rams linebacker Mike Jones's grip had slipped. Steve McNair and Co. have lived off that woulda, coulda moment for years, reminisced that their effort was gutsy and valiant, and blah, blah, blah.

Here's a more healthy perspective: the Titans didn't deserve to win that game. They had no answer for Kurt Warner's pyrotechnics. They gave up the biggest play of the game at the worst possible moment. If they had only played smarter, especially on defense, it would not have been necessary for another miracle finish to win.

Warner, the MVP of Super Bowl XXXIV, was 24 of 45 for 414 yards with two touchdown passes, including a lightning strike of 73 yards to Isaac Bruce with 1:54 remaining in the fourth quarter for the game-winning points. Yes, the Titans held Marshall Faulk to just 17 yards rushing on 10 carries, but he was misused, and thus disappeared, in both his Super Bowls. (Faulk had 76 yards on 17 carries against the Patriots two years later.)

That feel-good moment at the end of Super Bowl XXXIV (cue Al Michaels's great call of Dyson's catch and Jones's tackle) created this myth about the 1999 Titans that doesn't hold up. Even before they got to the Super Bowl, they weren't a very good team. Coach Jeff Fisher could beat Jacksonville—he did it three times that year, including the AFC Championship game—but the Titans had one of the easiest regular-season schedules of any Super Bowl participant. Their opponents' combined record was .461 that year. The Titans finished 13–3 but then needed the Music City Miracle play to beat the 11–5 Buffalo Bills—in Nashville—in the wild-card playoff game.

Dyson's 75-yard return after a lateral on a kickoff for the winning touchdown with three seconds remaining on an overcast Saturday afternoon at Adelphia Coliseum "will go down in history," as team owner Bud Adams said. But this team should not.

The Titans' leading receiver during the regular season was tight end Frank Wycheck. They ranked 13th in the league on offense and 17th on defense. In the four games of the postseason, McNair was mediocre at best, earning a completion percentage of 57.9, with just one touchdown pass and two picks. His quarterback rating was 65.7.

The Titans of 1999 had some pretty highlights that have become celebrated celluloid moments. But the rest of it was just pretty ordinary…and overrated.

Postscript: The Titans lost 23–16. The Rams were favored by a touchdown. It was the last Super Bowl that was a push. Had Kevin Dyson scored, a lot of bookies would've been looking for another line of work.

5. THE 2005 PITTSBURGH STEELERS

Here's what Steelers defensive lineman Casey Hampton said when he landed in Hawaii for the Pro Bowl after Pittsburgh prevailed in a very controversial Super Bowl XL in Detroit: "People crying about what happened, that's crazy. It doesn't matter. You can't talk about what might have happened. Two or three years from now, people won't remember who we beat in the Super Bowl. Just that we won."

Well, enough time has passed for people to forget. But they haven't. And that's why the 2005 Steelers, a wild-card team with not one skill player selected to the Pro Bowl, makes this overrated list.

The number that stands out is 22.6. That was Ben Roethlisberger's quarterback rating in Super Bowl XL, making his performance the worst by a quarterback to win a Super Bowl. Big Ben had just nine completions in 21 attempts, no touchdown passes, and two picks. And he never really scored the game's first touchdown. Every replay from every angle showed that with 1:55 remaining in the first half, Roethlisberger's dive into the end zone fell short. But the challenge by Seahawks head coach Mike Holmgren was denied.

In all, the officials took away 14 points from Seattle. Seattle wide receiver Darrell Jackson apparently scored the game's first touchdown when he caught a 16-yard pass from Matt Hasselbeck. Jackson was called for offensive pass interference in the end zone—the first time that penalty negating seven points was ever called in a Super Bowl.

Yes, the Steelers were a wild-card team that won four straight road games in the postseason to win the title—that run gave them a big Cinderella factor. But let's go through it: in the first round of the playoffs, defensive end Kimo von Oelhoffen knocked Bengals quarterback Carson Palmer out of the first-round playoff game by rolling into his left knee. Then, against the Colts the following week, one of the most accurate kickers in the game—Mike Vanderjagt—missed a 46-yard field goal that would have sent the game into overtime. In the AFC Championship game in Denver, Broncos quarterback Jake Plummer could not buy a clue for most of the first three quarters. For a conference that was supposed to be so strong, the Steelers' opposition came up lame.

What's more, the guy most celebrated in Detroit for his homecoming during Super Bowl week—Jerome Bettis—did not play a major role in the postseason. He averaged just 3.2 yards per carry, never going more than 52 yards in any of the four games. And he nearly cost Pittsburgh the game in Indy, with a fumble near the goal line. Only Roethlisberger's game-saving tackle of Colts cornerback Nick Harper prevented disaster.

In the end, this Steelers team—bridesmaids for so many years under Coach Bill Cowher—was celebrated for too much pluck, when it was really the beneficiary of an unprecedented string of incredibly well-timed post-season luck.

Postscript: After winning the Super Bowl, Bill Cowher should have stepped down. Bettis said at the beginning of the 2006 season that he knew Cowher was a lame duck. Instead, Cowher played coy about his future in Pittsburgh, and the season-long charade further tarnished his already-mixed record in the 'Burgh.

The Most Underrated Super Bowl Team in NFL History

THE 1976 OAKLAND RAIDERS, WINNERS OF SUPER BOWL XI

Picking a Lombardi Trophy *winner* to be the most underrated Super Bowl team is certainly a risk. But it's not a stretch when you put the 1976 Oakland Raiders into the historical context of the game and the perspective of that decade.

In the 1970s the Raiders were the stepchild of the Pittsburgh Steelers. The greatest post-merger dynasty in pro football history eclipsed just about every other pro football accomplishment of that decade—unless, of course, you happened to be the first team ever to go undefeated (Miami Dolphins, 1972). And the Steelers seemed to have had the Raiders figured out, from the standpoint of both tactics (the Steel Curtain defense) and luck (the Immaculate Reception).

What's more, when it was their year, the 1976 Raiders had to fight to get a headline. The country was celebrating the Bicentennial. Tall ships sailed into Manhattan. The Democratic National Convention caused a big stir at Madison Square Garden. Jimmy Carter was elected president, changing the guard at the White House. Big history and bigger political changes dominated the cultural landscape. The Raiders, a team playing in the second city in San Francisco's Bay Area—who cared?

But the 1976 Raiders were a truly great Super Bowl team that simply never got much recognition. And their accomplishment is fading over time. And that's why they headline this list.

In 1976 the Oakland Raiders finished 13–1 and captured their first Super Bowl title, drubbing a Minnesota Vikings team that went to four Super Bowls in the 1970s. During the 1976 season, the Purple People Eaters surrendered just 176 points—second only to the Steel Curtain (138 points). Indeed, in the AFC Championship game that year, the Raiders beat Pittsburgh, scoring 24 points off a team that gave up an average of just 9.9 points per game.

In Super Bowl XI, on a brilliantly perfect day at the Rose Bowl in Pasadena, the Raiders—having driven down from Oakland and trained in tony Newport Beach—were a supremely confident bunch. They rode that confidence to a 32–7 lead until the Vikings added a meaningless fourth-quarter touchdown—otherwise it would have been the most lopsided Super Bowl to date. Against one of the most celebrated defenses in league history, Raiders quarterback Ken Stabler had a quarterback rating of 111.7—better than the Super Bowl MVP performances of John Elway, Kurt Warner, Tom Brady (twice), and Peyton Manning.

And the 1976 Raiders had real star power. Six players from that team would go on to the Pro Football Hall of Fame: wide receiver Fred Biletnikoff (MVP of Super Bowl XI), cornerback Willie Brown, guard Gene Upshaw, offensive left tackle Art Shell, tight end Dave Casper, and linebacker Ted Hendricks. So would the man who put the team together, owner and general manager Al Davis, and the head coach, John Madden.

Granted, this team had just one meteoric flash of brilliance. But in the 1974 and 1975 AFC Championship games, they lost to one of the best football teams ever assembled—with a little divine intervention thrown in, courtesy of Frenchy Fuqua and Franco Harris. In 1977 they were poised to go back to the Super Bowl, but in the AFC Championship game against Denver, the Raiders were victimized by divine stupidity. They had three turnovers, losing to the Broncos 20–17 after not scoring a touchdown until the fourth quarter.

So this was another team that had dynasty written all over it but failed to close the deal. Still, the 1976 Raiders make the *underrated* list because they've never been compared to the 1985 Bears. They've never been talked about in that context. Although they should be.

It was a team that was just as dominant for just as short a period of time. Both teams had only one loss. Both teams thoroughly dominated the post-season. And the Raiders had much tougher playoff opposition. In fact, it's not even close. In the AFC Championship game, Oakland had to finally bring down the Steel Curtain. The Bears in 1985 had to play the mighty Los Angeles Rams, who never reached the Super Bowl that decade.

Then the 1985 Bears, which had only three players go to the Hall of Fame, had to beat another perennial powerhouse, the New England Patriots, in Super Bowl XX. The Patriots' quarterback was Tony Eason. The Raiders faced future Hall of Famer Fran Tarkenton, who finished his career in 1978 with an

NFL-record 342 touchdown passes. Against the Raiders defense in Super Bowl XI, Tarkenton was just 17 of 35 with one touchdown pass and two interceptions.

In 2006 the NFL Films panel voted the 1976 Raiders the 10th best Super Bowl team in history. So a morsel of respect was finally thrown their way. They should get much more.

Postscript: The 1976 Raiders could easily have two more Hall of Famers: Phil Villapiano, who played defensive end in Super Bowl XI but went to four Pro Bowls as a linebacker later in his career, and Ray Guy, considered the greatest punter of all time.

John Madden and his burly band, the 1976 Oakland Raiders, had to fight through other celebrated AFC dynasties in the 1970s, including the Miami Dolphins and Pittsburgh Steelers, to stake their claim as one of the best teams ever. (Photo courtesy Getty Images)

The Rest of the Most Underrated

2. THE 2002 TAMPA BAY BUCCANEERS, WINNERS OF SUPER BOWL XXXVII

What the Tampa Bay Buccaneers did in 2002 is a blur. They finished 12–4, tied for the best record in the league with the Green Bay Packers and Philadelphia Eagles, and then pulled off an improbable ride through the post-season. Traveling to snow-covered Philadelphia for the NFC Championship game, the warm-weather Bucs pulled off an upset that few predicted. In the last game played at old Veterans Stadium, the Bucs embarrassed the Eagles 27–10. Then Jon Gruden's team destroyed the high-powered Oakland Raiders (the team Gruden built) in Super Bowl XXXVII, 48–21, in San Diego.

But the 2002 Bucs make this list because that team and that Super Bowl performance have been nearly forgotten—for two reasons. First, blame the New England Patriots. The Bucs' title was sandwiched in the middle of the Patriots' three Super Bowl victories in four years, an NFL record that gave the Pats card-carrying dynasty status. Second, Super Bowl XXXVII itself was all but forgotten. It was overshadowed when the Raiders imploded in a controversy of their own making. The day before the game, Barrett Robbins, the linchpin of their offensive line, suddenly and inexplicably disappeared. Robbins—later it was revealed that he suffers from bipolar disorder—went on a drinking binge in Tijuana, Mexico, and never made it to the game. And before we knew it, Gruden (affectionately known as "Chuckie" for the faces he makes resembling the horror movie character) was pumping his fist, running down the sideline, exhorting linebacker Derrick Brooks on a fourth-quarter interception return for a touchdown to seal the blowout.

What people forget is just how dominant that Raiders team was. During the 2002 season, the Raiders led the league by scoring 450 points. Rich Gannon, in the offense designed by Gruden, was a machine. In the Super Bowl, Gruden and his defensive coordinator, Monte Kiffin, seemed to know Gannon's every move in advance. Through three quarters of the Super Bowl, Gannon's offense had been held to just nine points. Gruden and Kiffin pulled off one of the best coaching jobs in Super Bowl history. That year Kiffin's defense—featuring Brooks, defensive tackle Warren Sapp, defensive end Simeon Rice, and cornerback Ronde Barber—led the league in points allowed, just 196.

The NFL Films panel did not include the Bucs among the top 20 Super Bowl teams of all time. The 1999 St. Louis Rams made it—at number 19. Mistake. That year, the Rams struggled to beat the Bucs—then coached by Tony Dungy—in the NFC Championship game, winning 11–6. Kurt Warner and the so-called Greatest Show on Turf were shut down by Kiffin's defense. Then the Rams barely beat a far inferior Tennessee Titans team in Super Bowl XXXIV. Without a game-saving tackle on the goal line, the Rams are not in this conversation at all. The Bucs, like the Rams, won only one championship. But the Bucs were a far more dominant team.

Another thing has held back recognition of the Bucs—the perception that quarterback Brad Johnson was one of the worst Super Bowl quarterbacks ever. Not true. That season, Johnson completed 62 percent of his passes for 22 touchdowns and just six interceptions. By anybody's standard, that's a terrific year. In the Super Bowl, he was 18 of 34 with two touchdowns and a pick. Again, pretty good.

Postscript: Against that Bucs defense in the 1999 championship game, Kurt Warner threw three picks.

3. THE CLEVELAND BROWNS OF THE 1950s

All right, don't go calling the publisher, demanding a refund for a gross inaccuracy. The Cleveland Browns of the 1950s have been deliberately shoehorned into this chapter for a good reason. What Paul Brown did with that franchise was nothing short of monumental, and his accomplishment is a spectacular piece of pro football history that had a vast impact on the current game and has been all but erased from memory.

Why? All those grainy, black-and-white home movie–looking highlights just don't make for sexy, late-night classic TV viewing. And Art Modell, like a South American dictator, once tried to make the franchise disappear. He moved it to Baltimore in a dispute over (of all things) stadium funding. When a team relocates, it usually brings its history. But Modell tried to rewrite it. What's worse, the Ravens, his new team, have been wildly successful, actually playing in and winning a Super Bowl, which is all the more reason to stop right here and recognize the old Browns. Because the new

Browns are, well, awful and definitely not to be confused with the old Browns.

The old Browns were just flat-out good. But that was a long, long time ago, like, how about 1948? Now that was a very good year in Cleveland. The Indians won the World Series right before the New York Yankees said *fuhgetaboutit* and rattled off five straight world titles. It was the last time the Indians won the fall classic.

That victory obviously had a profound effect on the city's football psyche because that same year the Cleveland Browns—coached by the aforementioned Paul Brown (that's how they got their name, by the way)—went 14–0. That's 24 years before the Miami Dolphins went undefeated. Why doesn't anybody talk about it? Because in 1948 the Browns played in a league called the All-America Football Conference. In fact, Cleveland thoroughly dominated the AAFC, going 47–4–3 and winning four straight titles, from 1946 to 1949, when the struggling league folded.

Three teams were absorbed by the NFL: the San Francisco 49ers, the Baltimore Colts, and the Browns. The NFL fathers thought they were getting a new set of patsies. Wrong. The Browns were for-real good. Imagine for a moment if in 1986 the NFL had absorbed a handful of teams when the United States Football League folded. Then imagine the Denver Gold reached the Super Bowl in its first six years in the NFL. That's exactly what happened in 1950. The move to the NFL was supposed to spell the end of the Browns' dominance. Instead, the Browns reached the title game in each of their first six seasons, winning the NFL championships in 1950, 1954, and 1955. The Browns were virtually unbeatable from 1946 to 1955, going 105–17–4.

There was no magic formula, just the tried-and-true American way: ingenuity and guts. Brown, the Thomas Edison of pro football, started it all. He liked to tinker, and he stayed in the laboratory until he got it right: the off-season training programs, the heavy-duty film study, and the obsession with punctuality and order. Brown learned his organizational skills in the military, so he instituted everything from a strict training camp regimen—three-ring binders outlining every move by every coach and player—to making sure his roster was color blind. He recruited Otto Graham to be the quarterback of his innovative T formation offense, but he also gave a bruising black fullback named Marion Motley a shot in the bigs. (When the Browns traveled to Florida, Motley was left behind because segregation laws there prohibited blacks and whites from competing on the same field.)

Brown also cut back on physical practices, believing that his teams would practice smarter and be fresher down the stretch, an innovation that is often attributed to Bill Walsh in the 1980s. (Walsh learned that from Brown, who was his boss in Cincinnati in the 1970s.) Said Brown, "We're getting the guesswork out of football. We're making a science out of what is called a game." Sounds like Bill Belichick, doesn't he?

The result: the Browns are one of only four franchises in professional sports history to win five consecutive league titles, along with the Yankees (1949–1953), Celtics (1959–1966), and Canadiens (1956–1960). The roster was filled with future Hall of Famers: Doug Atkins, Len Ford, Frank Gatski, Otto Graham, Lou Groza, Marion Motley, Dante Lavelli, and Bill Willis.

It all came to screeching halt in 1956, the year a defensive wizard in New York named Tom Landry developed the 4-3 defense and installed a rookie linebacker named Sam Huff in the middle. Huff's first year was his best, and the Giants finally toppled the Browns to become NFL champions.

So what did Paul Brown do? In 1957 he drafted a running back out of Syracuse to fix the problem. His name was Jim Brown.

Postscript: In 1963, in one of the league's great ironies, the new owner of the Browns, Art Modell, fired Paul Brown. The following year, Jim Brown led the Browns to their final NFL title, a 27–0 beat-down of the Baltimore Colts. Since the franchise was revived in 1999, the new Browns have made one trip to the postseason.

4. THE 1981 CINCINNATI BENGALS, LOSERS OF SUPER BOWL XVI

You take an innovative mastermind like Paul Brown and a tough taskmaster like Forrest Gregg, who played under and was a natural heir to Vince Lombardi. Then you put them together as general manager and head coach of a football team. That's what the Cincinnati Bengals did, and it got them to the Super Bowl in 1981 for the first time in franchise history.

With Brown at the helm, this expansion franchise had the sorry luck of being birthed in 1968 and, after the 1970 merger, placed in the AFC Central

Division, where the lord overseers were the relentless Pittsburgh Steelers of Chuck Noll. So, while the Bengals had fits and starts, they did not come of age until the decade turned the page, when they went 12–4 in 1981.

That season they scored 421 points, the second-most in the league behind the San Diego Chargers. They even scored more than the team they would meet in Super Bowl XVI, the San Francisco 49ers, coached by Bill Walsh, who used to work for Brown in Cincinnati. (How about a chorus of "Luke, I am your father" right here?) The Bengals' prolific passer, Kenny Anderson, finished the season with 29 touchdown passes—10 more than Joe Montana for the 'Niners. Cris Collinsworth averaged 15.1 yards per catch. Just to give you an idea how good that is, Terrell Owens's career average is 14.6, and Jerry Rice's is 14.8. So Collinsworth was in the high-rent neighborhood in 1981.

The Bengals dropped 28 on the Bills to prevail in the first round of the playoffs. Then Cincinnati drubbed the San Diego Chargers, who led the league that year in points scored with 478. Final score: 27–7 for the right to face San Francisco in the Super Bowl.

The Bengals had everything going for them. The offense could score at will. Anderson was hitting everything in stride. The defense had not played at a higher level all year. The team had all the momentum. Just two-point underdogs, the Bengals coulda, shoulda beat the 'Niners in that Super Bowl and made some history. That's why they make this select list of underrated teams. Of all the Super Bowl losers after the Steelers dynasty had run its course, this Bengals team was the one that had everything aligned to hoist the Vince Lombardi trophy. Seven years later, when the Bengals went back to the Super Bowl in 1988 to face San Francisco again, the 'Niners—especially Montana—had already figured out how to win the big game. But the 1981 'Niners were novices, ripe for bullying.

Unfortunately for the city of Cincinnati, the 1981 Bengals picked the first half of Super Bowl XVI to have their worst half that season, indeed the worst first half of Super Bowl football to date. And the 'Niners jumped to a record 20–0 halftime lead.

In the second half, Anderson and the Bengals stormed back. Anderson ran for one touchdown and threw for two more. Trying to come from behind,

Anderson set a Super Bowl record for completions (25) and completion percentage (73.5 percent). The Bengals had 356 total yards to 275 for the 'Niners—the first time in Super Bowl history that the team that gained the most yards from scrimmage lost the game.

History has judged the Bengals harshly. It shouldn't. They just had one really bad half of football.

Ironically, the outcome of the game was decided by 'Niners kicker Ray Wersching, who had four field goals. Final score: 26–21. And instead of Paul Brown finally hoisting the trophy named for the coach who tormented him in the 1960s, it went to Brown's estranged protégé, Bill Walsh.

Postscript: Some will say, what about the 1988 Bengals? Aren't they more underrated? No. They were favored by seven points going into Super Bowl XXIII. And they had the lead and lost. Unforgivable. And obviously overrated.

5. THE BUFFALO BILLS OF THE 1990s

Anybody who's seen the movie *Patton* can recite one of the general's enduring lines: "America is a nation of winners." We like to win. That's why, as a nation, we never could get our arms around the Buffalo Bills, the team that will always be remembered for losing four consecutive Super Bowls, a legacy of failure unmatched in professional sports history. And that failure happened in sometimes dramatic, sometimes embarrassing fashion on the world's biggest stage.

Scott Norwood kicked an agonizing few feet wide right from 47 yards out in Super Bowl XXV. Jim Kelly threw four picks in Super Bowl XXVI. Troy Aikman burned the Bills for four touchdown passes in Super Bowl XXVII. And Emmitt Smith plowed through the Buffalo defense in Super Bowl XXVIII.

"The Buffalo Bills are a punch line," said Steve Tasker, the Bills' special teams star who went to seven Pro Bowls. "We were always the team that couldn't win the big game. But we kept getting to the big game."

So why are they in the category of the most underrated Super Bowl teams in history? Well, for starters, there is no *underachieving* section in this book. So our best option is underrated. And Buffalo is the only team in history to reach four straight Super Bowls. Since the Dolphins in 1973, nobody else has even reached three in a row. That counts for something.

Head coach Marv Levy, a Rhodes Scholar with a degree in English literature, became a master at leading his team through the annual Super Bowl devastation and getting them motivated to crank it up and try again six months later. Think Susan Lucci with a clipboard. Of course, his poor coaching and questionable tactics significantly contributed to the Super Bowl losses, but we'll deal with that in a future chapter.

The Bills won in large part because, in the early days of free agency, they figured out how to keep their best players. The mighty offensive nucleus stayed intact, with Kelly, wide receiver Andre Reed, and running back Thurman Thomas playing together from 1988 through 1997. And the defense was almost as good, ranking in the top six in the NFL twice during that four-year Super Bowl run. Hall of Famer Bruce Smith was the fierce, tireless pass rusher; athletic linebackers Darryl Talley, Shane Conlan, and Cornelius Bennett were the key figures in the Bills' 3-4 defense; and Nate Odomes and Henry Jones manned the secondary quietly but effectively.

From 1990 through 1993, the Bills won 49 games and lost 15. They averaged 12 wins per year during that stretch, the sixth-most wins in NFL history over a four-year span. And they won the AFC East all four seasons.

So dominant were the Bills in their own conference that they won their four AFC Championship games by an average of 22 points, with the last three of those titles coming against three of the greatest quarterbacks in history: Hall of Famers John Elway, Dan Marino, and Joe Montana.

It is remarkable that a team that kept getting knocked down had the inner strength to keep getting back up and come back for more.

"By the third Super Bowl, there was a real sense on our team that we just didn't know how to do anything but win," Tasker said. "You only know one way to do things, and that's like a champion. We had so much character on that team with leaders like Jim [Kelly], Andre Reed, and Thurman Thomas that nobody ever considered letting up. There was never a sense, no matter how tough it became, that we would stop fighting. That's why we were able to keep going back there."

The Super Bowl jinx has been a powerful force. Teams that lose in the Super Bowl typically fall to pieces the next year. No team has lost a Super Bowl and made it back to the next one since the Bills. And they did it three times in a row.

Levy—who will make a prominent, ignominious appearance in an overrated category later in this book—has the fourth-best winning percentage (.579) in history among head coaches who won 10 postseason games or more, behind only Belichick, Joe Gibbs, and Chuck Noll.

"I don't know if you can label us a great team since we didn't win a Super Bowl," Tasker said. "But we were a very good team."

And a vastly underrated one.

Postscript: Even after the Super Bowl streak ended, the Bills didn't disappear. They reached the playoffs four of the next six years, at one point losing three straight wild-card games by a combined 16 points.

The Worst Super Bowl Ever

SUPER BOWL XLI

There will always be those images of that final scene in Miami of Tony Dungy and Peyton Manning, the NFL's two lost souls, finally finding their way to the promised land of pro football immortality—hoisting the Lombardi Trophy, awash in multicolored confetti and, on this night, an unrelenting South Florida rain.

Dungy, who lost his son to suicide in 2005 and who had labored like a gentleman farmer in a sallow field of missed opportunities, became the first black head coach to win an NFL title.

Manning, fast becoming a shameless corporate pitchman who happened to put up the biggest numbers of any quarterback in a generation, finally validated his place in the record books, shedding the Marino label for the Elway legacy.

And it is that image and those significant milestones which threaten to overshadow one undeniable conclusion: Super Bowl XLI, between the Indianapolis Colts and Chicago Bears, was the worst ever.

It was a disappointment because both football teams came into the game with very high expectations, and neither team could have fallen shorter.

Let's start with the biggest star of the game: Manning. He came into Super Bowl XLI as the third-highest-rated quarterback in Super Bowl history. His quarterback rating of 101.0 for the 2006 season was just a shade lower than Kurt Warner's 101.4 rating in 2001 and Jim Kelly's 101.2 in 1990. So, just like Warner and Kelly, the expectations for Manning's performance were extraordinarily high. This was not Earl Morrall in Super Bowl V, a comparison a lot of people like to make.

The conventional wisdom is that the Colts of Super Bowl XLI were not even the worst Colts team in a Super Bowl, that the Colts of 1970 season were much worse. Well, that's exactly the point. Not much was expected from the 1970 team. Not true of Manning's Colts. Not true of Manning.

And, in the end, Manning was pedestrian. He opened the game with an interception and then dinked and dunked his way to a championship. It was a boring performance. Of course, you could blame the rain, but four times Manning had great field position but his offense stalled, failing to get into the red zone. His conservative approach kept the Bears in the game. Indianapolis should have won by 30.

Manning completed 65.8 percent of his passes, but his quarterback rating of 81.8 was the worst of any Super Bowl MVP. He had one touchdown pass and one interception. Only three other quarterbacks were given the MVP trophy with an equal or lower ratio: Elway had one touchdown and one interception in Super Bowl XXXIII (and was given the trophy for sentimental reasons), Len Dawson had one touchdown pass and one interception and threw a Super Bowl MVP low of 17 passes in Super Bowl IV (but was MVP because the voters gave the trophy to the first four quarterbacks), and Joe Namath had no touchdown passes or interceptions in Super Bowl III (but he won because, well, it was *his* Super Bowl).

In Super Bowl XLI, the MVP should've been Colts running back Dominic Rhodes, whose 21 carries and 113 yards kept the Colts offense on schedule, while the normally potent passing game slogged unceremoniously through the soggy night.

The Colts offense just had no rhythm right from the start. Take Manning's interception. It was on a play that the Colts had run all year, had practiced all week in Miami, knowing that the Bears' cover-two defense would be vulnerable to it. The play called for tight end Dallas Clark, who had been the Colts' leading receiver in the postseason because Marvin Harrison was getting

Peyton Manning finally got his ring in Super Bowl XLI, but the game and the weather failed to live up to the hype.

double-covered so much, to run a seam route underneath the Bears safeties. But Clark broke too far to the inside, giving Bears middle linebacker Brian Urlacher a chance to get his giant paw up to deflect the ball—interception.

After the game, Manning pinned the blame for the interception squarely on Clark. But a study of the game film shows that Manning clearly had time to pull back on the ball. *He* threw the pick.

And Manning's only touchdown pass? Reggie Wayne was wide open because of a major breakdown in the Bears secondary, something Chicago had avoided all season. Bears free safety Danieal Manning was in man coverage, while his teammates were in zone. Manning to Wayne for 53 yards was the MVP's only touchdown pass of the night—from the game's most prolific passer.

Time now to talk about the other quarterback. Calling this Super Bowl the worst ever without bringing up Rex Grossman is, of course, dumb. After his performance in Super Bowl XLI, Grossman did not quite achieve Steve

Bartman status in Chicago, but he came pretty close. *Sports Illustrated*'s Rick Reilly put it best: Grossman "seemed to be playing in ski boots and oven mitts."

Grossman's numbers are obvious: one fumble lost, two interceptions. But it was more than that. His general inability to generate any offensive momentum was demoralizing to a Bears defense that was playing well enough to keep Chicago in the game.

About halfway through the third quarter the Bears only trailed by five points, 19–14, despite Grossman's awful showing. Chicago had the ball at first-and-10 on its 46-yard line—four yards shy of midfield. Great field position. At that point, the game was very much in doubt.

As the field began to resemble some kind of South Florida swamp, Bad Rex surfaced like the Loch Ness monster to snatch the Bears from a possible comeback. He tripped, lost 11 yards. He muffed the snap. The ball squirted backward. He fell on it. Lost another 11 yards. On fourth and 23, the Bears wisely punted.

But then Bears head coach Lovie Smith missed another obviously wise move: remove Grossman for Brian Griese. That was at 5:36 in the third quarter. From that point on, the Colts offense managed just three points: one Adam Vinatieri field goal. The rest of the Indianapolis scoring was provided by Grossman. He threw two interceptions. One wobbly pass that looked like a punt was snagged by reserve cornerback Kelvin Hayden, who returned it 56 yards for a touchdown.

Thank you, Grossman, for delivering Manning's legacy and Dungy's place in history.

Then, there was the rain. The NFL can control a lot. Not the weather. In 2005, Super Bowl XL was held indoors at Ford Field in Detroit. But outside, the fan experience was doused by frigid Michigan weather—all to reward Detroit's fathers for erecting another domed palace for the NFL. The year before, Jacksonville, Florida, proved too chilly and too unprepared. Another downer for the league's fans, who again were getting cheated because Jacksonville's high rollers were getting rewarded for upgrades to Alltel Stadium.

So Super Bowl XLI was supposed to be a return to South Florida's sunshine. But on Super Bowl Sunday, drizzle arrived early and turned into a long, heavy rain. It was the first weather event in Super Bowl history, and it helped to make Super Bowl XLI the worst ever.

CHAPTER 3

Quarterbacks

The Most Overrated Quarterback of All Time

JOE NAMATH

If you're a boomer and grew up in the 1960s, you probably had a life-size poster of Joe Namath on your bedroom wall. He was your hero, a counterculture icon. He was Joe Cool. Broadway Joe.

He had the biggest contract. The best-looking girlfriends. He owned a bar in New York. Named it Bachelors III, and if he didn't get rid of it, NFL Commissioner Pete Rozelle was going to throw him out of football.

Namath came from immigrant roots in Western Pennsylvania. He was coached by a legend at the University of Alabama, Bear Bryant. Then he signed the richest deal in professional sports with a showbiz impresario who happened to own the New York Jets in the renegade American Football League. Four years later, the Jets were AFL champions.

Namath did it—with the hair and the booze and the broads. He was the toast of New York. And then, on January 9, 1969, at the Miami Touchdown Club, the rebel image was completed. At an annual awards dinner at the Playhouse catering hall in Miami Springs, Florida, Namath was asked about the Baltimore Colts being an 18-point favorite in the AFL-NFL Championship game after the 1968 season. His reply? "Most people don't give us a chance. I think we have a chance. Matter of fact, I think we'll win it. I'll guarantee it."

The legend of Broadway Joe Namath has much more to do with his Super Bowl III performance and prolific off-field antics than his career stats.

Three days later, 60 million people watched the Jets stun the Colts 16–7 at the Orange Bowl in a game that would soon be known as Super Bowl III.

It was the greatest upset in the biggest game in pro football history. The Jets had an incalculable impact on not only professional football but all of professional sports. Two years later the leagues merged, leading to the greatest sports entertainment empire the planet has known.

That's why Namath is in the Pro Football Hall of Fame. Not because he was a good quarterback—for most of his career he wasn't. And that's why he not only makes this list but gets the prize as the most *overrated quarterback* of all time.

Look beyond the blow-dried hair, the Super Bowl guarantee, the rebel personality, the celebrity friends, and the pantyhose commercials, and what's left? Just a lot of bad passes.

His career passer rating was 65.5, which after the 2006 season ranked him 129th out of 148 quarterbacks in NFL history who threw 1,500 or more passes. Just below Billy Joe Toliver, Don Majkowski, Bubby Brister, Eric Hipple, and Joey Harrington.

This is not to diminish the legend of Joe Namath, just dissect the legacy. In a career that lasted nine years beyond Super Bowl III, Namath lost 31 more games than he won and threw 47 more interceptions than touchdowns. In his eight seasons following the Super Bowl, Namath started 33 games against teams that finished the season with a winning record. He won two. That's a cool 6 percent winning percentage. And in those 33 games, Namath threw 29 touchdowns and 70 interceptions.

Granted, he struggled with wretched knees most of his career, but a lot of quarterbacks have bad knees. They don't go 2–31 against winning teams over the final eight years of their careers.

Namath didn't go into the Hall of Fame because of his numbers. Only twice in his 13-year career did Namath throw more touchdown passes than interceptions. He had one season with more than 20 touchdowns and five seasons with more than 20 interceptions. He was MVP of the Super Bowl, but even on that historic day in Miami he didn't do anything special against the Colts. The Jets' only touchdown came courtesy of a four-yard run by Matt Snell. It was Snell who dominated the game, with 121 rushing yards, four receptions, and 161 total yards of offense—to this day, the seventh-most total yards in Super Bowl history by a running back.

So Namath is essentially in the Hall of Fame for one game in which *he didn't even throw a touchdown.*

Namath's greatest accomplishment as a passer came in 1967, when he became the first AFL or NFL quarterback with 4,000 passing yards in a season. But even that year he threw two more interceptions (28) than touchdowns (26), something no other 4,000-yard passer in NFL history has done. He also completed just 52.5 percent of his passes that season, the second-worst completion percentage ever by a 4,000-yard passer. Jay Schroeder of the Redskins completed 51 percent during his 4,000-yard season in 1986.

In NFL history, 75 quarterbacks have thrown at least 150 touchdown passes. Of those 75 quarterbacks, only one, Norm Snead, has a worse ratio of touchdowns to interceptions than Namath. Snead will not be going into the Hall of Fame.

In NFL history, 126 quarterbacks have completed 1,000 passes. Only seven had a lower completion percentage than Namath's 50.1 percent.

If the Jets lose to the Colts in Super Bowl III, the Hall of Fame probably laughs at Namath. He was inducted into the Hall in 1985, his third year as a finalist—so the debate about whether he belonged was genuine. In the end, he belongs. You cannot tell the history of the NFL, indeed the history of sports in America, without Namath.

Namath put the AFL on the map. No other league in more than half a century had successfully challenged the authorities in professional football—or any other major sport, for that matter. In essence, Namath helped to create the current worldwide phenomenon that is the National Football League. He will be remembered as the John, Paul, George, and Ringo of pro football. With one major exception. He was a one-hit wonder.

Postscript: How big of a '60s cultural icon was Joe Namath? Consider these two items from Namath, *the critically acclaimed biography by Mark Kriegel:*

After winning Super Bowl III, Namath was drinking at Jilly's South, a Miami nightclub, when Frank Sinatra came in to congratulate him. Namath, partying like he was known to do, got up to greet Sinatra and knocked a table full of drinks all over the chairman of the board. Normally, Sinatra would have been less than pleased. But as Broadway Joe tried to stammer out an apology, Sinatra said, "Ah, Joe, don't worry about it."

Sometime later, Namath was in Vegas, where Elvis Presley held court. When Namath arrived to see the show, the King stopped and led the audience in a standing ovation for the man who had become bigger than Sinatra and Elvis.

The Rest of the Most Overrated

2. BRETT FAVRE

Who's next, Johnny Unitas? No, No. 19 does not make this list. But No. 4 does.

Brett Favre is a Super Bowl winner, a certain first-ballot Hall of Famer, the most durable player in NFL history. No argument.

So how can he be overrated? Because his image in the media has been hyperinflated. The good ol' boy routine. The gunslinger mentality. The hard-drinking life in the backwoods of Mississippi—complete with perpetual five-day-old stubble. It's a powerful TV image. Favre's been made into a folk hero by his friends in the broadcast booth.

John Madden had this to say during a Packers-Bears game in December of 2006: "Brett Favre loves to play the game. That's why America loves him."

Really? Interesting. He loves to play the game. Is there a quarterback in the NFL who *doesn't* love to play the game? Now *that* would be news. Chris Weinke loves to play the game just as much as Favre. He's just not as good.

Let's interrupt the deification of Favre for a moment to examine his recent career. Since beating the 49ers in the 1997 NFC Championship game, Favre has won just two of eight playoff games, with 14 touchdowns and 17 interceptions in those postseason games.

Favre has won exactly as many postseason games over the past decade as Michael Vick has. *But it's blasphemy to compare Vick and Favre!*

Maybe not. Since Vick entered the NFL in 2001, he's won 58 percent of his starts (41–30). During the same period, Favre won 57 percent of his starts (58–44). Vick has thrown an interception every 33 attempts so far in his career. During the same period, since 2001, Favre has thrown an interception every 27 attempts.

So the guy who supposedly can't read defenses has had a better winning percentage, has thrown interceptions less frequently, and has as many postseason wins as the Canton-bound Wild West gunslinger who loves to play the game. Yet the football hype machine paints Favre as this hallowed icon of Americana and a symbol of all that is right with sports. Meanwhile, Vick is portrayed as an overmatched bumbler who's constantly scrambling down the field because he doesn't know what he's doing in a structured offense.

"I don't see commentators and reporters saying certain things about other quarterbacks that they say about me when they're making mistakes," Vick said. "It's like I'm the worst person in the world when I throw an interception.

Other guys go out, throw four or five interceptions in one game, and it's all good. Nobody talks about it. I throw one, and I'm not doing my job."

Who might he be speaking of?

Favre has thrown four or more interceptions twice in the playoffs, including once in 2001 against a Rams team that hadn't intercepted more than two passes in a game *all year*.

Vick? He's thrown three interceptions in four career playoff games.

Favre was the best in the game once upon a time. Those days are gone, even if nobody wants to admit it. And that's why he makes this list of the most overrated quarterbacks.

Postscript: Favre is the only NFL quarterback to throw six interceptions in a playoff game in the last 50 years.

3. TERRY BRADSHAW

Terry Bradshaw gets conveniently lumped in there with Tom Brady, Joe Montana, and Troy Aikman because of his four Super Bowl rings, which are a tremendous accomplishment. But while Bradshaw deserves a lot of credit for winning four Super Bowls—and playing very well in two of them—he was ultimately an average quarterback who was surrounded by the greatest cast of talent ever assembled on one NFL roster.

He had a Hall of Fame running back behind him, Hall of Fame receivers on either side, and a Hall of Fame center snapping him the ball. You can make the argument that Bradshaw helped put them in the Hall of Fame. But you can't make that argument about the defense. And the defense in the years the Steelers won Super Bowls never had fewer than four future Hall of Famers on it. Heck, Rex Grossman could win four Super Bowls with eight Hall of Fame teammates. (In his short career, the hapless Grossman has a *higher* career passer rating than Bradshaw, a *higher* completion percentage than Bradshaw, and a *better* career touchdown-to-interception ratio than Bradshaw.)

Bradshaw's four Super Bowl rings obscure the fact that other than a handful of big playoff games, he was largely a mediocre passer. His 70.9 career passer rating places him 108th out of 148 quarterbacks in NFL history. His

51.9 completion percentage is even worse. Only 28 of the 148 quarterbacks in NFL history who've thrown 1,500 or more passes have completed a lower percentage than Bradshaw. For his career, he threw only two more touchdowns than interceptions.

Of the 17 Hall of Fame quarterbacks whose careers began in 1950 or later, only Namath completed a lower percentage of his passes than Bradshaw did. In fact, of the eight quarterbacks who have started 20 or more games for the Steelers, Bradshaw ranks seventh in franchise history in completion percentage (ahead of only Mark Malone) and sixth in passer rating (ahead of Malone and Bubby Brister). Which puts him behind the likes of Kordell Stewart, Neil O'Donnell, Ben Roethlisberger, Tommy Maddox, and Mike Tomczak in both categories.

Was Bradshaw indispensable to the Steelers during their unprecedented Super Bowl run, or was he just lucky to be along for the ride? In 1974 Chuck Noll benched Bradshaw to open the season, and backup Joe Gilliam went 4–1–1 in six starts before Noll went back to Bradshaw. In 1976 Bradshaw missed six games with injuries, and backup Mike Kruczek went 6–0. During the Steelers' six-year run from 1974 through 1979, the period including four Super Bowl titles, Bradshaw went 46–19 and his no-name backups were 11–1–1.

Bradshaw has a well-deserved reputation as a big-time postseason performer, and he was twice a Super Bowl MVP. But his final tally in 19 playoff games was a pedestrian 30 touchdowns and 26 interceptions. In his four Super Bowls, Bradshaw completed just 49 passes, fewer than Kurt Warner completed in just two Super Bowls.

How did the Steelers win four Super Bowls? Franco Harris ran the ball 101 times—17 more times than Bradshaw threw it. And the Pittsburgh defense allowed just 60 total points, 15 per game to the best teams the NFC could come up with.

Certainly Bradshaw played a huge role on those teams. But without him would the result have been any different?

Postscript: Bradshaw had only four 300-yard passing performances in 168 regular-season games.

4. KEN STABLER

Here's how critical Kenny Stabler was to the Oakland Raiders: they traded him after the 1979 season and proceeded to win two Super Bowls in the next four years with a middle-aged journeyman who had never taken a postseason snap or made it to a Pro Bowl in nine NFL seasons.

Stabler was a talented enough quarterback to manage a Super Bowl win with the Raiders in 1976. He completed 12 passes in that game, four of them timely throws to Fred Biletnikoff, who was named MVP. Stabler's quarterback rating in that game was terrific: 111.7. But the Raiders ran the ball 52 times, and their defense stifled Fran Tarkenton. That's why they won.

The Raiders were actually more successful once they jettisoned the Snake.

Tom Flores replaced Hall of Fame coach John Madden after the 1978 season, and one year later, the Raiders shipped Stabler to the Houston Oilers for Dan Pastorini. When Pastorini broke his leg five games into the 1980 season, with the Raiders sputtering along at 2–3, Flores turned in desperation to Jim Plunkett, who was with his third team in six years and had thrown 85 touchdowns and 118 interceptions in his eight previous seasons. All Plunkett did while Stabler was toiling in anonymity in Houston and New Orleans was lead the Raiders to Super Bowl triumphs over the Eagles in 1980 and the Redskins in 1983, compiling what was at the time the highest Super Bowl passer rating in history and which, nearly a quarter of a century later, remains second-best ever behind Montana.

Meanwhile, Stabler only won one postseason game in his last eight seasons after that 1976 Super Bowl, and he never won a playoff game in five seasons after leaving the Raiders.

Stabler threw more touchdowns than interceptions in only four of the 11 seasons in which he threw at least 75 passes. When his career ended, he had thrown 28 more interceptions than touchdowns—the 17th-highest differential in NFL history.

Stabler was a shaggy-haired, bearded wild man whose exploits with women, fast cars, late parties, and booze were the stuff of legend and were eventually detailed in his 1986 autobiography, *Snake*. As the years have gone by, Stabler's reputation has grown larger than life. But his stats haven't.

Postscript: Ken Stabler was drafted in 1968 by Oakland Raiders scout Ron Wolf, who 23 years later acquired Brett Favre from the Atlanta Falcons while he was with the Green Bay Packers.

5. TONY ROMO

When Tony Romo replaced Drew Bledsoe in the second half of a Cowboys game against the Giants in October 2006 and threw a couple touchdowns, the TV hype machine kicked into high gear. When he passed for 270 yards in a win over the Panthers a week later, the buzz got louder. When he toppled the undefeated Colts at Texas Stadium in mid-November, it was out of control. And when he passed for 306 yards and five touchdowns over Tampa on national TV on Thanksgiving Day, it became a full-blown frenzy.

"I thought it was Aikman out there," Buccaneers coach Jon Gruden said after the game.

It was actually Cowboys hotshot quarterback Romo, and by the time he won his fourth-straight game, there was no turning back. The hype was out of control. Romo had been tagged the Next Great Thing, and nothing was going to change it.

How meteoric was Romo's rise to the top of the football universe? During the Tampa game, a fan sitting in a luxury box hung a *faux* Ring of Honor banner with Romo's name alongside the real ones honoring Bob Hayes, Tony Dorsett, Bob Lilly, and 14 other all-time Cowboy greats. Romo was named to the NFC Pro Bowl team after just eight NFL starts—a first. He even landed himself a famous girlfriend, *American Idol*–winner Carrie Underwood.

Not so fast.

Once Romo's reputation had been established, he plunged steadily and helplessly back toward mediocrity. He lost four of his last five starts and generated just 37 points in his last three games against winning teams. After tying a franchise record with those five touchdowns against Tampa and the Bucs' 19th-ranked pass defense, Romo threw more interceptions (eight) than touchdowns (seven) in his last six games.

Romo has plenty of talent and a big arm, and even with his late-season reunion with reality he still led all NFL quarterbacks with a beefy 8.6 yards per pass. But he also ranked 13th in the league in interceptions despite throwing only the 25th-most passes. Romo only had to play one NFC East team twice, but in that one rematch with the Giants, he didn't throw a touchdown and was intercepted twice by the only team that got to prepare for him twice.

Maybe Romo will become a consistent winner and do something no Cowboys quarterback since Aikman has done—win a playoff game. The Cowboys' 2006 wild-card loss to the Seahawks had more to do with Romo's inability to hold a field-goal snap than his quarterbacking.

After one season, Romo became a full-fledged superstar without really accomplishing anything to deserve it. And that's something Underwood can certainly understand.

Postscript: Tony Romo was the fourth-string quarterback in Cowboys training camp in 2004 behind starter Quincy Carter, veteran Vinny Testaverde, and rookie Drew Henson, and he was in danger of being released. But the Cowboys released Carter when he was admitted into the NFL's substance-abuse program, and Romo made the team.

The Most Underrated Quarterback of All Time

BART STARR

The Packers were one yard from the 1967 NFL Championship. They trailed the Cowboys 17–14 at arctic Lambeau Field, and they had just used their final timeout. The field was a slippery sheet of ice, the wind was blasting in off Lake Michigan. It was so cold that the officials couldn't use their whistles because the metal would freeze to their lips.

The clock was stopped with 16 seconds left. Plenty of time for a field goal. But in those conditions? No way. Coach Vince Lombardi decided that the Packers would either win in regulation or lose in regulation and called a running play for burly Chuck Mercein. But quarterback Bart Starr had other ideas. He changed the play but told no one in the huddle. Center Ken

Bowman snapped the ball, Starr kept it, ran behind Jerry Kramer's block, and scored the winning touchdown.

It was one of the greatest plays in NFL history, and it shows up in the record books as a simple one-yard run.

Stats don't even begin to tell the story of Starr, who played in the shadow of Johnny Unitas but outperformed even the Colts' great, winning more championships than any quarterback in NFL history and, in the end, proving himself superior to even Johnny U.

Back in the 1960s, Starr was dismissed as simply a caretaker of the great Packers teams that made an annual habit of winning NFL championships. He never passed for 2,500 yards in a season, never threw more than 16 touchdowns in a season, and he averaged just 16.5 attempts per game during his 14 years as a starter. But forget the numbers for a second and consider this: Starr won five NFL championships in his career—as many as Unitas, Brett Favre, Steve Young, and Dan Marino *combined.*

Unitas was considered the greatest quarterback of his generation, and during the 16 years their careers overlapped, from 1956 through 1971, Unitas was by far the bigger name. Starr was supposedly the beneficiary of a team that had 10 different Hall of Famers in uniform during the championship years, while Unitas was perceived as the engine that made those great Colts teams go.

That perception is wrong.

Starr is the only quarterback in history to win five NFL championships and the only one to win three in a row. He lost just one of 10 career playoff starts, and that was the first one, the 1960 NFL Championship game against the Eagles at Franklin Field. His .900 career playoff winning percentage is the best in NFL history. And he compares favorably in every way to Unitas. This isn't just about winning titles, it's about playing extraordinarily well in huge games.

Unitas played in two NFL Championship games and two Super Bowls. He completed 44 percent of his passes in those games, with two touchdowns and six interceptions.

Starr played in six NFL Championship games and two Super Bowls. He completed 59 percent of his passes in those games, with 13 touchdowns and three interceptions.

Unitas posted a career playoff passer rating of 68.9, with seven touchdowns and 10 interceptions. Starr posted a career playoff passer rating of 104.8, the highest in NFL history, safely ahead of number-two Joe Montana (95.6) and light-years ahead of Unitas. Starr threw just three interceptions in 213 career postseason attempts, and when Tom Brady of the Patriots threw four interceptions during the 2006 playoffs, Starr reclaimed the career record for fewest interceptions per pass attempt in NFL postseason history.

Who else has shattered an NFL record *35 years after throwing his last pass?*

Starr's 58 percent regular-season career completion percentage might not sound that impressive in an era when David Carr is completing 68 percent of his passes. But when Starr retired, that 58 percent completion percentage was an NFL record.

Even though Starr played most of his career before the merger, he's one of only six quarterbacks to win more than one Super Bowl, and his average of 9.6 yards per pass is second-highest in Super Bowl history.

Starr may not be the greatest quarterback in history, but he's the most underrated. And he's not to be forgotten.

Postscript: Bart Starr finished his career with more NFL titles (five) than Pro Bowl appearances (four).

The Rest of the Most Underrated

2. LEN DAWSON

Okay, try to keep a straight face. It's time to compare Len Dawson and Joe Montana. Seriously.

- Dawson led the league in passer rating four times. Montana led twice.
- Dawson led the league in completion percentage eight times. Montana led five times.
- Dawson averaged 7.7 yards per pass in his career. Montana averaged 7.5 yards per pass.

- Dawson led the league in touchdown passes four times. Montana led twice.
- Dawson had six seasons with 20 or more touchdowns, the same as Montana.
- Dawson started every one of his team's games 11 times. Montana started every game in a season three times.
- Montana won four championships. Dawson won three.

Dawson's name is rarely suggested when the greatest quarterbacks in NFL history are discussed, but he was Montana before Montana, the most accurate passer of his generation and a champion in two leagues. This is not to insult Joe, but to help us remember Len.

When Dawson retired after the 1975 season, his 19th in pro football, his 57.1 completion percentage was second-best in NFL history, his 239 touchdowns were fourth-most in history, and his 82.6 passer rating was third-best.

Dawson served as a backup with the Steelers and Browns in his first five seasons, and he didn't even start a game until he was 27 years old and with his third team, the Dallas Texans of the AFL. But once he finally got his chance, he was unstoppable.

In 1962, his first year as a starter, Dawson became the first player in history to throw 29 touchdowns and complete 60 percent of his passes in the same season, and he led the Texans to the AFL Championship with a double-overtime win over the Oilers. After the franchise moved to Kansas City, Dawson added a second title, with two touchdown passes against the Bills in the 1966 AFL title game before losing to the Packers in Super Bowl I.

In Super Bowl IV, after the 1969 season, Dawson helped the Chiefs stun the heavily favored Vikings, with Dawson selected MVP of the final game played before the AFL-NFL merger. In his two Super Bowls, Dawson completed 63.6 percent of his passes, still fourth-best in Super Bowl annals behind Aikman, Montana, and Brady. Thirty years after he retired, Dawson still ranked 16th in NFL history with his 239 touchdowns.

Was Dawson Montana's equal? Of course not. Nobody is. But the comparison isn't at all far-fetched. Yet Dawson wasn't inducted into the Hall of Fame until five years after he became eligible, and he has never been accorded the same elite status as many quarterbacks whose accomplishments pale in comparison. He should be.

Len Dawson commanded the attention of his teammates, won three championships, and has the stats to rank among the greatest quarterbacks ever. (Photo courtesy Getty Images)

Postscript: Len Dawson backed up Earl Morrall and Bobby Layne in Pittsburgh and Milt Plum in Cleveland before finally becoming a starter with the Texans/Chiefs.

3. KENNY ANDERSON

Kenny Anderson and Terry Bradshaw both spent their largely overlapping careers in the AFC Central, with Anderson quarterbacking the Bengals from 1971 through 1986 and Bradshaw leading the Steelers from 1970 through 1983. And while Bradshaw has been immortalized as a four-time Super Bowl champion, a Hall of Famer, and supposedly one of the greatest quarterbacks of all time, Anderson has been largely forgotten, although he was actually far more accurate, threw for more yards, had fewer interceptions, compiled a far higher passer rating, and was even picked to more Pro Bowl teams than Bradshaw was.

What Anderson didn't have was a Super Bowl team around him.

Bradshaw played alongside eight Hall of Fame teammates and spent his entire career with a Hall of Fame coach, Chuck Noll. Anderson played for five different coaches and had the luxury of just two Hall of Fame teammates, offensive tackle Anthony Muñoz, who didn't join the Bengals until Anderson's 10th season, and Charlie Joiner, who didn't begin to establish his All-Star credentials until he left for San Diego after three-and-a-half mediocre seasons with Cincinnati.

Yet despite all this, Anderson's numbers not only hold up against Bradshaw's, they surpass his. After his final year as a starter, 1984, Anderson owned the seventh-best passer rating in NFL history at 82.0. After Bradshaw's final year as a starter, the strike-shortened 1982 season, his passer rating was 70.7, which didn't even put him in the all-time top 20. Only twice in their overlapping 12 years as starters did Bradshaw have a better passer rating than Anderson did.

Only seven quarterbacks have led the league in passer rating twice in a row. Anderson did it twice in a row *twice*—the only quarterback in NFL history to do that. And only Hall of Famers Steve Young and Sammy Baugh led the league in passing more than Anderson did.

Anderson's career passer rating was 82.0. Bradshaw only reached 82.0 in a *single season* three times in 13 years as a starter.

Anderson led the NFL in best interception percentage three times, the second-highest in NFL history, and set NFL records for both highest completion percentage in a season (still standing) and in a game (now number two of all time).

Despite operating in an offense built around the short passing game and designed by the Bengals' first quarterbacks coach, West Coast offense architect Bill Walsh, Anderson still averaged 7.3 yards per attempt in his career—higher than Bradshaw's 7.2.

Anderson and Bradshaw were both athletic and mobile. Bradshaw had more than 2,200 rushing yards and a gaudy 5.1 average, but Anderson also had more than 2,200 rushing yards and an even gaudier 5.6 average.

What about the playoffs? Bradshaw was the Man in the playoffs, right?

Here's the most shocking part of the Anderson-Bradshaw comparison: Bradshaw has those four Super Bowl rings, but Anderson was a *far* better postseason passer. In fact, more than 20 years after he retired, Anderson still holds the NFL record for the highest career postseason completion percentage at 66.3 percent. Bradshaw completed 57.2 percent of his passes in the postseason. That's pretty good and considerably higher than his 52 percent regular-season mark, but it's a far cry from Anderson's figures.

Anderson also owns the fourth-highest postseason passer rating in NFL history at 93.5, higher than 21 of the 23 modern-era quarterbacks in the Hall of Fame, including Bradshaw and his solid but unspectacular 83.0 rating.

Anderson made the list of Hall of Fame finalists in 1996 and 1998, but he hasn't been back since. He's the greatest eligible quarterback not in the Hall of Fame.

Put him in.

Postscript: On opening day 1981, Kenny Anderson threw three first-half interceptions against the Seahawks and was benched in favor of Turk Schonert with the score 21–0. Schonert rallied the Bengals to a win, but Anderson got his job back, threw only seven interceptions the rest of the season, and was named NFL MVP.

4. RANDALL CUNNINGHAM

Randall Cunningham was 35 years old when he finally found his way to a team that bothered to surround him with some offensive talent. And once he got a chance to play alongside real, live NFL players, he put together one of the greatest seasons any quarterback has ever had. Just imagine if

Cunningham had had the opportunity to play in a real offense earlier in his first 12 NFL seasons. Instead, Cunningham was incorrectly branded as an athletic marvel who wasn't smart enough to play quarterback.

Cunningham had a splendid career despite spending most of it with a team that had no running game, no capable wide receivers, and the worst offensive line ever assembled. Never in his first four years as a full-time starter did the Eagles have a running back with 700 yards or a wide receiver with 800 yards. Yet despite getting no help from the people around him and getting sacked at a record pace, he was already finding ways not only to win but to generate remarkable passing numbers. Cunningham went 38–22 during those four years, with 98 touchdowns and 56 interceptions. He was as close to a one-man show as there's been in modern NFL history, even leading the Eagles in rushing four straight years.

When the Eagles finally put some talent around him—they had a 1,000-yard rusher and a 1,000-yard receiver in 1992 for the first time since Cunningham started playing—the results were immediate. Cunningham won his first playoff game, beating the Saints in New Orleans.

But it wasn't until he retired to a life cutting granite, then unretired a year later to play with the high-octane Vikings, that Cunningham finally got to play in a big-time NFL offense—with Robert Smith, Randy Moss, and Cris Carter (who had played with Cunningham briefly in Philadelphia but was battling personal problems and had not yet emerged as a star).

In 1998, his one full season with that high-flying Minneapolis cast, Cunningham generated an NFL-record 556 points and earned his second MVP award. And if not for some dubious fourth-quarter coaching by Dennis Green and a missed 38-yard field goal by Gary Anderson against the Falcons in the 1998 NFC Championship game, Cunningham would have reached a Super Bowl and solidified his Hall of Fame credentials.

As it is, despite not playing with a Pro Bowl offensive lineman until his 12th season, Cunningham finished with a sparkling 82–52–1 won-loss record, which was second-best, percentage-wise, among active quarterbacks with 100 or more starts when he retired, behind only Brett Favre. Cunningham is in the NFL record book with the highest rushing average in NFL history. (His 6.4 mark is more than a full yard-per-carry better than Jim Brown's.) He also set an NFL record with 4,928 career rushing yards by a quarterback and scored 35 touchdowns on the ground to go with his 207 in the air. Cunningham even blasted a 91-yard punt on a quick kick against the Giants, the third-longest punt in NFL history.

The big knock on Cunningham was always that, yeah, he was a great runner, but he couldn't read defenses like all those brainy Super Bowl–winning NFC East quarterbacks—Troy Aikman, Phil Simms, and Mark Rypien. But Cunningham threw 42 more touchdowns and seven fewer interceptions than Aikman did and eight more touchdowns and 23 fewer interceptions than Simms managed, and he had a higher completion percentage and passer rating than Rypien did.

Cunningham retired with a touchdown-to-interception ratio of 1.5, the fourth-best in NFL history among the 28 quarterbacks with 200 or more touchdown passes, trailing only Joe Montana, Steve Young, Peyton Manning, and Dan Marino—the four greatest pure passers ever.

That's why Cunningham is so vastly underrated: he wasn't simply a brilliant scrambler who could use his legs to create something out of nothing, like conventional wisdom says. He was also a brilliant passer.

Postscript: Randall Cunningham was sacked an NFL-record 72 times in 1986 despite only 209 pass attempts. That's one sack every four times he dropped back to pass.

5. DAVID KRIEG

Journeyman. The word conjures up images of some hapless bottom-of-the-barrel lifetime backup scrambling from team to team as he desperately tries to squeeze another year of paychecks out of his fading career.

David Krieg played for the Seahawks and the Chiefs. He played for the Lions and the Cards. He played for the Bears and Oilers. He definitely qualifies as a member of the Journeyman Quarterbacks Club.

All of which has clouded what's really important: Krieg could play. His numbers compare favorably with just about anybody who's ever played the game. He just happened to play for a lot of teams.

Every quarterback in NFL history with more career passing yards or more touchdown passes than Krieg who was eligible for the Hall of Fame was inducted in either his first or second year.

Krieg's detractors like to point to his 494 sacks and 153 fumbles, which are both the second-most in NFL history. But those numbers had more to do with the fact that during his 12 years with the Seahawks, the team with which he spent most of his career, he *never* took a single snap behind a Pro Bowl offensive lineman.

Following the 1996 season, Krieg's final year as a starter, he ranked seventh in NFL history in pass attempts, seventh in completions, 16th in completion percentage, eighth in passing yards, and seventh in touchdowns. Only Montana, Elway, Marino, and Warren Moon ranked higher in each category, and all four of them were *first-ballot* Hall of Famers. Krieg has never even been a finalist in the round of 15.

Krieg threw 261 touchdown passes in his underrated career, more than all but six of the quarterbacks enshrined in the Hall of Fame. And his touchdown-to-interception ratio of 1.3 is tied for fourth-best of the 15 quarterbacks in history with 5,000 or more pass attempts.

He didn't win a Super Bowl, but neither did Dan Fouts, and Krieg threw more touchdowns and fewer interceptions than Fouts in overlapping careers. Krieg went to three Pro Bowls and won five playoff games—two more than Fouts managed.

Krieg was one of the most successful quarterbacks in NFL history even though nobody realizes it, and that's why he makes this list complete.

Postscript: David Krieg was inducted into Wisconsin's Milton College Athletic Hall of Fame in 1985, three years after Milton College closed.

CHAPTER 4

Wide Receivers

The Most Overrated Wide Receiver of All Time

LYNN SWANN

In his best season—his *best* season—Lynn Swann ranked seventh in the NFL in receiving yards and tied for seventh in catches. Wesley Walker, John Jefferson, and Reggie Rucker had more yards. Rickey Young, Tony Galbreath, and Pat Tilley had more catches. Not quite elite company. And that was his best season.

Swann was an important member of the Steelers' Super Bowl dynasty, and until Jerry Rice came along, he was the Super Bowl yardage record holder. He's one of only five wide receivers named Super Bowl MVP, and he had a knack for finding the end zone, scoring 51 career touchdowns, with nine more in the playoffs.

Swann made some of the most graceful, acrobatic catches anybody has ever seen, notably during the last three of the Steelers' four Super Bowl triumphs in the 1970s. There was the 64-yard touchdown in the fourth quarter of Super Bowl X, when Swann outran Cowboys cornerback Mark Washington for the clinching touchdown. And the 32-yarder down the right sideline in the same game to set up Randy Grossman's touchdown. There was the 18-yarder way in the back of the end zone in Super Bowl XIII against the Cowboys. And the 47-yard touchdown against the Rams in the third quarter of Super Bowl XIV, when Swann out-leaped Nolan Cromwell and Pat Thomas at the 2-yard line on his way into the end zone. Clutch plays. *Historic* plays.

We all have those plays etched in our collective memory banks. That's what we know about Swann: an all-timer. The problem with Swann is that there's nothing beyond those Super Bowl plays that separates him from the pack. Look past a few games—indeed, look past a few *catches*—and Swann suddenly becomes a mere mortal, a serviceable receiver and little else.

Set aside the Super Bowls for a moment. Swann never approached 1,000 yards in a season. He caught 50 passes once. He caught fewer passes in his career than Rice once had in a three-year span.

Swann averaged 37 catches, 607 yards, and 5.7 touchdowns in his nine NFL seasons. Great numbers—for a nickel receiver. Comparable to Drew Bennett, who has averaged 46 catches, 672 yards, and 4.2 touchdowns in his first six NFL seasons.

Robert Brooks of the Packers once had more 100-yard games in a single *season* (nine) than Swann had in 116 regular-season games (eight).

And this: Swann caught fewer passes in his career than Torrance Small, the poster boy for wide-receiving mediocrity. That alone should be grounds for impeaching him from the Hall of Fame.

Drew Bennett? Robert Brooks? Torrance Small?

Going into the 2007 season, Swann ranked 243rd in NFL history with 336 catches, 167th in NFL history with 5,462 yards, and 84th with 51 touchdowns. Yet, he's among only 18 wide receivers whose bust sits in the Hall of Fame gallery.

Reggie Langhorne, Marty Booker, Frank Sanders, Brett Perriman, Darnay Scott, and Bobby Engram all have more career catches and yards than Swann.

Bobby Engram?

Even the perception of Swann as a postseason legend isn't accurate. Outside Super Bowls X and XIII, Swann averaged just 2.6 catches for 44 yards in 14 postseason games.

Although he had a flair for the dramatic and a dynamic personality that made him one of the most popular members of the Steelers during their 1970s championship run, he wasn't even the best receiver on his own team. John Stallworth had three 1,000-yard seasons and four years with at least 900 yards—a plateau Swann never reached. And Stallworth was also the superior postseason receiver. Swann had two career playoff 100-yard games. Stallworth had five, an NFL record when he retired and still the third best in history. Stallworth—not Swann—holds the Super Bowl career record for yards per catch and is the only player in history to catch a touchdown in eight straight postseason games.

If not for a handful of Super Bowl catches, nobody would perceive Swann as a superstar, nobody would have considered him for the Hall of Fame, nobody would have voted for him for governor.

Three games—no matter how brilliant, no matter how important—don't make a career. And Swann's is the most overrated of any receiver in history.

Postscript: Lynn Swann received 39.6 percent of the vote in the 2006 Pennsylvania gubernatorial election to 60.4 percent for incumbent Democrat Ed Rendell.

The Rest of the Most Overrated

2. TERRELL OWENS

The one time in his 11-year career his team reached a Super Bowl, it got there without him, which speaks volumes about Terrell Owens.

Owens has piled up some remarkable stats since entering the NFL with the 49ers in 1996. Lots of catches, tons of yards, reams of touchdowns. He's also managed to render all those catches, yards, and touchdowns meaningless by single-handedly destroying every team he's been with. By 2003, Owens had alienated three-time Pro Bowl quarterback Jeff Garcia and worn out his welcome with the 49ers. By the middle of 2005, he'd alienated five-time Pro Bowl quarterback Donovan McNabb and worn out his welcome with the Eagles. And it took him only one year in Dallas to drive Hall of Fame coach Bill Parcells into retirement.

Owens was actually fairly normal early in his career. He was a humble, soft-spoken kid, respectful to his teammates and coaches. As he became more dangerous on the field, however, he became more unpredictable off it. In 2000 and 2001 he had consecutive 1,400-yard seasons, something only Jerry Rice and Marvin Harrison also achieved. He sure looked every bit like a budding Hall of Famer. But he had changed. He started to believe his image. And he began to value that image more than the reality on the field.

And that meant he was blasting his coaches, ripping his teammates, and shredding team chemistry, which effectively neutralized all the on-field pyrotechnics. That's why Owens is so overrated. No matter how many passes

Terrell Owens's dubious style has eclipsed his substance, and while he may have piled up some decent stats during his career, his impact on the teams he has played for has not always been positive. One of his coaches with the 49ers said, "At first, he was 90 percent Terrell Owens and 10 percent T.O. By the end, he was 10 percent Terrell and 90 percent T.O."

he catches, no matter how many touchdowns he scores, no matter how many Pro Bowl teams he's picked to, he ends up damaging his team. He can't help it.

"He's like a wild bronco," longtime NFL quarterback and TV analyst Boomer Esiason said. "Every cowboy thinks he can control him, but there are some broncos that nobody can saddle."

Owens began his career playing alongside Rice, who didn't have to brag to convince people he was the greatest receiver of all time. With Rice and Owens together, the 49ers won playoff games in 1996, 1997, and 1998, advancing to the NFC Championship game in 1997. But without Rice, Owens hasn't won a thing. During the eight-year period from 1999 through 2006, Owens was in uniform for one postseason victory. His lifetime playoff record is 4–6, but without Rice it's 1–4, and in three of those five games he had 40 or fewer receiving yards.

The 2004 Eagles were forced to play their first two postseason games without an injured Owens, and they won both easily. With Owens back, they lost to the Patriots in the Super Bowl.

So during the last eight years, Owens's teams have won more postseason games *without* him than *with* him.

Owens got his catches in the Super Bowl—nine for 122 yards—but he always gets his catches. He just never wins anything.

Owens led the NFL with 15 dropped passes in 2006, according to Stats Inc. In the Cowboys' wild-card loss to the Seahawks and their 19th-ranked defense, Owens caught two passes for 26 yards. And for the seventh time in eight years, his season ended without so much as a single playoff victory.

"When it comes to this game, I'm the best in the field," Owens yelped in a 2006 rap single.

If being the best means ignoring your coaches, infuriating your teammates, and dropping more passes than anybody in the league, he's absolutely right.

Postscript: In 2005 Terrell Owens told Eagles offensive coordinator Brad Childress not to speak to him, according to testimony during his suspension hearing. He's quoted as saying, "Why do you talk to me? I don't talk to you. You don't talk to me. There's no reason for you to talk to me."

3. CRIS CARTER

Few wide receivers in NFL history did less with more than Cris Carter, who took the concept of possession receiver to an absurd extreme.

Carter was a dependable pass catcher with tremendous leaping ability and a knack for scoring touchdowns that nearly matched his knack for discreetly pushing off opposing cornerbacks. Marvin Harrison will catch him soon, but entering 2007 Carter was number two in NFL history in catches and touchdowns. He'll almost certainly be in the Hall of Fame one day, and rightfully so.

Carter's fatal flaw, and what separates him from the truly magnificent wideouts of his generation, is his microscopic yards-per-catch figure. In NFL history, there have been 526 1,000-yard seasons turned in by wide receivers. In only six of those 526 seasons has a receiver averaged 11.2 yards per catch or less.

Carter is responsible for *two* of those six seasons.

In 1995 he averaged 11.2 yards per catch, the sixth lowest ever by a 1,000-yard receiver. One year earlier, he averaged 10.3 yards per catch, the worst ever.

So Carter owns two of the six worst per-catch averages in a 1,000-yard season in NFL history. Carter finished his career with 12.6 yards per catch. Of the 489 wide receivers in NFL history who had at least 100 career receptions through 2006, Carter ranked 451st, just behind James Thrash and just ahead of Derrick Mayes. James Lofton caught 337 fewer passes than Carter, but he had more yards. And Carter played 12 of his 14 seasons as a starter with the Vikings, which means half of his career games were in a dome, with controlled conditions and a fast surface that should have been conducive to long plays down the field.

One of Carter's underrated teammates was Steve Jordan, whose career overlapped for five years with Carter in Minnesota. Jordan had a higher career receiving average than Carter at 12.7.

Jordan was a tight end.

Carter never ranked in the top six in the NFL in receiving yards and never had more than 1,371 yards in a season, a plateau 39 receivers have topped, including such household names as Yancey Thigpen, Rob Moore, and Marcus Robinson.

Carter was a terrific underneath receiver, and his 130 touchdowns are second-best in history. He was a critical piece of one of the most electrifying offenses in NFL history and a clutch big-game player. But the popular notion that his sheer volume of receptions automatically makes Carter one of the handful of best receivers ever is flawed. He caught them. He just didn't do that much with them.

Postscript: Cris Carter pleaded guilty in 1988 of lying to a grand jury during the racketeering and mail fraud trial of sports agent Norby Walters. When the Eagles faced the Lions in a preseason game in August 1988, the fans at the Silverdome began a rhythmic chant of, "Norby, Norby, Norby," when Carter took the field.

4. RANDY MOSS

Six years into his NFL career, Randy Moss was doing the unthinkable. He was outplaying Jerry Rice.

Moss amassed 525 catches, 8,375 yards, and 77 touchdowns *all before his 27th birthday*. After six seasons, Moss claimed 79 more catches, 509 more yards, and eight more touchdowns than Rice had after his first six years.

"To me, he's better than Rice," Cowboys defensive coordinator Mike Zimmer said on ESPN's *Sports Century* series. "Moss has more speed, more size, and just as much shake. He can be the best ever."

He should have been the best ever. He had the pure talent. He had the fire. With his stunning leaping ability, rangy frame, pulsating speed, and superb hands, he simply could not be covered. And after six years he was on track to one day unseat Rice as the top wide receiver in history.

Moss was in the perfect system in a bombs-away offense with the Vikings. He played in the perfect stadium, the Metrodome speedway ideally fitting his speed and cutting ability. He was blessed with cannon-armed quarterbacks Randall Cunningham, Jeff George, and Daunte Culpepper, who each loved to chuck the ball down the field. Moss had that aura of greatness. He won battles before the ball was snapped. Defensive backs were in such desperate fear of Moss that they routinely provided a soft cushion to prevent the huge play. So Moss caught mid-range passes and then exploded past them anyway.

Then something happened. Moss turned 27 and lost interest in football. He got into trouble. He started sulking. The aura disappeared. His numbers plummeted. In 2004, his last season with the Vikings, he was overshadowed and outplayed by teammate Nate Burleson, and for the first time Moss didn't reach 1,000 yards. Didn't even reach 800. In 2005 Moss went to the Raiders and struggled through an even worse season. And in 2006 he not only stopped catching passes, he admitted that he didn't play hard if he didn't feel like it—despite an $8.25 million base salary.

"My concentration and focus level tend to go down when I'm in a bad mood," Moss said.

He must have been in a lot of bad moods, because in 2006 Moss ranked 78th in the NFL with 42 catches, 73rd with 553 yards, and 60th with three touchdowns.

And those comparisons with Rice? You don't hear them anymore. After outperforming Rice in his first six years, Moss became a pedestrian player the next three. In seasons seven through nine, Moss had 111 fewer catches, 1,585 fewer yards, and 15 fewer touchdowns than Rice did.

By opening day 2007, Moss will have turned 30 years old and will be four years removed from his last Pro Bowl. He's not getting younger, and he's not getting better.

And he's not getting any less overrated.

Postscript: Randy Moss was fined $25,000 in 1999 after squirting an official with a water bottle during the Vikings' playoff game against the Rams.

5. KEYSHAWN JOHNSON

Maybe his book should have been called *Just Give Me the Damn 7-Yard Out!* Keyshawn Johnson has spent the last decade demanding the football, blasting his quarterbacks, feuding with his coaches, and bragging about his own vast playmaking ability to anybody who will listen. But when you call your autobiography *Just Give Me the Damn Ball*, you better be able to back it up.

Johnson yaps like a superstar receiver, but he catches the football like a big ol' lumbering fullback. Although he did make three Pro Bowl teams and win a Super Bowl ring early in his career, Johnson has now gone five straight years without a Pro Bowl nod and four straight years without a 1,000-yard season.

But the most amazing thing about Johnson is how rarely he's actually turned in big plays during his career. He's played 167 games and has just one career touchdown catch longer than 43 yards. Lee Evans had two touchdowns longer than 80 yards in the span of *six minutes* against the Texans in 2006. Johnson has had one touchdown catch longer than 43 yards in 11 years. That hasn't stopped him from hosting a national radio show called *Taking It to the House.*

By the time the 2006 season ended, Johnson had gone more than 4.5 seasons without catching a pass longer than 40 yards. His last one came on October 6, 2002, when he was with the Buccaneers (three teams ago). With 4:32 left in the third quarter of a game against the Falcons at the Georgia Dome, he caught a 76-yard touchdown pass from Brad Johnson. Since then, 263 NFL players have made at least one reception of 41 yards or more. None are named Keyshawn Johnson.

During the last 11 weeks of 2002, 82 players caught passes longer than 40 yards, including Jason McAddley, Trevor Gaylor, and Cecil Martin.

In 2003, 99 players caught passes longer than 40 yards, including Justin Gage, Kassim Osgood, and Chris Hope.

In 2004, 118 players caught passes longer than 40 yards, including John Stone, David Kircus, and Randy Hymes.

In 2005, 119 players caught passes longer than 40 yards, including Shawn Bryson, Chris Horn, and Nathan Poole.

In 2006, 104 players caught passes longer than 40 yards, including Jason Wright, Malcolm Floyd, and Jamal Jones.

Since week five of 2002, Andre Johnson, Bethel Johnson, Bryant Johnson, and Chad Johnson have receptions of 40 yards. But *Keyshawn* Johnson doesn't.

Talking about big plays doesn't make them happen. Even in his one monster season, with Tampa back in 2001, Johnson became the only receiver in NFL history to catch 100 passes in a season without scoring at least four touchdowns. He had one—against the 2–14 Lions, who allowed an NFL-high 30 touchdown passes that year. Along with Michael Irvin in 1998,

Johnson is one of only two players in NFL history with 1,000 receiving yards in a season but just one touchdown.

Johnson's career average of 13.0 yards per catch ranks 426th of the 489 wide receivers in NFL history with 100 or more receptions through 2006. In the six years from 2001 through 2006, Johnson caught only 25 touchdown passes. Some 35 receivers (and five tight ends) had more during the same span. Johnson has never led the NFL in a major receiving category, and he's never even finished in the top three. He's only shown up in the top 10 in yards twice (seventh in 2001 and 10th in 1998), in touchdowns once (tied for sixth in 1998), and in catches three times (sixth in 1998 and 1999, and fourth in 2001).

Johnson has a book, he's got endorsements, he's had huge contracts, he's got the inflated reputation that comes along with being one of only two receivers taken with the first pick in the last 40 years. But that doesn't add up to stardom. He's a decent possession receiver and a willing blocker. Nothing more.

Postscript: Keyshawn Johnson is the only player in NFL history to catch a touchdown pass on Monday Night Football *with four different teams: the Jets, Buccaneers, Cowboys, and Panthers.*

The Most Underrated Wide Receiver of All Time

MARVIN HARRISON

Marvin Harrison's problem is that he's not an egotistical, loudmouth jerk. He hasn't bragged about his $10 million signing bonus in a rap CD, he hasn't invented an antagonizing end zone dance, he hasn't even been arrested yet. What's his problem? How does he expect to be accepted into the fraternity of obnoxious superstar wide receivers without an attitude?

Harrison is quiet, he's shy, he's humble, and he's a reluctant interview. With so many character flaws, it's shocking that he's even allowed to play wide receiver in the NFL.

All Harrison has done the last decade is to compile a set of receiving numbers that tower over the efforts of his more annoying contemporaries.

Marvin Harrison has quietly dominated at a position known for its brash personalities.

The one receiver who truly deserves to boast about how great he is seems to be the one guy who refuses to do it. Because of his reticence, Harrison has played in relative anonymity while loudmouths like Randy Moss, Keyshawn Johnson, and Terrell Owens are lavished with far more attention. But on the field, Harrison is by far their superior.

Harrison is so obsessive about shunning the spotlight that he once told *Sports Illustrated* that he'd rather not go into the Hall of Fame.

"If it doesn't happen, that will be fine with me because that means I'm not going to give a speech," he said.

Oh, he'll definitely be making that speech. Five years after he retires, Harrison will be a first-ballot Hall of Famer, an honor reserved so far only for Raymond Berry, Lance Alworth, Paul Warfield, and 1987 strikebreaker Steve Largent.

But Harrison has compiled his world-class numbers so quietly that they're easy to overlook. He's already number three in history in receiving touchdowns, number four in catches, and number six in yards. With 80 catches, 1,238 yards, and nine touchdowns in 2007—a typical year—Harrison will move into second place in NFL history (behind Jerry Rice) in all three categories.

During the eight seasons from 1999 through 2006, Harrison averaged 103 catches for 1,402 yards and 13 touchdowns. Ponder that for a moment.

Rice only had two single seasons where he outperformed Harrison's numbers during an eight-year span. Only four other receivers—Sterling Sharpe, Herman Moore, Isaac Bruce, and Randy Moss—have had one such season. And that's what Harrison averaged over eight seasons.

Harrison's 59 100-yard games are second-best in history, again trailing only Rice. Harrison has played 170 games and caught a pass in each one, an NFL record. He was fastest in NFL history to 600, 700, 800, 900, and 1,000 receptions. He has 80 more catches after 11 seasons (1,022) than Rice. Harrison had four straight 100-catch seasons. Only six other players have ever had two in a row.

Rice averaged 5.1 catches, 76 yards, and 0.65 touchdown catches per game in his peerless career. Harrison can top that. He's averaged 6.0 catches, 81 yards per game, and 0.72 touchdown catches per game.

Is Harrison merely a product of Peyton Manning's vast talent? In the two years before Manning arrived in Indianapolis, Harrison averaged 69 catches, more than 850 yards, and seven touchdowns per season playing with Jim Harbaugh, Kelly Holcomb, and Paul Justin. Is he merely a product of having Reggie Wayne opposite him? Wayne wasn't even around for Harrison's first five seasons, and Harrison already had surpassed 1,400 yards twice.

In 2002 Harrison caught 143 passes, breaking Herman Moore's NFL record by an unthinkable 20 receptions. Harrison has just one 100-yard game and two touchdowns in 14 postseason appearances, but he's actually averaged a respectable 4.3 catches and 60 yards in those 14 games. And, unlike Moss and Owens, Harrison now has a Super Bowl ring.

He may be the greatest ever by the time he retires, but unless he invents a celebratory touchdown dance or writes a self-aggrandizing autobiography or gets himself arrested for cocaine a couple times, few will notice.

"He doesn't need to be in the newspapers like T.O. He's not saying 'Just give me the damn ball,' like Keyshawn," said Donovan McNabb, Harrison's college quarterback at Syracuse. "He doesn't care about all that stuff. He's never cared about it. That's why he's so underrated. He doesn't care about himself or his stats, and he doesn't do anything to draw attention to himself. He just wants to win. That's enough for him."

Postscript: Marvin Harrison was the fourth wide receiver taken in the 1996 draft. The Jets made Keyshawn Johnson the first pick, the Patriots selected Terry Glenn seventh, and the Rams picked Eddie Kennison 18th.

The Rest of the Most Underrated

2. JIMMY SMITH

Jimmy Smith has made a living out of being underrated and unappreciated. Not just during his 11-year career with the Jaguars but all his life. How else can you explain one of the most accomplished wide receivers in NFL history not even getting a chance to catch a pass until he was nearly 27 years old?

Smith played his college football at Jackson State, which, despite producing Walter Payton and Oil Can Boyd, is hardly an athletic powerhouse. Smith was drafted by the Cowboys but never caught a pass for them and was released after two years. He was signed by the Eagles, only to be released before opening day so head coach Rich Kotite could keep Jeff Sydner on the final roster instead. Yes, Jeff Sydner.

Any team could have had Smith for nothing that summer, but nobody bothered, and he spent the season out of football, his career seemingly dead before he caught a pass. But the Jaguars were about to enter the league the following fall, and pro personnel director Ron Hill and wide receivers coach Pete Carmichael were looking everywhere for long shots to fill the expansion roster.

"Pete kept saying to me, 'There is something about this kid. There is something about this kid,'" said Giants coach Tom Coughlin, the Jaguars' head coach during their formative years. "He rose from a young man who, within a three-year period, was on his third team and had nothing but disappointment and failure to look back upon. But to his credit he just got better and better and better. And by the second half of the 1996 season, he was as good a receiver as there was in the National Football League."

Smith's name rarely comes up when the top receivers in NFL history are discussed, only because his entry into the NFL was so inauspicious and his emergence took so long. But before he was finished, he had more catches than Steve Largent, more yards than Michael Irvin, and more touchdowns than Lynn Swann. When Smith retired, only five receivers in NFL history had more catches and yards. All this even though he didn't catch a pass until the ninth game of his third season, when he was three months shy of his 27th birthday.

When Chad Johnson turned 27, he already had 282 catches. When Smith turned 27, he had 288 *yards*.

But once he got started, Smith quickly made up for lost time. He generated two seasons with 112 or more catches and at least 1,300 yards. Only seven other players have ever had *one* such season.

During the 10 years from 1996 through 2005, Smith averaged 84 catches for 1,200 yards. Only Jerry Rice and Marvin Harrison have ever averaged more receptions and yards during a 10-year span.

But Smith wasn't just putting up hollow numbers during the regular season. He helped the Jaguars grow from a lowly 4–12 expansion franchise in 1995 to an AFC powerhouse that reached the playoffs five times in the next 10 years. And Smith shined in the postseason, averaging 4.5 receptions for 72 yards with seven touchdowns in nine playoff games. It was Smith who caught what proved to be the winning touchdown pass from Mark Brunell in Denver when the Jaguars stunned the Broncos in a 1996 conference semifinal playoff game, the most important play in franchise history.

Smith might be the best player in NFL history to be released by two teams. And Jeff Sydner's final career numbers? Three catches. Or 859 fewer than Smith.

Postscript: Jimmy Smith challenged the Cowboys after they refused to pay him for the 1993 season, which he missed after suffering a dangerous infection following an appendectomy. Cowboys owner Jerry Jones claimed that because an appendectomy is not a football-related injury, the Cowboys were not responsible for Smith's salary. An arbiter ruled in Smith's favor.

3. ANDRE REED

Andre Reed never had that one massive season that landed him a bunch of big-money endorsements and late-night TV appearances. He never quite made it to the magical 100-catch plateau that seems to elevate so many receivers into the realm of superstardom. He never led the NFL in a major statistical category, although he came close several times. No, Reed's career with the Bills was one of dogged consistency, not fleeting brilliance. He rarely dazzled, but when he finished playing football in 2000 after 16 seasons, the numbers had somehow become dazzling when nobody was looking.

There are several reasons Reed has flown under the radar despite being one of the finest receivers in history. He played college ball off the beaten path at Kutztown State in remote Northeastern Pennsylvania. He was a lightly regarded day two draft pick. He spent 15 of his 16 seasons playing somewhere along the Canadian border in western New York State, so he never received the media attention those who ply their trade in New York, Chicago, or Washington receive. And there were those four Super Bowl losses.

All Reed did was put together one of the most productive careers of any wide receiver in NFL history, despite playing all but six of his 112 home games in Orchard Park, New York, in some of the most bitter conditions in the NFL.

Reed played on four Super Bowl teams, performed at a consistently high level in the postseason, and generated career numbers that rival the best receivers in history. He was bypassed by the Hall of Fame selection committee in both 2005 and 2006 and had to endure watching Michael Irvin's enshrinement in 2006, even though Reed finished with 201 more catches,

1,294 more yards, and 22 more touchdowns than Irvin and had almost identical postseason numbers.

Only Rice has more seasons (17) with 50 or more catches than Reed (13). During the 15-year period from 1985 through 1999, Reed had more yards and more catches than anybody in the league other than Rice. Although Reed only managed four 1,000-yard seasons during his 10 healthy seasons, from 1988 through 1998, he actually averaged *more than* 1,000 yards per season. And his 13.9 per-catch average is second-best of the six receivers in history with 900 or more catches (behind Rice, naturally).

The Bills may have lost four Super Bowls, but don't blame Reed. He caught 27 passes for 323 yards in those four-straight Super Bowl defeats. Only Rice has caught more Super Bowl passes than Reed, and only Rice and Swann have more Super Bowl yards. In 19 postseason games, Reed caught 85 passes and topped 100 yards five times. Both marks are third-best in NFL history, behind Hall of Famers Rice and Irvin. Reed's 1,230 postseason receiving yards rank number four of all time behind Rice, Irvin, and Cliff Branch.

Reed is one of the best to play the game, and all the Super Bowl losses in the world can't change that.

Postscript: When the Bills rallied from a 35–3 third-quarter deficit in a 1992 wild-card game to beat Warren Moon and the Oilers 41–38 in the biggest comeback in NFL history, Andre Reed caught touchdowns of 26, 18, and 17 yards from Frank Reich.

4. LIONEL TAYLOR

A generation before modern receivers like Jerry Rice and Marvin Harrison were putting up huge receiving numbers, a quarter of a century before Herman Moore and Torry Holt were catching 90 passes per season, and decades before wide receiver evolved into the glamour position it is today, Lionel Taylor was providing a glimpse of the future.

Four days after joining the Broncos one month into the 1960 season, Taylor caught 11 passes against the Raiders. By the time the season ended just 10 weeks later, he had an NFL-record 92 receptions in just 12 games, a pace that nearly half a century later has been exceeded only twice.

Taylor spent most of his career with the premerger Broncos, and although the NFL absorbed all the AFL stats and records, Taylor had retired by the time the two leagues combined in 1970. Unlike many AFL stars, he never had the chance to display his considerable skills on the larger stage of the NFL, and he never earned the reputation he deserved.

Taylor wasn't fast, but he had the softest hands in the game. He obsessively studied opposing cornerbacks, and he knew how to find and exploit their weaknesses. And in an era when nobody else in either the AFL or NFL was catching 80 passes in a season, Taylor averaged 85 per season from 1960 through 1965, the first six years of the AFL.

During that same six-year period, the NFL receiving leader—and it was a different player each season—averaged 78 catches per season. Taylor caught 508 passes from 1960 through 1965—95 more than anybody in either the AFL or NFL. From 1960 through 1966, only one other player, Johnny Morris of the Bears, had as many receptions in any season as Taylor *averaged.* Morris caught 93 passes in 1964.

Taylor led all of professional football—the AFL and NFL—in receptions four straight years, from 1960 through 1963, and again in 1965. And because all AFL performances were adopted by the NFL, Taylor is officially in the record books as one of only two players in NFL history to lead the league in catches five or more times. Don Hutson, who played in the 1930s and 1940s, did it eight times. Taylor and Hutson are also the only players to lead the league in catches at least four straight years.

In 1960 Taylor became the first to catch 90 passes. A year later, he became the first to catch 100. It was another 23 years before anybody in the NFL reached the 100-catch plateau. He reached 300 career receptions in just 54 games, a record that stood until Anquan Boldin got there in 47 games.

Taylor played long before ESPN, before nightly highlight shows, before mammoth contracts, before 'round-the-clock NFL coverage. But the numbers don't lie. Taylor was a pioneer. No matter how few people recognize his name.

Postscript: Lionel Taylor was an assistant coach with the Steelers on two of their Super Bowl teams in the 1970s. Colts coach Tony Dungy, moments after becoming the first African American head coach to win a Super Bowl, singled out Taylor as one of the African American assistant coaches who should have had the opportunity before he did.

5. STERLING SHARPE

Sterling Sharpe's brilliant career should have ended with a halftime celebration at Lambeau Field, tens of thousands of fans roaring their appreciation, Brett Favre throwing one more ceremonial pass his way, and then five years later another ceremony, this one in Canton. Instead, it ended with a press release.

On March 1, 1995, the Packers issued a six-paragraph statement announcing that Sharpe's neck injury would make it impossible for him to play football again. The statement read, "We therefore are terminating his contract, with reluctance."

Sharpe's career was severely shortened. Thus Sharpe is not considered one of the all-time greats. But he should be. And not by projecting what *could* have been had he stayed healthy but merely by examining what Sharpe accomplished before he was forced to retire.

Sharpe averaged 85 catches, 1,162 yards, and nine touchdowns in his seven seasons with the Packers. He was playing at such a remarkable level when his career ended that he caught 18 touchdown passes in his final season. Only Jerry Rice has ever caught more touchdown passes in *any* season.

Despite never playing a game after his 30th birthday, Sharpe led the NFL in catches three times—more than Jerry Rice, more than Cris Carter, more than Andre Reed, and more than Tim Brown. Nobody else since the AFL-NFL merger in 1970 has led the NFL in catches three times, and only Don Hutson (eight times in the 1930s and 1940s) and Lionel Taylor (five times in the AFL in the 1960s) have led their league more than Sharpe did in half a career.

Sharpe was the first and second player in NFL history with at least 108 catches in a season. And for the first 60 years that the National Football League existed, Sharpe was the only wide receiver who had 108 or more catches twice. Nobody else did once. And he was also the first player with consecutive 100-catch seasons.

Sharpe was also huge in both his playoff appearances—11 catches, 229 yards, and four touchdowns. And although Sharpe did enjoy some masterful seasons playing with Favre, he actually averaged 70 catches for 1,070 yards and made an All-Pro team in four seasons *before* Favre arrived in Green Bay, playing mainly with Don Majkowski and Mike Tomczak.

If Sharpe hadn't gotten hurt, he may have rivaled Rice. He may have *surpassed* Rice. Sharpe had 75 more catches than Rice had after seven years.

Forget projecting what could have been. Even in half a career, Sharpe accomplished more than nearly anybody else in a full career. But he only played seven seasons. He didn't speak with the media, and he predated the Packers' Super Bowl seasons, so Sharpe has never gotten the credit he deserves for all he was able to squeeze into seven short seasons.

Postscript: Sterling Sharpe's career ended the year before the Packers won the Super Bowl in 1996. After his brother Shannon won his first Super Bowl with the Broncos two years later, Shannon gave Sterling his Super Bowl ring. When Broncos owner Pat Bowlen heard about this, he had a new ring made for Shannon.

CHAPTER 5

Defensive Backs

The Most Overrated Defensive Back of All Time

JASON SEHORN

He carried himself like a superstar, he married like a superstar, and he made the gossip pages like a superstar. The only problem was that Jason Sehorn rarely played football like a superstar.

Sehorn spent eight of his nine NFL seasons with the Giants, and the largest media market in the Western Hemisphere served him well. He was likable and well-spoken. He was bright and quotable. He was good-looking and hung around with the Madison Avenue cognoscenti. The camera loved him and so did the fans. Back in the late 1990s, the sporting goods stores made a fortune selling Sehorn's No. 31 Giants jerseys to kids from Syosset, New York, to Secaucus, New Jersey.

He had the looks and the reputation and a celebrity wife in actress Angie Harmon of the hit TV show *Law and Order*, and all that outside stuff overshadowed something kind of important: Sehorn wasn't very good. He recorded just 19 interceptions in nine NFL seasons—a little more than two per year. He was always hurt, averaging just 8.4 starts per season and managing a full 16 starts only once.

There were occasional moments of brilliance early in Sehorn's career. In a playoff game against the Eagles in 2000, Sehorn made a juggling sideline interception off Donovan McNabb while lying on the ground, righted himself, and ran 32 yards for a touchdown that sealed the Giants' 20–10 win. A week later, in the NFC Championship game, Sehorn limited Vikings All-Pro receiver Randy Moss to two catches—a 13-yarder and a five-yarder—and intercepted a Daunte Culpepper pass intended for Cris Carter in the fourth quarter of a game the Giants won 41–0 to reach the Super Bowl.

But the highlights were few and far between. And one of Sehorn's lowest moments came when the lights shone the brightest, in his only Super Bowl, Super Bowl XXXV, against the Ravens in Tampa two weeks after that win over the Vikings.

With the game still scoreless in the middle of the first quarter, Trent Dilfer spotted Sehorn trying to cover Brandon Stokley. Dilfer fired Stokley a pass inside the Giants' 10-yard line. Sehorn attempted to make a touchdown-saving tackle at the 5-yard-line, but Stokley broke free and scored. The 38-yard touchdown got the Ravens rolling on their way to a 34–7 rout.

In Sehorn's last 63 games, he had just eight interceptions. He was so bad that after the Rams beat the Giants in a 2001 game, Rams coach Mike Martz told reporters, "We just keep running by Jason, that's all I know," and, "I'd like to line up against Jason Sehorn every day of the week."

Strangely, Martz actually signed Sehorn two years later and tried to convert him into a safety, an experiment that lasted 10 games before Sehorn finally retired.

Despite playing in an era when the NFC East was jammed with outstanding cornerbacks—Darrell Green, Troy Vincent, Aeneas Williams, Deion Sanders—Sehorn led the league in hype. But even during his two decent seasons, 1996 and 1997, Sehorn only finished 11th and fifth in the league in interceptions.

If you're going to propose to your girlfriend on *The Tonight Show with Jay Leno* while Leno cackles along, you better have at least one Pro Bowl on your résumé. Sehorn didn't.

His play on the field never measured up to his play off it. And that's why he's the most overrated defensive back in NFL history.

Jason Sehorn, the most overrated defensive back in NFL history, watches Deion Sanders, one of the most underrated defensive backs in NFL history (playing wide receiver on this play), make a touchdown catch against him in a 1996 game.

Dolphins safety Brock Marion was once asked by *The Miami Herald* who the most overrated player in the NFL was. "I've got two, actually," he replied. "Jason Sehorn. He does all this stuff off the field, and he isn't that good. And I should say Warren Sapp, too, but I've got to take that back. He talks a lot, but he produces, so let's leave Sehorn alone there."

Postscript: While at Shasta College in Redding, California, in 1991, Jason Sehorn set a national junior college football record with 506 all-purpose yards in a game against Solano Community College of Fairfield. The record stood until 2001, when Jonathan Smith of Pasadena City had 515 against Cerritos.

The Rest of the Most Overrated

2. ROY WILLIAMS

It's called the Roy Williams rule, and it was approved after the 2004 season in a vote of the NFL owners for the sole purpose of banning the dreaded horse-collar tackles made famous by the Cowboys safety. In 2004 alone Williams single-handedly caused serious injuries to future teammate Terrell Owens of the Eagles (broken leg, torn ligaments), Tyrone Calico of the Titans (torn anterior cruciate ligament), Jamal Lewis (sprained ankle), and Musa Smith of the Ravens (broken leg) by grabbing the inside of their shoulder pads and slamming them to the ground while Williams crow-barred his leg into the ankle or lower leg of his victim.

The Cowboys voted against the proposal. But 27 of the 31 other NFL teams voted in favor of it, enough to officially outlaw the horse-collar, which now draws a 15-yard penalty.

Fifteen yards is a bargain considering the yardage Williams usually gives up.

Williams is an outstanding hitter, a physical if inconsistent tackler, and an intimidating presence in the Dallas secondary at his strong safety post. The only problem is that he can't cover. He makes a couple of bone-crushing hits each game and an occasional highlight-reel interception, and that's enough to guarantee him an annual ticket to the Pro Bowl.

But what about that one other little tiny thing defensive backs are supposed to do? *Cover people?* That's a problem.

Before strong safety Darren Woodson retired with a neck injury after the 2003 season, the Cowboys were able to hide many of Williams's deficiencies because Williams could hang out along the line of scrimmage and use his might as a virtual linebacker. But the last three years, with Woodson gone, Williams has been forced to roam more in the deep secondary. And he's been exposed.

With their alleged superstar Pro Bowl strong safety, the Cowboys in 2006 allowed 25 touchdown passes—the second-most in the NFL. With the season on the line, the Cowboys gave up 16 passing touchdowns and an average of 279 aerial yards in their last five games, losing their grip on first place in the NFC East. Then they allowed two more passing touchdowns in their wild-card loss to the Seahawks.

Let's watch some film from 2006.

In a loss to the Eagles in October, Williams was matched up against rookie wide receiver Hank Baskett, who had four receptions in his career entering the game. But Baskett, who went undrafted because of his lack of speed, beat Williams down the sideline for an 87-yard touchdown—the longest touchdown catch by an undrafted rookie in 56 years.

In a loss to the Giants in October, Eli Manning completed a 50-yard touchdown pass to Plaxico Burress when Williams *ran into one of the officials in the end zone*. Then Manning completed a 13-yard pass to Jeremy Shockey, who beat Williams for the touchdown.

In a three-point loss to the Redskins in November, Williams was called for a 48-yard pass interference penalty on Brandon Lloyd, setting up a fourth-quarter touchdown.

In a crushing 42–17 home loss to the Saints in December, Williams bit on a fake reverse, and Drew Brees took advantage, hitting Devery Henderson for 50 yards down to the 2-yard line, setting up a touchdown.

In the Cowboys' wild-card loss to the Seahawks, Williams missed a tackle on Bobby Engram's 36-yard catch-and-run that set up a field goal, got beat for a 15-yard touchdown by tight end Jerramy Stevens, and was late to help linebacker Bradie James on Stevens's 37-yard game-winning touchdown catch.

Williams can deliver monster hits, although he does use poor judgment, often going for the big hit instead of the sure tackle and allowing extra yards. He doesn't have great timing, often misjudging his leap. And the 10 or 15 pounds Williams has gained to help him smash opposing players has slowed him down a step in coverage. A significant step.

Williams turns in plenty of big plays, but he allows more. Far more than you'd expect from somebody whose $11.1 million signing bonus was the largest in NFL history for a safety and who, in 2006, was picked to his fourth-straight Pro Bowl team.

Postscript: Roy Williams was engaged to singer Kelly Rowland of the Grammy Award–winning R&B group Destiny's Child, but the couple broke up when Williams realized that he didn't know her very well. Rowland appeared on the cover of an issue of Modern Bride *magazine that hit the streets days after they called off their engagement.*

3. ROGER WEHRLI

They must be "the finest the game has produced," the Pro Football Hall of Fame tells its selectors when they're evaluating candidates for the highest honor in the land.

Roger Wehrli was a very slick player, smart and technically proficient, well respected around the NFL during the 1970s. But was he among "the finest the game has produced"?

The facts: Wehrli never had more than six interceptions in a season. He never led his conference in interceptions. He never even finished in the top five. Wehrli only outright led his own team in interceptions twice in 14 seasons, and he shared the lead two other times.

Teammate Norm Thompson only spent six years with the Cards—from 1971 through 1976—but he led the team in interceptions just as many times as Wehrli did in 14 seasons. In their six years playing together, Wehrli never had more interceptions than Thompson had. And from 1977 through 1982, Carl Allen had as many interceptions (16) as Wehrli. During those six years, Wehrli only had more interceptions than Allen had once.

Now, interceptions shouldn't be the only criteria to measure a cornerback. Wehrli's supporters claim he shut down the opposing team's best receivers so thoroughly that teams never even threw at him.

But the Cards ranked in the top 10 in the NFL defensively just twice in Wehrli's 14 seasons and never won a playoff game during that period. They were 0–3 in the postseason with Wehrli in uniform, allowing 30, 35, and 41 points and allowing seven passing touchdowns in those games to three quarterbacks (Fran Tarkenton, Ron Jaworski, and Lynn Dickey) who combined for just 29 passing touchdowns in those particular seasons.

Compare Wehrli with Bengals cornerback Ken Riley, whose career began the same year as Wehrli's (1969) and ended one year after Wehrli's (1983). In almost exactly the same time frame, Riley had 25 more interceptions, almost twice as many return yards (596 to 309), and more than twice as many touchdowns (five to two). Wehrli never had more than six interceptions in a season.

Riley had seasons with eight and nine. Yet Wehrli is in the Hall of Fame and Riley has never even made the final 15.

Wehrli never led his conference in interceptions. Riley led his conference three times.

Even the Hall of Fame's own official bio of Wehrli includes this unintentional slap in the face: "He registered an interception in all but two seasons during his career."

In other words, in two seasons he didn't have any interceptions.

Wehrli shouldn't be in the Hall of Fame, and by virtue of his surprising induction into the hallowed Hall in Canton, Ohio, in 2006—his 20th year of eligibility—Wehrli immediately cemented his status as one of the most overrated defensive backs in history.

Postscript: Roger Wehrli scored a touchdown in his final NFL game but not as a defensive back. Wehrli was the Cards' holder on place-kicks, and in the first quarter of a 24–21 win over the Giants at Busch Stadium on December 26, 1982, he scored on an 18-yard run on a fake field goal. Wehrli, who planned to retire after the season finale a week later, suffered a knee injury that ended his career later in the game.

4. DeANGELO HALL

"I'm the best."

Along with the boast comes the responsibility of backing it up. And by the second half of 2006, young Falcons cornerback DeAngelo Hall began to realize that calling himself the best cornerback in the league and actually playing like it were two entirely different things.

Hall's career got off to a hot start when he had a couple of interceptions as a rookie in 2004 and then earned his first Pro Bowl berth in 2005 after picking off six more passes. But he really excelled at bragging.

"I always feel like I'm the best guy out there," Hall told an Associated Press reporter after a game against the Eagles, a game in which he limited Terrell Owens to 112 yards. "When a guy catches a pass, it almost seems like luck to me. If a guy makes another catch, I'm like, 'Two? How did that happen?'"

Two? Try two dozen. By the end of 2006, Hall was invisible as the Falcons plunged toward the bottom of the NFL pass-defense rankings. He picked up four interceptions in the Falcons' first five games but had none in the next 11 games. He finished the season in a 15-way tie for 18th place in the NFL with his four interceptions.

Opposing quarterbacks had stunning success throwing deep against the self-professed best cornerback in football. Marques Colston caught a 45-yard touchdown against Hall in the first Saints-Falcons game, and Devery Henderson had a 76-yarder in the rematch. Hines Ward of the Steelers *lost a shoe* and still outraced Hall to the end zone for a 70-yard touchdown. Roy Williams of the Lions beat Hall on a 60-yard touchdown. T.O. beat Hall on a 51-yard catch just after teammate Terry Glenn beat Hall for 34 yards.

In the final seconds of the first half of the second Saints game, Drew Brees unloaded a Hail Mary from near midfield that Hall appeared to be in position to knock down. Instead, he tried for a stat-padding interception.

"I was being kind of lazy," Hall explained.

Terrance Copper of the Saints came down with the football and a 48-yard touchdown that turned a 14–6 lead into a spirit-crushing 21–6 advantage as the first half ended. The Saints went on to win 31–13.

"Everybody pumps him up like he's Deion Sanders," the Lions' Williams said. "But he's not Deion Sanders. He's DeAngelo Hall. He's not the shutdown type of corner that everybody expects him to be."

The Falcons in 2006 allowed an NFL-high five receivers to catch 138 yards or more in a game. Ward had 171 yards against the Falcons, the most of his nine-year career. Joey Galloway got 161 yards, second highest in his 12 NFL seasons. Henderson had 158 yards, his second-best game ever. Williams's 138 yards were the third-most of his career. Hank Baskett had 177 on the last day of the season—158 more than he averaged the first 15 games.

After Eagles third-string quarterback A.J. Feeley torched the Falcons for 324 yards on the last day of the season, Atlanta finished the year ranked 29th in the NFL in pass defense, ahead of only the Cardinals, Bengals, and Vikings. Yet Hall made his second-straight Pro Bowl team—and started!

That's what reputation gets you. Hall is fast and athletic, but what he does best is trash-talk. His penchant for getting personal with opposing receivers got him into feuds with Williams, Terrell Owens, Donte Stallworth, Chad Johnson, Steve Smith, and even Lions center Dominic Raiola, who, after Hall cheap-shotted Lions quarterback Jon Kitna, fumed, "I promise that if I see him on the field again, I'll take his head off. He's a cheap-shot artist."

After the Eagles beat the Falcons, Stallworth called out Hall, who had been taunting him on the field all day.

"He called me a bum," Stallworth said. "He kept saying he's been to two Pro Bowls and I haven't been to any. Well, this bum is going to be in the playoffs next week while that two-time Pro Bowler is out on the golf course or somewhere."

Postscript: When DeAngelo Hall recorded his first career interception on November 28, 2004, against Aaron Brooks of the Saints, he was 21 years and nine days old, making him the youngest player in NFL history to record an interception.

The Most Underrated Defensive Back of All Time

DEION SANDERS

You hear it all the time: Deion Sanders wasn't a great cornerback because he never tackled anybody. That's like saying Dan Marino wasn't a great quarterback because he couldn't run.

Sanders was the best cover corner in NFL history. Who cares how many tackles he made?

When you can stalk opposing receivers the way Sanders did, you can live with those few extra yards the running back just picked up.

With his astonishing makeup speed, remarkable instincts, and knack for reading quarterbacks, Sanders routinely blotted out the best receiver on the other side of the line of scrimmage. And once he got the football in his hands, Sanders became a magician. He was better than any defensive back in NFL history at transforming himself into an offensive weapon and going the other way with the football.

"There's two kinds of corners in the NFL," Bengals receiver Chad Johnson said. "Regular corners play not to get beat. Deion Sanders played the game to make a play."

The thing about Sanders is that there was always so much going on with him that tended to overshadow his performance on the football field. He played major league baseball, too, and wasn't bad. Sanders hit .263 in nine seasons and had a .533 average for the Braves in their 1992 World Series loss to the Blue Jays. He recorded a rap album that played off his nickname, Prime Time, with song titles like "House of Prime," "Time for Prime," "Prime Time Keeps on Ticking," "Must Be the Money," and "Y U NV Me?"

U can't spel!

Anyway, Sanders also hosted *Saturday Night Live*. He appeared in commercials for Nike, Burger King, Visa, and Pizza Hut. For a while there, he was everywhere, and the focus drifted away from Deion Sanders the cornerback to Neon Deion and Prime Time.

The image—the designer suits, the controversial interviews, the celebrity appearances—all served to distract people from just how astounding a player Sanders really was. And although he often came across as a cartoon character whose unparalleled speed and athleticism made up for his lack of true football ability, Sanders actually was a serious student of the game. His combination of preparation and physical skill made him the greatest shutdown cornerback ever. Even though opposing quarterbacks tried to throw nowhere near Sanders, he still finished his career with 53 interceptions in 189 NFL games, or one every 3.6 games.

And once the ball was in his hands, Sanders truly became Prime Time. His 1,331 career return yards are the second-most in NFL history, as are his nine touchdown returns. His average of 25.1 yards per interception return is an NFL record.

And, true to his nickname, he really was a prime-time player. He's one of only five cornerbacks in NFL history to win Super Bowls for two different teams, the 49ers in 1994 and the Cowboys in 1995. He had an interception in the 49ers' Super Bowl win over the Chargers, and he shares the NFL postseason record for at least one interception in three consecutive games.

Sanders was such a skilled cornerback that when he came out of retirement with the Ravens in 2004—*four years after he last played a game*—he had three interceptions in nine games, playing almost exclusively in nickel situations, then two more a year later at age 38.

Postscript: Despite playing in just 97 games, Deion Sanders led the National League with 14 triples while playing for the Atlanta Braves in 1992. He fell three short of the club record of 17 set in 1974 by Ralph Garr.

The Rest of the Most Underrated

2. KEN RILEY

Ken Riley is the greatest player in NFL history to never make a Pro Bowl team. His career measures up favorably with the best defensive backs in history. He should be a legend. He's not. Why has Riley never gotten his due?

He was only a sixth-round draft pick. Strike one.

He spent his entire career playing in obscurity in Cincinnati. Strike two.

He was quiet and humble and not given to talking about himself. Strike three.

The Bengals were a second year expansion team in 1969, and, other than the 1981 Super Bowl season, they just weren't very good during Riley's 15-year stay in Cincinnati. Strike four.

Wait, you can't have a *strike four!* Well, yes, but in Riley's case, everything is a little out of whack. Except how he played.

Riley was as consistent and productive as any cornerback during the 1970s, even though nobody really noticed. His 65 interceptions still ranks fifth in NFL history behind three Hall of Famers and Rod Woodson, a sure Hall of Famer as soon as he's eligible in 2009.

Riley had great hands, rarely dropped the football, and could have been a decent wide receiver if he wanted to be. He had five or more interceptions seven times, including in 1983, his final season, when he had eight at age 36. In 1977 he intercepted Joe Namath twice in Namath's final NFL game (and also picked off Richard Todd the same day).

Riley's finest season was 1976, when he led the NFL with nine interceptions, including one off the Packers' Lynn Dickey that he returned 53 yards for a touchdown. But somehow, even after that season, Riley was ignored by the Pro Bowl voters.

Why soft-spoken Bengals cornerback Ken Riley has not been inducted into the Hall of Fame, while those with much lesser stats have been enshrined, is a mystery. (Photo courtesy Getty Images)

While Riley was being ignored, his high-profile teammate Lemar Parrish was getting invited to the Pro Bowl just about every year. Parrish was terrific, but let's compare the two.

In 1974 Riley had five interceptions and Parrish had none. Parrish went to the Pro Bowl. Riley didn't.

In 1975 Riley had six interceptions and Parrish had one. Parrish went to the Pro Bowl. Riley didn't.

In 1976 Riley had nine interceptions and Parrish had two. Parrish went to the Pro Bowl. Riley didn't.

During that three-year span, Riley had 20 interceptions and Parrish had three, yet Parrish was picked to three Pro Bowl teams and Riley none.

Of the 27 players in NFL history with more than 50 interceptions, Riley is the only one who was never selected to a Pro Bowl team. The four players in the history of professional football with more interceptions than Riley were selected to a combined 35 Pro Bowls. Riley made none.

Riley was beyond underrated. He was criminally ignored.

Postscript: Riley spent the 1986 through 1993 seasons as head coach at his alma mater, Florida A&M, where he led the Rattlers to two Mid-Eastern Conference Athletic Conference championships and was twice named MEAC Coach of the Year.

3. DERON CHERRY

He started out as a walk-on at Rutgers. (Pause for dramatic effect.) A walk-on *punter!*

Stop right there for a moment and think about this. When Deron Cherry graduated from high school, there wasn't a single college that projected him as a Division I defensive back. And by the time he left Rutgers, there wasn't a single team that projected him as an NFL safety. So after he was ignored in the draft, Cherry signed as a punter with the Kansas City Chiefs.

As a punter, Cherry was overrated. As a safety, he was really underrated. *He wasn't rated at all.*

Not a single NFL team thought Cherry was worth even a 12th-round draft pick. For the record, here are some players who were drafted in 1981: Bob Shupryt, Major Ogilvie, Jairo Penaranda, Forrest Valora, Larry Friday. (An aside—Friday never played for the Browns, but he did get on the field six years after he was drafted as a 29-year-old rookie with the Bills' 1987 replacement team during the players' strike.)

It took Cherry a couple of years to convince somebody in Kansas City that he should actually be playing defense. But once he settled in at free safety, he quickly established himself as one of the league's best defensive backs.

Cherry's 50 interceptions are the most ever by an undrafted player, and he recorded 49 of them in his last eight seasons after playing sparingly in 1981 and 1982. He also had six 100-tackle seasons.

So why is Cherry's name rarely mentioned when people talk about the best safeties in football history? It didn't help that he played for a Chiefs team that only made the playoffs three times in his 11 seasons and won just one postseason game. Plus, in terms of major markets, Kansas City is somewhere just above Fort Wayne and just below Sacramento. Guys playing in Missouri in the pre-Internet age weren't getting a whole lot of media attention.

Ronnie Lott is considered the greatest safety of his generation and may be the greatest of all time. He's not only a Hall of Famer but also a first-ballot Hall of Famer. And deservedly so. Let's compare Cherry and Lott.

Both were rookies in 1981. Lott was the eighth player drafted. Cherry was not among the 332 players drafted. During the eight-year period from 1983—when the Chiefs finally let him actually play on defense—through 1990, Cherry had 45 interceptions. Lott had 42. Got that? Deron Cherry had three more interceptions than the great Ronnie Lott.

Cherry wasn't Lott's equal, but Lott is the measuring stick for defensive backs of the 1980s and 1990s and one of the greatest safeties ever. Cherry is right there. And he's been ignored. And that's why he prominently and deservedly makes this list.

Postscript: Deron Cherry intercepted four passes against the Seahawks on September 29, 1985. From 1979 through 1997, he was the only NFL player with four interceptions in a game.

4. DAVE BROWN

No, not *that* Dave Brown. Not the Dave Brown who was a lousy quarterback with the Giants and Cardinals in the 1990s.

Different guy. This Dave Brown played cornerback (and a year of free safety) at an extraordinary level during his 15 NFL seasons in the 1970s and 1980s but had the misfortune of being yanked off the Steelers roster in the 1976 expansion draft. He then spent most of his career with a fledgling Seahawks team that didn't even reach the playoffs until its eighth season.

Things could have been so different for Brown. The Steelers made him the final pick in the first round of the 1975 draft, and for one magical year, there he was, part of a dynasty that was on its way to winning four Super Bowls in six years. He played alongside Mel Blount, Jack Lambert, and Jack Ham, and two days after his 23rd birthday, he won a Super Bowl ring as a rookie when the Steelers beat the Cowboys 21–17 at the Orange Bowl.

But the NFL was changing. Two expansion teams paid a then-record sum of $16 million to join the NFL after the 1975 season, and on March 10, 1976, the league held a veteran allocation draft to help the expansion Buccaneers and Seahawks stock their rosters. Each existing NFL team was allowed to protect 29 players, but the Steelers, bursting at the seams with All-Pros and Hall of Famers, couldn't protect Brown. The Seahawks snapped him up.

And that's about the last anybody heard of Dave Brown. Instead of spending his career winning Super Bowls with one of the game's most historic franchises, Brown was sent to NFL Siberia, where he toiled in virtual anonymity for the next 11 years.

But while he was there, Brown set a franchise record that still stands: 50 interceptions, including five he returned for touchdowns. Of the 13 other defensive backs in NFL history with 57 or more interceptions, only one—Rod Woodson—returned more for touchdowns.

Brown finished his career with the Packers, where he added 12 more interceptions in three seasons. When he retired, he ranked fifth in NFL history, with 62 interceptions. Going into the 2007 season, 18 years after he played his last game, Brown still ranked seventh on the all-time interception list.

Brown had as many as eight interceptions in a season and nine years with four or more interceptions, but he was picked to only one Pro Bowl. From 1976 through 1986, he started 159 of a possible 165 games, and he still holds every major Seahawks interception record.

If not for the expansion draft, Brown would have been a sure-fire Hall of Famer with three Super Bowl rings. Instead, he's one of the most underrated defensive backs ever.

Postscript: On November 4, 1984, Dave Brown tied an NFL record by returning two interceptions for touchdowns of 90 and 56 yards in a 45–0 win over the Chiefs. Kenny Easley and Keith Simpson also returned interceptions for touchdowns for the Seahawks, whose four total interception returns for touchdowns set an NFL record that has not been matched. The Seahawks had 325 return yards in the game, still an NFL record.

CHAPTER 6

Offensive Linemen

The Most Overrated Offensive Lineman of All Time

RON YARY

It was the Vikings' turn to pick, but they weren't quite ready and had to skip a turn. So NFL Commissioner Pete Rozelle stood at a microphone and announced, "The Vikings pass."

Without skipping a beat, a fan in the audience at the 1975 NFL draft in New York immediately yelled, "And L.C. Greenwood knocks it down."

Everybody laughed because they remembered what Greenwood had done to the Vikings a few months earlier.

In Super Bowl IX, Greenwood dominated Vikings All-Pro offensive right tackle Ron Yary, knocking down three Fran Tarkenton passes in the Steelers' 16–6 win. Greenwood also busted past Yary to tackle Dave Osborn for a five-yard loss in the third quarter. The Vikings managed only 119 yards that day, still the fewest ever in a Super Bowl. They gained only 17 yards on 21 runs.

"They dominated us," Yary said after the game.

They dominated *you*.

Yary was a perennial All-Pro offensive lineman for the Vikings during their late 1960s and 1970s glory years, and in 2001 he was inducted into the Pro

Time after time, Minnesota Vikings offensive lineman Ron Yary seemed to play small in big games.

Football Hall of Fame. But in big game after big game, Yary was dominated by an opposing defensive end.

The Vikings reached four Super Bowls with Yary, but they scored only 34 points in those games and actually averaged just 7.0 points on offense. In their 11 postseason losses from 1968 through 1980, the Vikings averaged an abysmal 10.9 points per game.

Greenwood wasn't the only defensive end to give Yary a rough time in a Super Bowl. Everybody did. In Super Bowl VIII, after the 1973 season, Dolphins defensive end Vern Den Herder manhandled Yary, beating him for one sack of Tarkenton to help Miami's defense limit the high-powered Vikings offense to no pass plays longer than 30 yards and no runs longer than nine yards in a 24–7 win.

Three years later the Vikings faced the Raiders in Super Bowl XI. After Fred McNeill blocked Ray Guy's punt late in the first quarter of a scoreless game, the Vikings had a first-and-goal on the Oakland 3-yard line. Yary lined up at tight end opposite Raiders defensive end Phil Villapiano, who blasted past Yary so fast he reached running back Brent McClanahan at the same time as Fran Tarkenton's handoff, and Villapiano knocked the ball loose. Willie Hall recovered for the Raiders, who went on to a 32–14 win.

In Super Bowl IV, it was Chiefs defensive end Jerry Mays's turn to expose Yary. On the sixth play of the game, Mays beat Yary and stuffed Vikings running back Bill Brown for a one-yard loss after a short completed pass. With the Chiefs protecting a 3–0 lead in the second quarter, Mays blew past Yary and sacked Joe Kapp for a six-yard loss. By the time the Chiefs had finished off the Vikings 23–7, Minnesota had managed just 239 total yards and committed four turnovers.

Yary was a six-time All-Pro and a seven-time Pro Bowl starter. He annihilated people in the run game and was a generally overwhelming pass blocker who had to protect a quarterback who skittered around unpredictably. And Yary was durable, missing only five games in his 14 years with the Vikings.

But in the Super Bowl, Yary fell short. Not once, not twice, not three times, but all four times the Vikings got there.

Postscript: Ron Yary was versatile enough to play defensive tackle in the NFL. After his senior year at USC, he played offensive tackle against Indiana in the Rose Bowl and defensive tackle in the Hula Bowl all-star game.

The Rest of the Most Overrated

2. JIM LANGER

Jim Langer was an outstanding center, a stalwart on the Dolphins' offensive line during their heyday, a starter on two Super Bowl teams and on the NFL's last unbeaten team.

Was he a legend? Was he an icon? Was he one of the two or three greatest centers who ever lived? Was he dominating enough to be one of only two centers ever voted into the Pro Football Hall of Fame on the first ballot? Not even close.

Langer spent 10 years—the entire decade of the 1970s—with the Dolphins before finishing with a couple years in Minnesota. He was voted an Associated Press All-Pro three times. Outstanding credentials. All this after being undrafted out of South Dakota State.

But consider the company he's in. The only other center invited into Canton in his first year of eligibility was the incomparable Jim Otto of the Raiders, who earned first-team All-AFL or All-Pro honors for 11 consecutive years.

Other than Langer and Otto, only five offensive linemen have ever been admitted into the Hall of Fame in the first year of their eligibility. They are absolute giants of the game: Forrest Gregg, Gene Upshaw, John Hannah, Anthony Muñoz, Jackie Slater.

The first ballot should be reserved for only the immortals.

Langer simply does not belong in that group. But by finding his way into the Hall of Fame in 1987, the first chance he had, Langer's already-inflated reputation grew even more. First-ballot? He *must* be an all-timer.

It took Mike Webster two tries to get into the Hall of Fame. It took Dwight Stephenson five attempts. Jim Ringo was a finalist six times before he cobbled together enough votes. Yet Langer coasted in on his first try even though nobody believes he was in the class of Webster, Stephenson, or Ringo, the top centers in football history.

Mick Tingelhoff of the Vikings actually earned first-team All-Pro honors twice as many times as Langer—an unprecedented six straight years. Yet he's never even been a Hall of Fame finalist. Forrest Blue of the 49ers was a first-team All-Pro center three consecutive years, but nobody's even heard of him.

So why has this happened? The Dolphins' perfect 1972 season has been so thoroughly romanticized over the past three-and-a-half decades that there's been a tendency to romanticize nearly everybody on that roster. Langer wasn't a superhero, but because he played on that legendary team, he's been treated like one.

Langer started in Miami for only seven-and-a-half years, or nearly a decade less than Tinglehoff, who didn't miss a game for 17 years, from 1962 through 1978.

Three All-Pro seasons during a short career is hardly grounds for first-ballot induction into the hallowed grounds of Canton, Ohio. It is grounds for being overrated.

Postscript: The Jim Langer Award is given annually to the best offensive lineman in NCAA Division II, even though Langer was a linebacker when he was at South Dakota State.

3. LEONARD DAVIS

When Steelers offensive coordinator Ken Whisenhunt was named head coach of the Arizona Cardinals in January 2007, one of his first major decisions was what to do with Leonard Davis.

The massive but underachieving Davis was scheduled to become a free agent in a month, and Whisenhunt had to figure out whether the Cards should spend the money to keep the 28-year-old offensive lineman.

They certainly had the money—$24.8 million was available under the $109 million salary cap, the fourth-highest figure in the NFL. If they wanted Davis, they'd have no problem affording him.

But a few weeks after taking over the Cards, Whisenhunt issued a statement that, in effect, said there's no way Davis was worth the money he was about to make. The statement read, "When you look at the situation on the whole and take everything into account, we don't feel that the investment that would be required to keep him is equal to the performance."

Ouch.

In other words, *he's overrated.*

Davis certainly *looks* like a stud. He stands a colossal 6′6″, 365 pounds. He's a smart player and a durable one, with 91 starts out of a possible 96 games in Arizona. But he doesn't *play* like a stud. His footwork is average. He doesn't work hard enough. He's not as motivated as he should be. He's never made a Pro Bowl team. In his contract year of 2006, he committed 10 penalties.

Davis played right guard his first three years in Arizona and left tackle his last three years. During that span the Cards allowed 41 sacks per season. During that six-year period, they ranked 24th in sacks allowed and never ranked in the top half of the league in offense. Not all his fault, naturally, but if he really deserved the largest contract ever for a lineman, you'd expect something better than 24th-best in the league.

Nonetheless, Davis certainly has a reputation as a first-rate lineman. He was the second pick in the 2001 draft—behind only Michael Vick—and on March 4 he signed a contract with the Cowboys that included $18.75 million in guaranteed money, the most ever given an offensive lineman. If he plays out his entire seven-year contract with Dallas, he'll earn $49.6 million—*more than $7 million per year.*

But even the Cowboys' official team website said that Davis is overrated, acknowledging in a story that when he signed with Dallas, Davis had "never lived up to advance billing."

How often does a team give out nearly $20 million in bonus money to a player that the very team admits on its own website is overrated? So his former team and his current team both labeled him as overrated in the span of a few weeks. They're right. Davis is an average player with the reputation of a stud.

Postscript: Leonard Davis's nickname is "Big." He was 6', 205 pounds by the time he reached fifth grade, and he'd grown to 6' 4", 300 pounds as a seventh grader. He reached 360 pounds while he was still in high school.

The Most Underrated Offensive Lineman of All Time

JERRY KRAMER

His name has become synonymous with one of the most historic plays in NFL history. Packers right guard Jerry Kramer's block on Cowboys defensive tackle Jethro Pugh paved the way for Bart Starr's game-winning, one-yard touchdown plunge in the final seconds of the 1967 NFL Championship game, the legendary Ice Bowl.

In a way, that single play, that single block, may have done more damage than good to Kramer's reputation. That play has grown so iconic that the rest of Kramer's brilliant career has been, to a large degree, forgotten. But Kramer is one of the finest offensive linemen in history, and his career as a ferocious blocker and one of the giants of the Packers dynasty extended far beyond one miracle play in the final seconds of one mythic game.

Kramer spent his entire 11-year career with the Packers, walking away on his own terms after the 1968 season. He was tough. He was smart. He was fearless. He was an immovable force on all five of Vince Lombardi's NFL Championship teams, the last two of which won the first two Super Bowls. Kramer's specialty was pulling out on the power sweep, the Packers' signature running play under Lombardi. He overcame a litany of injuries that is simply unbelievable, undergoing more than a dozen operations during his career. But

Offensive lineman Jerry Kramer, shown here escorting Paul Hornung downfield on a sweep, was a cornerstone of the great 1960s Green Bay Packers. (Photo courtesy Getty Images)

his level of play never wavered, and he is, without question, one of the greatest guards in the game's history.

Kramer was versatile enough to kick three field goals in bitter conditions to help the Packers win the 1962 NFL title game over the Giants at Yankee Stadium, 16–7. He was powerful enough to help Jim Taylor become the first player in NFL history to rush for 1,000 yards five straight years. He was dominating enough to be the only guard named to the Hall of Fame's 50-Year Anniversary team in 1969. And he was respected enough to be picked to the Super Bowl Silver Anniversary team in 1991.

Despite an astonishing array of accomplishments and an overwhelming résumé, Kramer has been snubbed by the Pro Football Hall of Fame more than anybody in history. He has been a finalist 10 times—most recently as a senior committee nominee in 1997—but remains the best lineman in football history not enshrined in Canton. The only players to reach the round of 15 even more than Kramer are Lynn Swann, Carl Eller, Paul Hornung, and Tom Mack, and all four of them eventually were inducted.

Kramer is the only player selected to the 50-Year Anniversary team who is not in the Hall of Fame, which, when you think about that for a second, is absolutely stupid. And it must be corrected.

"Nobody deserves it more," Hornung told the *Milwaukee Journal Sentinel* in 1997. "He was the best guard during that whole era, not only on the Packers, but he was the best right guard in the business at that time. He defined his position for over 10 years as the best."

Why haven't the Hall of Fame voters accorded one of the most outstanding guards in history the greatest honor possible? There are already 11 players and a coach from those Packers teams of the 1960s in the Hall of Fame, and some voters believe that's enough. Certainly some of the old-guard selectors held it against Kramer that he wrote several insightful books about the Packers, including the best-selling *Instant Replay*, published in 1968.

Kramer has given the game so much, only to have his accomplishments inexplicably ignored year after year. Yet he isn't bitter. In fact, Kramer in 2007 established a charity to benefit aging former NFL players who can't afford the medical care they need to take care of themselves.

Seems he's underrated as a humanitarian, too.

Postscript: Jerry Kramer made four field goals in the Packers' win over the Steelers at County Stadium in Milwaukee on November 3, 1963, tying the Packers franchise record set by Paul Hornung. Kramer owned a share of the record for 27 years, until Chris Jacke made five field goals against the Raiders on November 11, 1990, at the L.A. Coliseum.

The Rest of the Most Underrated

2. JOE JACOBY

To win three Super Bowls during the 1980s and early 1990s, the Redskins didn't just have to be the best team in football, they had to be the best team in their own division. That meant they had to find a way to neutralize Giants linebacker Lawrence Taylor, the most feared pass rusher in the game. Without slowing down Taylor, the Redskins couldn't beat the Giants. And without beating the Giants, they couldn't win the NFC East. And without winning the division, they had little chance to get to the Super Bowl.

The man they picked for the impossible task was Joe Jacoby, who went undrafted out of the University of Louisville in 1981. But by the middle of his rookie year, Jacoby was starting at the critical left-tackle position, blocking quarterback Joe Theismann's blind side. Coach Joe Gibbs knew it would take a special player to deal with Taylor. Jacoby was 6′7″, 300 pounds, and unusually athletic for an offensive lineman. With a stud opposite Taylor, the 'Skins had a chance.

"We put him at left tackle for one reason, to match up against Lawrence Taylor," Redskins offensive line coach Joe Bugel said in Michael Lewis's book about left tackles, *Blind Side*.

How did it go?

During Jacoby's career, the Redskins swept the Giants four times and reached the Super Bowl each time—1982, 1983, 1987, and 1991—winning all but the second.

Taylor didn't play in the two Giants-Redskins games in 1987, but Jacoby held Taylor without a sack in four of the six other showdowns and limited him to one sack in a fifth game.

That's how critical Jacoby was to the Redskins.

Jacoby was one of the original Hogs, along with Mark May, Russ Grimm, Jeff Bostic, and George Starke, who had been with the Redskins since the early 1970s. Everybody knew about Theismann, running back John Riggins, and All-Pro receivers Art Monk, Gary Clark, and Ricky Sanders. But the Hogs were the heart of an offense that, in 1983, set an NFL record with 541 points and, from 1982 through 1992, ranked among the top six in the NFL in offensive yards eight times.

Once the Redskins got to those Super Bowls, they averaged 426 yards of offense and 193 rushing yards. Jacoby and Bostic were the only Hogs to start in all four. And it was Jacoby (along with Otis Wonsley) who sprung Riggins on his historic 43-yard touchdown run on fourth-and-1 five minutes into the fourth quarter of Super Bowl XVII against the Dolphins. That run gave the Redskins the lead for good at 20–17 on the way to their first Super Bowl triumph.

Jacoby only missed 12 non-strike games from 1981 through 1991, but when Taylor ended Theismann's career in 1985, gruesomely shattering his leg during a sack, Jacoby was on the sideline in street clothes with a bad knee.

Taylor was a first-ballot Hall of Famer and is considered by some the greatest defensive player ever. So what about the guy who shut him down in so many critical games?

Jacoby, who moved to right tackle when the Redskins acquired Jim Lachey in 1988, was named to the NFL's Team of the 1980s, but like the other Hogs, he's been ignored by the Hall of Fame. He superbly blocked Taylor, a Hall of Famer, and he blasted out holes for Riggins, another Hall of Famer. He was perhaps the best player on perhaps the best line in football history and a three-time Super Bowl winner. Yet Jacoby has flown under the radar from the start of his career, when no NFL team believed he was worth drafting, through retirement, where he's failed to receive the accolades he so richly deserves.

Postscript: When Redskins coach Joe Gibbs first saw the 6'7", 300-pound Joe Jacoby, he mistook him for a defensive lineman and told him he'd give him a shot at defensive tackle. Jacoby was so awed by Gibbs that he didn't correct him.

3. DONNIE MACEK

If Donnie Macek had stayed at right guard, he would have been picked to a handful of Pro Bowl teams and recognized not only as one of the key elements on the Chargers' record-shredding offense in the 1980s but also as one of the finest offensive linemen of his day.

Unfortunately, the Chargers didn't have a center.

So after a ho-hum 7–7 season in 1977, they went out and traded for three-time Pro Bowl right guard Ed White, who was in the middle of a contract dispute with the Vikings. White arrived, saw Macek, and was confused.

"They brought me in to play right guard, but when I saw the guy they had, I wondered why," White said. "The guy was great."

Macek was also versatile. With White on board, Macek swung inside to center, and the stage was set for an offensive explosion the likes of which the NFL had never seen before or since.

Under coach Don Coryell, who replaced Tommy Prothro four games into the 1978 season, the "Air Coryell" Chargers rampaged through opposing defenses for nearly a decade. They led the NFL in offense five times in six years, including 1980 through 1983, when they joined the Bears of the early 1940s as the only teams to lead the league in total offense four years in a row.

At one point over the 1982 and 1983 seasons, the Chargers surpassed 400 yards an NFL-record 11 straight games. They led the NFL in passing an astonishing six straight years, from 1978 through 1983, and again in 1985. Since 1940, no other team has led the league in passing more than three years in a row.

Those Chargers made four trips to the playoffs—their first since the AFL days in the mid-1960s—and sent quarterback Dan Fouts, receiver Charlie Joiner, and tight end Kellen Winslow to the Hall of Fame.

Behind the scenes was the Chargers' criminally underrated offensive line, with Billy Shields at left tackle, Doug "Moosie" Wilkerson at left guard, Macek at center, White at right guard, and Russ Washington and later Dan Audick at right tackle.

White, Wilkerson, and Washington took the Pro Bowl bows—Washington five times, Wilkerson three times, and White once after three nods with the Vikings. White should probably be a Hall of Famer and could easily be on this underrated list, but Macek's got him beat.

Stuck behind Mike Webster of the Steelers all those years, Macek had no shot at the Pro Bowl.

"Donnie held everything together," Fouts said. "In those days a lot of teams played a 3-4 defense with a big nose guard like Rubin Carter or Fred Smerlas, and Donnie could handle snapping the ball and then blocking those big monsters. He was a great athlete."

Fouts could barely move in the pocket, but he enjoyed phenomenal protection. From 1978 through 1987, Fouts threw 4,510 passes but was sacked only 219 times—less than 22 times per *year.* Yet in a story on the Pro Football Hall of Fame's official website about those incredible Chargers offenses, the offensive line isn't even *mentioned.*

Macek embodied everything football is about. He sacrificed individual honors and recognition for the good of the team. He toiled in anonymity, his remarkable career recognized only by those who played alongside him.

Postscript: Donnie Macek spent all 14 of his NFL seasons with the Chargers. Only Dan Fouts and Russ Washington, with 15 seasons of service, played longer with the Chargers.

CHAPTER 7

Coaches

The Most Overrated NFL Coach of All Time

NORV TURNER

Here's the dictionary definition of the word overrated: "to rate too highly." Simple enough. Overrated then is brother to overstated, which means "to state in too strong terms," or exaggerate. If you're labeling something as overrated, then you are trying to set the record straight—not denigrate. Being called overrated is often taken as a putdown. That's not what's intended, especially in this book.

Why talk about this now? Well, because Norv Turner is a decent man, a very likable man, a man who was wildly successful in his career as an assistant coach. In the early 1990s Turner was the offensive coordinator on a team that won multiple Super Bowls: the Dallas Cowboys. His star pupil, Troy Aikman, one of the most respected quarterbacks of his generation, so admires Turner that he asked him to make his induction speech into the Pro Football Hall of Fame in 2006. There is no higher praise than that.

In 2006 Turner nearly landed his dream job, returning to the Dallas Cowboys as head coach, taking over for Bill Parcells. Aikman implored owner Jerry Jones to hire Turner. For whatever reason, the two sides could not agree. Instead, Turner was hired to replace Marty Schottenheimer as the head coach of the San Diego Chargers. The Cowboys did not make a mistake.

As a head coach in the NFL, Turner has been, well, disastrously overrated, mostly by the people who have hired him (but also by some of his friends in the media who continue to wrongfully defend him).

The numbers simply don't lie. Turner has been an NFL head coach for nine years—seven with the Redskins, two with the Raiders. His career record is 58–82–1. He has had just one year with 10 or more wins (10 in 1999), when he led the Redskins to the playoffs. In all, he's had just three winning seasons. His teams have made the playoffs only once, winning one game before being knocked out. Turner is one of just 11 head coaches in NFL history to have coached in at least 100 games with just one playoff appearance.

He doesn't even beat up on the league's losers. Against teams that finished the year with a losing record, Turner is 33–27, barely treading water. Against teams that finished the season at .500 or better, Turner was abysmal—19–43–1, or an average of .310. That might get you into Cooperstown, but not Canton.

As the offensive coordinator in Dallas, Turner turned Aikman, Emmitt Smith, and Michael Irvin into Hall of Famers. Of course, even Tina Turner could have coached the Triplets to a Super Bowl.

Without that mother lode of talent in Washington, none of Turner's teams in his seven years there reached the top 10 in total yards of offense in a single season. This sort of shoots down the theory that Turner is a marvelous tactician. Either that or he forgets how to coach offense.

Here's the book on Turner's teams: they're soft, they fade down the stretch, and they're less prepared for adversity. Here's what the greatest wide receiver of all time, Jerry Rice, said about his experience with Turner in Oakland: "He could not motivate the players. He had no control." Ouch.

Inexplicably, Turner was given another chance—as the head coach of the Chargers. Schottenheimer had a long feud with the team's general manager, A.J. Smith, even though the Chargers had the best record in the AFC last season. Turner and Smith do get along.

So, it's only fair to give Turner one more shot. This is America, right? Okay, let's see how he does. The Chargers were 14–2 in 2006. They have the best offensive player in the NFL, LaDainian Tomlinson, and the best defensive player, Shawn Merriman. Turner inherits a hotshot young quarterback

(Philip Rivers) playing in a system Turner practically invented. (He served briefly as the Chargers' offensive coordinator in 2001, and San Diego's offense went from 28th in the league to 11th.)

Now, you could argue that Turner is as least as good a head coach as Barry Switzer is, right? So, let's see if Turner can do what Switzer did. In 1994, the year after the Cowboys won the Super Bowl, Switzer took over as head coach after Jimmy Johnson and Jones had their falling out. The Cowboys went 12–4 in 1993 under Johnson. Under Switzer in 1994, the Cowboys went 12–4. In 1995 the Cowboys under Switzer went 12–4 again and returned to the Super Bowl and won it.

Now, for this comparison to be fair, Turner doesn't have to take the Chargers to the Super Bowl and win it in two years. Let's say, too, that he doesn't necessarily have to go 14–2 in the 2007 season. Doing that in back-to-back seasons is rough. Let's just say that Turner's Chargers must finish the season with a winning record and go to the playoffs. That's it. Then he deserves another chance. If that happens, the overrated label can be amended. Not removed, just tweaked. If San Diego wins the Lombardi Trophy on Turner's watch, this chapter will be rewritten. If he fails, the overrated label is indelible.

Postscript: Norv Turner was 7–6 with the Redskins in 2000 when owner Daniel Snyder relieved him of his command. In 2001, ironically, Marty Schottenheimer replaced Turner as the Redskins head coach. That year under Schottenheimer, Washington was 8–8. Schottenheimer lasted one season.

The Rest of the Most Overrated

2. JEFF FISHER

At the start of the 2007 season, Jeff Fisher of the Tennessee Titans was the longest-tenured head coach in the NFL. Why?

If you count 1994, when he finished out the year for Jack Pardee, Fisher is beginning his 14th season as head coach of the Oilers/Titans franchise. And yet, he's gone to the playoffs just four times. Let's say the 1994 season doesn't count (he went 1–5 to finish the year, yet got the permanent gig anyway). Fisher has gone to the postseason in four of his 12 full seasons as a head coach. Four winning seasons. Four losing seasons. Four seasons of 8–8. And how exactly is this good?

Fisher's won-loss record of 105–93 (.530) barely cracks sea level, and his playoff record is 5–4. Yet he is continually deified as one of the bright, young coaches in the league. When Bill Parcells retired from the Cowboys, it was rumored that Dallas owner Jerry Jones would pay any price to get Fisher down in Big D. Again, why?

Yes, he's a photogenic boomer with an ex-cheerleader wife. He looks like a country music star prowling the sideline. His NFL pedigree is undeniable: USC, Chicago Bears defensive back. The players love him. He lets them stay home during training camp. All part of the glossy, good ol' boy image.

But strip away the carefully crafted veneer, and you get one mediocre head coach who doesn't deserve the constant doting of the national media.

In his head coaching career, Fisher has feasted on lowly competition, beating teams that finished the season with a losing record at a .684 clip—65–30. But his record against teams that finished the season with winning records? Almost the polar opposite: 30–53 for .361.

Oh, Fisher has made a living bragging about owning Jacksonville—even though he's only 13–11 against the Jaguars. But put him in the same cage with a real tiger—Peyton Manning—and it's no contest. Fisher is 4–7 against Manning. And forget long road trips, Fisher's teams just come up small. He's 6–14 against the AFC West, 0–5 against Seattle, has won one of three from the 'Niners, and it's the same story against the Cardinals. And he's 1–3 against New England.

Fisher grew up in Buddy Ryan's 46 defense. Yet, in all his years with the Oilers/Titans, Fisher's teams finished better than 10th in points allowed in the league just twice, in 1995 and 2000. Same story on offense. Only in two seasons did Fisher's teams finish in the top 10 in points scored: 1999 and 2003.

Let's compare Fisher to another head coach who doesn't get nearly the same lavish praise: Dennis Green. As of 2006, Green, too, had 13 seasons as a head coach. His record was 113–94—eight more wins than Fisher. But he made the playoffs in eight of those 13 seasons (of course, his record in the

Despite a mediocre win-loss record, Jeff Fisher has somehow managed to beat the heat to become the NFL's longest tenured head coach.

postseason was 4–8). So, about the same. Yet, Green is unemployed. Fisher is in demand. Again, why?

While Green's poor showing in the playoffs is constantly regurgitated, Fisher's failures in big games are rarely discussed. Let's look at the four biggest games of Fisher's head coaching career.

In 2003 the Titans finished 12–4, went to New England in the divisional playoffs, and lost to the Patriots 17–14.

In 2002 the Titans finished 11–5 and lost to Oakland in the AFC Championship game. Jon Gruden's offense stomped all over the defensive genius: 41–24 Raiders.

In 2000 Fisher's Titans finished 13–3 and won the old AFC Central for the first time. Don't forget, that year Tennessee finished second in the league in points allowed and total yards. Trent Dilfer, Ray Lewis, and company just came into Nashville and stripped Fisher's team of its manhood: 24–10 Baltimore.

And in 1999 the Titans finished 13–3 and advanced to Super Bowl XXXIV against the Rams. Kurt Warner played pitch and catch all day. Fisher's defense had no answer, allowing the game-winning 73-yard touchdown pass from Warner to Isaac Bruce with 1:54 left. Even with Steve McNair's late-game heroics factored in, Fisher's coaching performance should go down as one of the most overrated in Super Bowl history.

Postscript: Jeff Fisher is Teflon.

1. It was general manager Floyd Reese who drafted Vince Young over Matt Leinart. Leinart had been the preferred choice of Fisher and offensive coordinator Norm Chow, who coached Leinart at USC, Fisher's alma mater. Young was the 2006 Rookie of the Year. Reese was let go.

2. Two words: Pacman Jones. It was Fisher who demanded that the Titans draft Jones in the first round over the objections of his scouting staff. Jones has become the poster child for NFL bad-boy behavior.

3. BUDDY RYAN

The week before their 1989 wild-card game against the Rams, as snow piled up in Philadelphia, the Eagles practiced at the Falcons' facility in Suwanee, Georgia. One afternoon a writer from Los Angeles asked Eagles head coach Buddy Ryan how concerned he was with Rams running back Greg Bell, who had rushed for more than 1,100 yards during the regular season. Ryan babbled something generic, then, while he passed the Eagles writers on his way out of the room, he laughed and said, "Greg Bell, my *ass!*"

That Sunday in Philadelphia, Bell ran for 124 yards and a touchdown, and the Rams upset the Eagles 21–7.

It was typical of Ryan. He had plenty of bluster, but he rarely backed it up. As a head coach in Philadelphia, Ryan talked tough and had a defense jammed with all-stars, but he never won anything.

Total career Pro Bowls for the Buddy Ryan defense: 19.

Total playoff wins for the Buddy Ryan defense: 0.

The Eagles had one of the most astounding collections of defensive talent ever assembled, but they not only never won a championship, they never won a playoff game. In 1988 the mighty Eagles defense allowed 17 first-half points to the Bears before the fog rolled in at halftime, and the Bears coasted to a 20–12 win. In 1989 the Eagles allowed 14 first-quarter points in that 21–7 loss to the Rams. And in 1990 they allowed 20 unanswered points after the offense gave them a 6–0 second-quarter lead in a wild-card loss to the Redskins.

In those playoff games, the Ryan defense lost to three quarterbacks—Mike Tomczak, Jim Everett, and Mark Rypien—who were hardly superstars. It lost to three running backs—Thomas Sanders, Bell, and Earnest Byner—who were capable but hardly Hall of Famers. The Eagles got trampled in each game, giving up 164, 144, and 93 rushing yards, and their ballyhooed pass rush managed just three total sacks in those three playoff losses. The last two losses made the Ryan Eagles the only team in NFL history to lose home wild-card games in consecutive years.

While Ryan is credited with building that dominating Eagles defense, several of the players—including Reggie White, Wes Hopkins, and Andre Waters—were there before he was. And the year before Ryan arrived, the Eagles defense was ranked 10th in the NFL. In his five years with the Eagles, they never ranked higher than that (18th, 26th, 28th, 10th, 12th). When the Eagles finally did rank number one in the NFL in defense in 1991, Ryan was gone. Bud Carson was in charge of the Eagles defense.

Ryan is one of only four head coaches in NFL history to lose three or more postseason games without winning any. Among the three others is Wade Phillips, who was Ryan's defensive coordinator when that streak of postseason ineptitude began.

As an assistant coach, Ryan did accomplish two truly great things. During the Chicago Bears' championship season of 1985, Ryan whipped a cast of Pro Bowlers and future Hall of Famers, including middle linebacker Mike Singletary, into one of the most feared defenses in league history. His 46 defense put as many as 10 defenders at the line of scrimmage with near-criminal intent: to destroy the quarterback's intentions, his psyche, or his body.

That high-risk, high-reward defense—which was his downfall in Philly—has been somewhat modified by his two sons, Rex and Rob, who coach the defenses in Baltimore and Oakland, respectively. With unparalleled talent, Rex Ryan and the Ravens led the AFC in defense in 2006. The Raiders, with far less Pro Bowl–level talent, were third in the AFC under

Rob. The system works. Unfortunately, if you are a quarterback who knows what he's doing, the 46 will eventually break down. And you've got to have an offense to go with it. Peyton Manning and the Colts defeated the Ravens in the first round of the playoffs in 2006, 15–6. Rex kept Manning out of the end zone, but Ravens coach Brian Billick's offense couldn't score. That's been the story of the Ryan family football life—problems with the offense.

Go back to 1994. Buddy Ryan was running the defense for the Houston Oilers. Kevin Gilbride was running the offense. Here's Ryan's second big contribution to football. The Oilers were beating the Jets 14–0 with 37 seconds left in the second quarter—on ESPN. Instead of running out the clock, Gilbride, the architect of a dubious offensive system called the run-and-shoot, called two pass plays. The second one led to a fumble, which led to a turnover, which led to Ryan's defense having to go back on the field to defend deep in Oilers territory, which got Ryan pissed, which led to the old Oklahoma horse farmer throwing a punch at Gilbride, who grew up in the suburbs of Connecticut.

The punch wasn't much, but it had lasting impact. It cemented Ryan's image as a tumultuous character who probably should not be entrusted with another head coaching job. But it also pointed an unflattering spotlight on the run-and-shoot, which Ryan derisively had named "chuck-and-duck." The following year, the run-and-shoot—long criticized for putting too much wear and tear on defenses and being unable to protect a lead—died. Ryan put it out of its misery.

As a defensive coordinator, nobody was better. As a head coach—while he was spectacularly popular in Philly (still is)—Ryan was wildly overrated.

Postscript: By the way, after the Jets recovered that fumble on the Houston 18-yard line, New York missed a chip-shot field goal. The Oilers won the game 24–0. Ryan got his shutout.

4. JIM FASSEL

Whenever there is an NFL head-coaching vacancy, watch the list of prospective candidates. The name Jim Fassel always pops up. Fassel's got plenty of moles in the national media willing to float his name—even if his career as a head coach was vastly overrated by the New York hype machine and one highly successful season that went down in flames in Super Bowl XXXV.

As head coach of the New York Giants from 1997 to 2003, Fassel finished with a record barely north of .500: 58–53–1. But he cleaned up on bad teams. His record against teams that finished the season with a losing record was 39–14 (.736). When Fassel faced teams that were .500 or better, his record plummeted to .382 (19–31–1).

Yet Fassel is always mentioned for head-coaching vacancies, while Mike Martz—who started the 2007 season as the offensive coordinator in Detroit—is routinely dismissed. Why? Fassel has always been a media darling. His flamboyant press conferences are good TV. Martz is prickly and difficult to deal with. Yet, Martz's record as a head coach is 53–32—a .624 winning percentage! It's not even close. And Martz was 20–15 against teams that finished the season above .500.

Fassel and Martz both lost their head-coaching debuts in the Super Bowl. Martz's Rams lost to Bill Belichick and Tom Brady, winners of three Super Bowls in four years. There is no shame in losing to a dynasty. Fassel's Giants lost to the Ravens. The Ravens did have the best defense in a generation, but their quarterback was Trent Dilfer. After Dilfer's 38-yard touchdown toss to Brandon Stokley over Jason Sehorn in the first quarter, Dilfer was 11-for-24 and just 115 yards.

Fassel, the guy who essentially ran the Giants offense, was so thoroughly outcoached that his quarterback, Kerry Collins, played worse, throwing four interceptions.

Fassel finished his career in New York with three nondescript seasons and then announced his own firing to the New York media—with two games remaining in the season.

That embarrassment was later followed by this: his best friend fired him. After Fassel could not land a head coaching job anywhere else, Ravens head coach Brian Billick, who had known Fassel since their days together in college, put Fassel in charge of Baltimore's offense. It was a disastrous experiment.

After a two-game losing streak during the 2006 season, Billick concluded that Fassel had failed to generate any offensive cohesion or chemistry. Fassel was gone. After that, the Ravens went on a tear, averaging 27.8 points per game in a five-game winning streak. They finished 13–3 and won the AFC North.

Postscript: Back to Super Bowl XXXV. The Giants offense never got inside the Ravens' 29-yard line, a Super Bowl record. Even though offensive coordinator Sean Payton was calling the plays—it was the Super Bowl for crying out loud—Jim Fassel had a responsibility to get the team ready and then step in when things were falling apart.

5. MARVIN LEWIS

Why the constant gushing about Marvin Lewis?

In his four years as head coach in Cincinnati, Lewis has led the Bengals to just one season above .500. That was in 2005, when the Bengals were one-and-done in the playoffs. Granted, his star player, quarterback Carson Palmer, was knocked out of that wild-card playoff game by the Pittsburgh Steelers. But during that game, the Bengals defense—Lewis's supposed strength—allowed Ben Roethlisberger and company to just walk up and down the field at will. Big Ben fired three touchdown passes, the most he's thrown in a playoff game. And the Bengals collapsed 31–17.

Lewis largely got the job in Cincinnati on the strength of the reputation he built as the defensive coordinator in Baltimore. In 2000 the Ravens defense was ranked first in the league and set a record for points allowed in a season (165), shutting out the Giants offense in Super Bowl XXXV. But it's clear that Marvin Lewis had less to do with that defensive performance than Ray Lewis did—and still does.

In 2006 the Ravens defense was again ranked first in the league, giving up just 201 points. In the six years Marvin Lewis led the Ravens defense, it finished 30th, 27th, 23rd, second, first, and fourth in total yards. In the five years since, it has finished 22nd, fourth, sixth, fifth, and first. Not much difference.

And in Cincinnati, Lewis has a record of 35–29 as head coach. But he's only 15–19 against teams with a record of .500 or better. He's 20–10 against teams with a losing record. And he's had perennial Pro Bowlers at key positions—left tackle, quarterback, and wide receiver—every year he's been in Cincinnati. That, of course, includes perhaps the second-best quarterback in the league, Palmer. But three of Lewis's four teams have finished at .500.

Again, the question: why all the gushing over Lewis? He's just flat-out overrated.

Postscript: And then there is this rather embarrassing record. During the 2006 season, nine Bengals ran afoul of the law, prompting a personal visit by new NFL commissioner Roger Goodell, who asked what he could do to clean up the team and the league's image.

The Bengals' ignominious record of arrests was largely responsible for inspiring Goodell to institute new league behavior guidelines and punishments in March 2007.

When Goodell asked Marvin Lewis what he could do better to clean up the team, Marvin Lewis said he needed more help from the league. How about picking players with better character?

The Most Underrated Coach of All Time

WEEB EWBANK

We hear so much about Don Shula and Bill Walsh and Joe Gibbs and, of course, Vince Lombardi. But Weeb Ewbank did something none of those Hall of Fame coaches ever did. As a head coach, he won championships in both the NFL and the AFL. In the course of that accomplishment—which, of course, now can never be duplicated—Ewbank coached the winning teams in perhaps the two most historic games in pro football history.

Ewbank coached the Baltimore Colts to victory in the 1958 NFL title game—the Greatest Game Ever Played—when the Colts beat the New York Giants 23–17 in sudden-death overtime. Ewbank was overshadowed in the game by the brilliant performance of quarterback Johnny Unitas, whose unpredictable play-calling and field generalship sparkled on that cold winter night at Yankee Stadium. Ewbank's most memorable moment in the game—

Weeb Ewbank briefs his team for the next day's legendary title game against the New York Giants at Yankee Stadium on December 27, 1958.

one that endeared him to his players (and maybe some of the Giants, too)—came when Giants linebacker Sam Huff flagrantly hit Colts wide receiver Raymond Berry out of bounds—right in front of Baltimore's bench. Ewbank hauled off and slugged Huff in the mouth. (No wonder Ewbank hired Buddy Ryan as a member of the Jets coaching staff some years later.)

The following year, Ewbank's Colts beat the Giants again in the NFL title game, 31–16. After a messy divorce from Baltimore, Ewbank was hired by the fledgling New York Jets, and this time his quarterback was the opposite of Unitas in every way: the erratic, flashy Joe Namath.

In Super Bowl III, Ewbank had revenge against his old team and his old quarterback, piloting the Jets to the greatest upset in pro football history—and the only title in Jets history. The head coach he beat in the game? Only Don Shula, the most celebrated head coach of his generation, who finished his career with the most wins of all time (although he was 2–4 in the Super Bowl).

Ewbank's career has always been underrated because he finished his coaching career (including his AFL record with the Jets) at barely above .500 (130–129–7). That .507 record is the lowest among the 35 coaches who finished their careers with 100 or more wins. But Ewbank came up big in big games, always allowing his stars or his assistants to manage the game the way they determined it could be won. (See Unitas in 1958. See Buddy Ryan and Walt Michaels in Super Bowl III.)

Thus, Ewbank was 4–1 in the postseason. And how'd you like to have this on your résumé? Greatest Game Ever Played and Greatest Upset in Pro Football History. Win and win. Pretty good—and very underrated. Hopefully, when the Jets move from Weeb Ewbank Hall at Hofstra University, their home on Long Island for two generations, to New Jersey, they won't forget to honor Ewbank, who was inducted into the Hall of Fame in 1978 and died in 1998 at the age of 91.

Postscript: Weeb Ewbank's mediocre win-loss record was mostly due to his final four years with the Jets, from 1970 to 1973. Joe Namath broke his wrist in 1970, then the star quarterback was hobbled by agonizing knee pain. In those four years, Ewbank's Jets were 21–35.

The Rest of the Most Underrated

2. TOM MOORE

Tom Moore has labored in relative obscurity in his 30 years in the NFL. Yes, he started coaching in the NFL when Jon Gruden was still in elementary school, but who has been more recognized for his accomplishments? Well,

Gruden, of course. But Moore has been instrumental in helping three teams win a Super Bowl ring—Gruden only one. And Gruden has time to catch up—Moore turns 59 during the 2007 season, and Gruden will turn 59 in the 2022 season—if his career makes it that far.

Moore's longevity is historic, and his career underappreciated and underrated. Consider this: as the receivers coach in Pittsburgh in the late 1970s, Moore was instrumental in helping Pittsburgh win Super Bowls XIII (1978) and XIV (1979). In those two games, Terry Bradshaw threw five touchdown passes to Lynn Swann and John Stallworth, and the Steelers exploded for a combined 66 points (after scoring 37 total points in their previous two Super Bowl wins).

Then in 2006 Moore helped the Colts offense (with rookie running back Joseph Addai replacing the veteran Edgerrin James, who bolted for the Cardinals) win Super Bowl XLI. So 27 years separated Moore's last two Super Bowl rings—the largest gap for any assistant coach in league history. That's an impact that has lasted two generations of football players.

Moore joined the Indianapolis Colts in 1998 as offensive coordinator and assembled one of the most prolific offenses in NFL history. Yes, it helps to have Peyton Manning, Marvin Harrison, Reggie Wayne, Edgerrin James, Dominic Rhodes, Addai, and Dallas Clark. But Moore is like Joe Torre—he's got a stable of superstar talent that takes a lot of care and feeding (and coddling) to create a cohesive whole. No one works harder than Manning, but you wouldn't want to coach him at this point in his career. It takes Moore's unique blend of experience and steady demeanor to manage a superstar like that, just like Torre does in the Yankees clubhouse.

The result: Manning has had an NFL-record nine consecutive seasons with 25 touchdown passes or more, and a league-record seven straight seasons with 4,000 yards or more. And the Colts are the only NFL offense ever to have a 4,000-yard passer and a 1,000-yard rusher in three straight seasons (1999–2001). The first two years it was Manning, Harrison, and James; when James got injured in 2001, Rhodes replaced him, and the Colts didn't miss a beat.

In the rain in Super Bowl XLI, Moore was smart enough to realize that Manning needed to be reined in. The Colts running backs took over the game, and Moore won his third ring.

Postscript: Tom Moore was the offensive coordinator in Detroit for the 1995–1996 season. The Lions led the NFL in total offense in 1995, becoming the first NFL team to have two receivers with more than 100 catches in a season (Herman Moore and Brett Perriman). The Lions quarterback that year was not Peyton Manning. It was Scott Mitchell.

3. BUD CARSON

He's the man who molded the Steel Curtain defense, perhaps the most dominant defensive force in pro football history, the winners of four Super Bowls in the 1970s.

He's the man who created the cover-two defense—the defense used now more than ever around the NFL. Both teams in Super Bowl XLI, the Colts and the Bears, used it.

He was an innovator, a strategist, a coach truly loved by his players for his personal toughness and tactical cunning.

His name was Bud Carson. He died at the age of 74 on December 7, 2005. He should not be forgotten.

He's not in the Hall of Fame. And he's not going to get there because Carson had only one two-year stint as a head coach, with the Cleveland Browns in 1989. In his first season, he brought the Browns to the doorstep of the Super Bowl. Carson's Browns were a 9–6–1 team that squeaked through as winners of the AFC Central division and then lost the AFC Championship game to the Denver Broncos 37–21. The following year, when the Browns got off to a 2–7 start, Carson was gone.

But in Pittsburgh in 1972 it was Carson who implored Chuck Noll to stress quickness and athleticism on the defensive line. The foursome of Joe Greene, Ernie Holmes, L.C. Greenwood, and Dwight White was such a mobile, powerful, relentless force that it became known as the Steel Curtain. Carson also invented the cover-two defense, where the safeties play a deep zone covering the back half of the field. With that pass rush from those four down linemen, the cover-two's umbrella frustrated offenses—particularly Bill Walsh's burgeoning system in Cincinnati—with shifts and disguises.

It was all devised by Carson. A college quarterback playing defensive back in Pittsburgh named Tony Dungy learned the cover-two from Carson. Dungy brought it to Tampa, where Monte Kiffin redefined it and perfected it.

After Cleveland, Carson worked his magic in Philadelphia as the defensive coordinator under head coach Rich Kotite. In 1991 an underachieving defense partially built by Buddy Ryan finally finished first in the league in total defense under Carson. He never had Ryan's charisma with the press. He worked in the shadow of Noll in Pittsburgh. So his accomplishments have rarely been recognized and are vastly underrated.

Postscript: Bud Carson did not suffer fools gladly. He was gruff. He didn't like reporters. Also, he didn't like his players freelancing. In the AFC Championship game in 1974—the first time the Steelers had reached that level of the postseason in two generations—Carson had the temerity to bench future Hall of Famer Mel Blount. He didn't like the way Blount was checking Raiders wide receiver Cliff Branch. The Steelers won 24–13 and then went on to win their first Super Bowl.

4. MONTE KIFFIN

During the week leading up to Super Bowl XLI in Miami, longtime defensive coordinator Monte Kiffin was hanging out at his house on the beach near St. Petersburg, Florida, relaxing contentedly.

If you know anything at all about the crazy, maniacal, one-thousand-words-a-minute Kiffin, you know this scene is nearly impossible to imagine. But there he was, at rest, savoring the moment.

And why wouldn't he? In Super Bowl XLI, the two head coaches were Tony Dungy of the Colts and Lovie Smith of the Bears, two former Bucs coaches who learned the so-called Tampa-two defense from Kiffin at a bivouac of trailers within earshot of the Tampa International Airport. So loud are the airplanes coming and going a few hundred yards from the practice fields at One Buc Place (where the Bucs once were headquartered) that Kiffin has become nearly hoarse in the 11 years he's worked in Tampa.

In 10 of those 11 years, his defense finished in the top 10 in the NFL in both yards and points allowed. Kiffin's defense finished first in the league in both categories in 2002, the year the Bucs won Super Bowl XXXVII.

Let's compare for a moment. In the 10 years Kiffin has been defensive coordinator, his defense averaged seventh in the league in points allowed and fifth in the league in yards allowed. Buddy Ryan averaged 14th and 17th, respectively. Since the merger, Kiffin is the only defensive coordinator to lead the league in points allowed twice in a four-year period (2002 and 2005).

And Kiffin's defense has been adopted by no fewer than a dozen NFL clubs, including the two that played in Super Bowl XLI. What is the Tampa-two? Well, it's a basic pass defense where the two safeties are responsible for the deep half of the field—the cover-two that Dungy learned from Bud Carson in Pittsburgh. Kiffin's wrinkle was to have the inside linebacker run down the middle of the field with the inside receiver—first Hardy Nickerson, then, of course, the perennial Pro Bowler Derrick Brooks. In Chicago, it's Brian Urlacher running deep down what they call the chute, between the hash marks. You've got be a hybrid player: hit like a linebacker, run like a safety. Urlacher was a safety in college. In Tampa, Kiffin was able to develop two players who could've played both positions at once: safety John Lynch hit like a linebacker, and linebacker Brooks ran like a safety. The results were imposing.

If the Bucs had had an offense like Tony Dungy has (Dungy had a lot of Chuck Noll in him until he met Tom Moore and Peyton Manning in Indy) they might have beaten the Rams in the NFC Championship game in 1999. And Kiffin might have had two rings. In a deafening dome in St. Louis, the Bucs nearly pulled a monumental upset by holding the high-flying Rams to just one touchdown, losing 11–6. It was a Tampa loss, but it may have been Kiffin's finest moment.

Outside the football fraternity and the town of Tampa, few know of Kiffin's impact. And because he is often portrayed as a mad professor, Kiffin has grown into a caricature of himself, and he has gone underappreciated. That's why he makes this list. Maybe he'll get more recognition now that his son, Lane, is the head coach of the Oakland Raiders. Lane coaches the offense.

Postscript: "I think a lot of people have it wrong with Monte," Monte Kiffin's former general manager, Rich McKay, once told the St. Petersburg Times. *"They see his energy and they hear the stories, and they think what makes him good is that he has a screw loose. That's not Monte. The thing that makes*

Monte—attention to detail. He's unreal. He doesn't miss anything. And he continues to modify, to tinker with his defense, so it evolves a little each year."

5. CHUCK KNOX

Chuck Knox has got some bad numbers. It's tough to justify putting him on this list. Throughout his long career, Knox was put down mercilessly for not being able to win the big game. He became a catchword. When the Philadelphia Eagles lost three straight NFC Championship games—an unprecedented two consecutive losses at home in 2002 and 2003—head coach Andy Reid was described as the Chuck Knox of his era. So it's necessary to put Knox's career into better perspective to give him his due.

First the rap: after 22 seasons as an NFL head coach with three different teams (two different stints with the Rams), Knox compiled a regular-season record of 186 wins, 147 losses, and a tie—good for eighth on the all-time list. But in all his time in the league—including another near-decade as an assistant coach—Knox never coached in a Super Bowl. In the modern era, only Marty Schottenheimer has more wins (200) without going to the big game. Knox was 7–11 in the postseason. Schottenheimer, after the disastrous loss to New England in the 2006 playoffs, is 5–13.

The big-game losses have kept Knox out of the Hall of Fame. His "Ground Chuck" offensive philosophy of running the ball has also become synonymous with overly conservative play—a forefather, if you will, of Marty Ball.

So, why honor Knox by putting him on this list? Two reasons. First, longevity. Twenty-two years as a head coach should not be forgotten. He was the Associated Press Coach of the Year three times—the most of any head coach since the merger (Bill Parcells, Joe Gibbs, Mike Ditka, and Don Shula each won it twice).

Knox was a tough, loyal, well-liked head coach who may have battled with his owners but who left his mark on thousands of NFL players and the league. He was a great leader of men. He was the first NFL head coach to win division titles with three different teams. With the Rams, Knox won five straight NFC West titles with five different quarterbacks, including Joe Namath.

It was perhaps with Namath in a previous coaching incarnation that Knox made his greatest contribution to the game. In 1963 New York Jets head coach Weeb Ewbank hired Knox as the offensive line coach. The AFL was a wide-open league, and Namath wanted to throw the ball. But the pass rushers were getting bigger, faster, and stronger. And the referees were letting them get away with murder (Ben Davidson and the Raiders practically put Namath in the hospital).

Knox was responsible for training the guy who would play left tackle for the Jets, Winston Hill, the guy responsible for protecting the franchise player of an upstart league. Everybody wanted to take out Namath. Knox tried something different. For generations, pass blockers were instructed to keep their hands balled up in fists and pulled in toward their chests. That gave them no power, no leverage. Knox told Hill to build muscle in his biceps and forearms and extend them—and open up his hands. At that time, it was an illegal move for an offensive-line player, but the referees started to let it go. Why? It protected Broadway Joe. Joe had time. Remember all those deep, 20-yard square-ins and square-outs to Don Maynard and George Sauer Jr.? Nobody had 20-yard square-outs in their playbook. But the Jets did. And you've seen Namath high in the air, throwing that ball to the deep middle of the field, time after time. Got to have protection—four, five seconds—to complete those passes. Namath did. Knox gave it to him.

Knox opened up the passing game all over the AFL. Scoring points meant paying customers. More fans meant the league survived and flourished. Knox's technique would be the wave of the future. It led to protecting the passer and more points. Knox was a trailblazer. Protect the passer, protect the franchise, build your franchise, build your league. Funny all that would come from Ground Chuck.

In 1966 Namath attempted 471 passes—more than any other quarterback in either the AFL or NFL. He was sacked just nine times.

Give Knox a seriously large dollop of credit for the merger of the two leagues four years later. That's why he's on this underrated list.

Postscript: Chuck Knox never got to taste the fruit of his labor in New York. In 1967 he left to coach in the "real" league with the Detroit Lions. In 1968 Namath and the Jets conquered the whole football world, winning Super Bowl III.

The Worst Coach (But the Most Underrated Commissioner)

BERT BELL

As an NFL head coach, Bert Bell was very overrated. Check that—he was just bad. In five seasons coaching the Philadelphia Eagles, he managed just 10 wins.

As NFL commissioner, he was extraordinarily underrated. Pete Rozelle's vision for a lucrative national TV contract has been lionized over and over again. His successor, Paul Tagliabue, will be immortalized for labor peace and astronomical profitability. Rightfully so. But there is no Tagliabue, no Rozelle, without Bell.

For example, in 1946, in his first year as commissioner, all Bell did was save the reputation of the NFL. Here's the story.

Bell, who also owned the Eagles, forced the league to move its headquarters from Chicago to Philadelphia. But he really ran the league out of the living room of his home in the Philadelphia suburb of Narberth.

On the night before the NFL Championship game between the New York Giants and Chicago Bears, New York City Mayor William O'Dwyer woke Bell up at home to warn him of an impending crisis. The Bears were 10-point favorites over the Giants, even though New York had easily beaten Chicago earlier in the season 14–0. Giants quarterback Frank Filchock and running back Merle Hapes had been summoned to the mayor's residence, Gracie Mansion in downtown Manhattan, to quell suspicions about the spread. Detectives had heard the fix was in. O'Dwyer got Hapes to talk. He had indeed taken a bribe to fix the game. Filchock denied it. Bell heard the story over the phone. The next morning, he immediately suspended Hapes.

The Giants lost the game. Filchock threw six interceptions. Later, when the case went to court, Filchock again said he took no bribe. But this time, under oath, he admitted that gamblers had approached him.

Bell felt betrayed. He was a decent and honorable man who had been lied to. Both Hapes and Filchock were suspended indefinitely.

The following year Bell demanded and received full powers to clean up any perception of gambling, any hint of organized crime activity. The owners granted Bell the power to ban for life any player involved in fixing a game. And then Bell instituted a rule that still stands. The NFL would publish injury reports—official reports from each team—as a way of removing any hint that a player's availability was being manipulated by the team or outside influences.

That's why, to this day, it's so important that NFL head coaches not abuse this time-honored process, and why the league comes down hard on those coaches who do. That's why injury reports and updates are such an essential element of game reporting. Players get hurt. The game must be kept clean. Bell had the vision to see that in 1947.

But Bell's vision was much, much broader than that.

Before Rozelle got credit for it, it was Bell who saw that certain teams were dominating the league—not only big-market teams like the Bears and Giants but also the Packers and Redskins. From 1937 to 1946, those four teams accounted for 19 of the 20 berths in the NFL Championship games.

So Bell decided to take into account a team's record when devising the schedule—a practice that is followed to this day. He didn't have a word for it, but we do. Parity. Bell founded it. (He even authored this line, which became as famous as any in American pop culture: "On any given Sunday." Those

Bert Bell, center, receives congratulations in Chicago on January 20, 1949, from George Halas Jr. (left), and Charles W. Bidwell Jr. after being presented with a 10-year contract to continue to serve as commissioner of the NFL.

four words signify nothing less than what America was about, the land of opportunity. And it was what the NFL wanted to embrace.

To maintain equal opportunity in the NFL, Bell, a quarterback at the University of Pennsylvania who never had the skills to go pro, created the annual college player draft. Bell understood that this would stoke off-season hope among the fans of the have-nots. Perhaps he didn't envision Madison Square Garden filled with fans of the hapless New York Jets year after year, heckling their franchise's first-round draft choice—then staying through day two of the draft to catch chocolate chip cookies from ESPN analyst Mike Golic. But that's what Bell wrought—a way for the league to stay in the public eye before major league baseball took center stage.

Again, even though Rozelle is remembered as the one who fathered the NFL's national TV audience, it was Bell who negotiated the first national television network contract. Then he put in place a very unpopular blackout rule to encourage people to get out of the house and buy tickets to the games. The result: the NFL became a national draw and a local attraction at the same time. Next time your team's blacked out, either buy a ticket or blame Bert Bell.

Even though he was a blueblood from Philadelphia's Main Line, and a wealthy one at that, Bell established a pension plan for NFL players and then privately lobbied the owners not to attempt to stop the players' pursuit of a union. So the NFL Players Association was established on his watch.

It was Bell who understood that the NFL had to be married to the confines of TV. There was a show. It had a time slot. It came on the air and went off the air like any well-scripted drama. Thus Bell created sudden-death overtime. No other sport has it. He knew it would guarantee drama. It insured that TV would have a nice, clean, bold finish. Bell saw that first.

Postscript: Talk about sudden death. The last NFL Championship game Bell saw was the 1958 sudden-death overtime thriller, the Colts 23–17 over the Giants, which launched the modern marriage of television and the NFL.

The following October, Bell died. At age 65, at Franklin Field in Philadelphia, watching a game between the Eagles and the Steelers, Bell collapsed from a heart attack.

Three months later, Pete Rozelle was named to replace him.

CHAPTER 8

The Worst Team in Football History

The Columbus Panhandles

The expansion Tampa Bay Buccaneers won two of 28 games in their first two seasons in the mid-1970s. The Jets of the mid-1990s won four of 32 games in two years under coach Rich Kotite. The Raiders averaged 3.8 wins per year from 2003 through 2006.

That's some kind of preposterously bad football by some people who claimed to know football. Still, it's not enough to claim the title of Worst Team Ever.

Back when a ragtag band of Central Ohio railroad workers joined the American Professional Football Association in 1920, little could they have imagined that nearly 90 years later they would remain the benchmark for NFL ineptitude.

Meet the Columbus Panhandles.

First, a definition of terms. Even though the APFA didn't change its name to the National Football League until 1922, football historians consider the charter NFL franchises to be those 14 teams that played a full league schedule during the 1920 APFA season. Among them were the Decatur Staleys, who

The sport wasn't exactly a ballet of grace and power back in the 1920s, and during that era the Columbus Panhandles played some of the ugliest football in history. (Photo courtesy Bettmann/CORBIS)

later became the Chicago Bears, and the Chicago Cardinals, who continue today as the Arizona Cardinals.

But this was a time of great fluidity in professional football. Many teams were disorganized and poorly funded and often moved or shut down after a year or two. Several folded in midseason. Others simply stopped scheduling APFA opponents and returned to the sandlots. Most of those original 1920 franchises are long forgotten—the Akron Pros, the Muncie Flyers, the Dayton Triangles. The owners found players in the factories and steel mills of these rugged Rust Belt towns, and some of the wealthier teams supplanted the local boys with college players who actually earned a few dollars per game.

One of those original 1920 NFL teams was the Panhandles, which had existed off and on as a sandlot team since 1904. The Panhandles were operated by sports impresario Joe Carr, who was also a machinist with the

Panhandle Division of the Pennsylvania Railroad. Most of his players, including the seven burly Nesser brothers, were railroad men who squeezed practice time into their lunch break.

The Panhandles survived as an NFL franchise only three years, but during that brief period they produced a record that will never be challenged.

They played 22 games against NFL competition.

They won one.

They were outscored by a combined 509–78, got shut out 12 times—more than half their games—and never scored more than 13 points. Their only win was a 6–0 thriller on the final day of the 1921 season over the Louisville Brecks, a borderline professional bunch that played only two games against NFL opponents in 1921 and was shut out in both. Then the Brecks went out of business two years later when their stadium burned down. Save for a bad fire, the Panhandles might've won another game or two.

The Panhandles played 20 of their 22 games on the road—the downside to free train travel—and closed up shop after the 1922 season. They were reorganized under new management as the Columbus Tigers, who continued to operate with slightly better results until disappearing after the 1926 season.

But the Panhandles did leave a lasting legacy on the NFL landscape. Carr became NFL commissioner in 1921, and during his 17 years on the job he introduced several critical reforms that helped to create the National Football League landscape we know today. It was Carr who brought the NFL standard player contracts, a system of official league-wide standings, and, most important, rules banning college players from simultaneously playing for NFL teams, a practice that had been rampant. Carr actually banished the expansion Green Bay Packers from the NFL in 1921 for signing collegiate players using fake names, then he accepted a new Packers team into the league a year later. That is the Packers franchise we now know today.

So, how's this for irony? The man responsible for the worst record in pro football history was inducted as a charter member of the Pro Football Hall of Fame in 1963.

Postscript: Only teams that played a full league season in 1920 are now credited with NFL lineage, and only games between two such teams are now considered actual NFL games. Although nobody realized it until years later, the first NFL game ever played was between the Columbus Panhandles and the Dayton Triangles on October 3 at Triangle Park in Dayton. Dayton won 14–0.

The Most Underrated Premerger Unit

THE 1950 RAMS PASSING GAME

The Rams loved to fire the ball up and down the field. They shattered an array of NFL passing records. They scored points at an astonishing clip. And they rode their breathless aerial attack all the way to an NFL Championship game.

And this was 20 years before Kurt Warner was even born.

The Greatest Show on Turf, with Warner, Torry Holt, Marshall Faulk, and Isaac Bruce, was hardly the first high-octane, record-smashing passing attack in Rams history. Half a century earlier and 1,800 miles to the west, another Rams team was winning football games with an almost identical strategy: *throw*.

With an aerial assault that wouldn't have looked out of place in modern times, the 1950 Los Angeles Rams shattered virtually every NFL record for passing and offense—22 of them in all. Norm Van Brocklin and Bob Waterfield shared quarterbacking duties, and three Rams—Tom Fears, Elroy Hirsch, and Glenn Davis—each had 42 or more receptions. Only five other players in the entire league caught that many passes.

The Rams' 3,709 passing yards broke the existing NFL record set by Sammy Baugh and the 1947 Redskins by nearly 400 yards and translated to 309 per game, a figure that's been surpassed only three times since. The rest of the NFL in 1950 averaged 176 passing yards per game.

The Rams had games of 45, 45, 51, 65, and 70 points. Their 466 total points set a record that, although surpassed by a couple AFL teams in the 1960s, wasn't broken by an NFL team until the 1981 Chargers scored 478. To this day, no team in NFL history has approached the 1950 Rams' 38.8

points per game. Even in their most explosive season, the peerless Colts of Peyton Manning, Marvin Harrison, and Reggie Wayne averaged about a touchdown less per game than the 1950 Rams did.

Van Brocklin, Waterfield, and Davis combined to throw an NFL-record 31 touchdown passes in 1950. Fears became the first player in NFL history to catch 77 or more passes with 1,000 or more yards two years in a row—an achievement nobody repeated for a decade.

Those 1950 Rams went 9–3 during the regular season and roared past the Bears in an NFL semifinal playoff game before losing 30–28 to the Cleveland Browns in the NFL Championship game at Municipal Stadium, where the franchise had won an NFL title five years earlier before moving west.

But in true Rams fashion, they went down guns a-blazing. In the loss, they netted 418 yards, 312 in the air.

Postscript: On December 3, 1950, Tom Fears caught 18 passes in a game against the Packers. That stood as an NFL record for more than 50 years, until Terrell Owens caught 20 on December 17, 2000, against the Bears.

CHAPTER 9

Specialists

The Most Overrated Specialist of All Time

SAMMY BAUGH

How could a quarterback whose career began when Franklin D. Roosevelt was president still be the greatest punter in NFL history? Sound a little fishy? It should. Here's why.

Sammy Baugh, better known as the greatest *passer* during the early years of the NFL, is also the greatest *punter* in NFL history. At least, that's what the numbers claim.

Baugh averaged 51.3, 48.7, and 48.2 yards per punt in 1940, 1941, and 1942, performances that more than half a century later remain among the six best single-season figures ever recorded. Not since Baugh's accomplishment 66 years ago has any NFL punter averaged 51 yards per punt over a full season. Or 50 yards per punt. Or 49 yards per punt.

Baugh, who was vastly underrated as a quarterback, was every bit as overrated as a punter. He finished his career with a 45.1 punting average, which stood as an NFL record until the equally overrated Shane Lechler finally surpassed it in 2002.

How could Baugh generate numbers that even the biggest, strongest, most powerful punters 60 years later can't approach? There's one simple reason. The Redskins in those days made a living punting on second and third down. So, many of the times that Baugh punted, *there was nobody on the other team back deep to field them.* Baugh's punts simply *bounced* their way into the NFL record books.

It's called the quick kick these days, and occasionally a team backed up in a third-and-26 or some such desperate down and distance will ask an athletic quarterback to punt to try to take advantage of an unsuspecting defense. In theory, the ball bounces endlessly, the team in trouble gets a huge field-position boost, and the game's momentum changes.

Randall Cunningham of the Eagles once blasted a quick kick 91 yards over Dave Meggett's head against the Giants, the fourth-longest punt in NFL history. In 2005 Steelers quarterback Ben Roethlisberger pinned the Ravens at their own 1-yard line with a 33-yard quick kick.

These days it's rare. Back then it was a fundamental component of the Redskins attack. Baugh had already grown accustomed to quick-kicking while at Texas Christian in the mid-1930s, and the Redskins' wing-T formation was a perfect fit not only for his marvelous passing skills but also for his surprise quick kicks. Pinned back deep? Let Slingin' Sammy boot it away.

Baugh had an 85-yard punt in 1940 against the Eagles and an 81-yarder against the Lions in 1943, both on quick kicks. In the Redskins' 14–6 win over the Bears in the 1942 NFL Championship game, Baugh unloaded another 85-yard quick kick. Baugh's 52.5 punting average in that game remains the second-highest in NFL postseason history, and according to a story in *The Washington Post* the next day, the Redskins "kept the Bears in the hole aided by Sammy Baugh's record-breaking punting, most of it the quick-kick variety."

Strategically, it was brilliant: aim the ball over everybody's head, watch it bounce around, and gain 70 yards in field position. Statistically, it was brilliant: Baugh still has the second-highest punting average in history. But his inflated average says far more about *when* Baugh punted than *how* he punted.

Postscript: Sammy Baugh was the quarterback on the losing end of the most lopsided NFL game in history, the Bears' 73–0 win over the Redskins in the 1940 NFL Championship game. With the Bears leading 7–0, a Redskins end dropped a sure touchdown pass in the end zone. After the game, Baugh was asked whether

Sure he could sling the ball downfield, as he prepares to do here in a 1942 game against the Bears, but Sammy Baugh wasn't the greatest punter in the history of the game, though his stats might otherwise indicate.

the game would have turned out differently if his receiver had caught it. Baugh replied, "Yeah. I suppose it would have made it 73–7."

The Rest of the Most Overrated

2. MIKE VANDERJAGT

He's the most accurate kicker in NFL history. You can't get any more overrated than that.

The Colts jettisoned kicker Mike Vanderjagt after the 2005 season even though, at the time, Vanderjagt was *by far* the most accurate kicker in history. He had made 87.5 percent of his field goals in eight seasons with the Colts, and nobody else who had made 100 or more field goals had converted 87 percent, 86 percent, 85 percent, or even 84 percent. In fact, Phil Dawson of the Browns was such a distant second to Vanderjagt that even if he had made 46 consecutive field goals without a miss, he would still be second in career accuracy to Vanderjagt. From 2003 through 2005, Vanderjagt missed just seven of 87 field goals.

That didn't help him with 21 seconds in the Colts' conference semifinal playoff game against the Steelers at the RCA Dome on January 15, 2006. Vanderjagt lined up for the biggest field goal of his life, a 46-yarder that would have tied the game at 21 and forced overtime. But Vanderjagt was wide right, and, after he was penalized 15 yards for unsportsmanlike conduct for slamming his helmet on the turf, the Steelers ran out the clock and went on to win the Super Bowl three weeks later.

In nine playoff games, Vanderjagt has made 79 percent of his field-goal attempts. Of the 20 most accurate kickers in NFL history, Vanderjagt's percentage decline from regular-season percentage to postseason percentage is the fifth-largest.

How valuable was Vanderjagt to the Colts? As soon as they released him, they won a Super Bowl.

Vanderjagt resurfaced with the Cowboys in 2006, where he made just 13 of 18 field goals (72.2 percent) and was released 10 games into the season with the second-worst field-goal percentage in the league, a fraction ahead of Sebastian Janikowski's 72.0 percent.

One of the reasons Vanderjagt has been so accurate is that he rarely tried long field goals over his last several NFL seasons. His last field goal longer than 50 yards was in 2002. Since then, 41 other kickers have made a field goal of 51 yards or more.

And for the last couple months of the 2006 season, while Vanderjagt's former team was steaming toward a Super Bowl championship, the most accurate kicker in NFL history was out of work.

Postscript: In the days leading up to the Colts' 2004 playoff game against the Patriots, Mike Vanderjagt told reporters that the Patriots were "ripe for the picking."

*Patriots safety Rodney Harrison replied by saying, "He has to a be a jerk. Vander*jerk.*"*

The Patriots won 20–3 on their way to a second-straight Super Bowl championship.

3. JAN STENERUD

Sure, Jan Stenerud deserves to be in the Hall of Fame. Here's the problem: as long as Stenerud is the only kicker enshrined in Canton, he's guaranteed to be overrated. Until he's got some company, he can't help it.

There are 41 running backs, 32 offensive linemen, 30 quarterbacks, 25 defensive linemen, 21 coaches, 17 defensive backs, 16 linebackers, and 16 old-time two-way linemen in Canton.

And one pure kicker. Stenerud.

As the only kicker admitted into Canton, he should be dramatically better than every other kicker in history. He should have some unique qualifications. He should be in a kicking universe all his own.

Stenerud was the NFL's second-leading scorer when he retired. But other than playing a few more years and scoring a few more points, Stenerud's numbers were hardly superior to those produced by his contemporaries.

Today, in an age of domes, artificial surfaces, and specialized snappers and holders, Stenerud's 66.9 field-goal accuracy would make him the worst kicker in football (unless Chris Boniol was around). On the all-time NFL list, he's not even among the top 50 most accurate kickers these days. But back in the late 1960s and 1970s, 66.9 percent wasn't bad. It wasn't top five, though, and it wasn't top 10, either.

Stenerud, a native of Fetsund, Norway, ranked only 14th in NFL history in kicking accuracy when he left the game. In 19 seasons he led the NFL (or premerger AFL) in field-goal accuracy outright only twice, and he tied with Don Cockroft one other time. During the same span, Cockroft led his league five times, Garo Yepremian led four times, and Ray Wersching led three times.

Here's what the NFL career kicking leaderboard looked like when Stenerud retired after the 1985 season, based on 100 made field goals:

Kicker	Field Goals–Attempts	Percentage
Eddie Murray	134–172	77.9
Nick Lowery	136–177	76.8
Rolf Benirschke	130–183	71.0
Rafael Septien	165–235	70.21
Jim Breech	120–171	70.18
Matt Bahr	118–173	68.2
Toni Fritsch	157–231	68.0
Efren Herrera	116–171	67.84
Uwe Von Schamann	101–149	67.79
Pat Leahy	184–273	67.40
Tony Franklin	126–187	67.38
Garo Yepremian	210–313	67.1
John Smith	128–191	67.0
Jan Stenerud	373–558	66.9

Stenerud needs some company in Canton, but it's not likely to happen soon. So Stenerud should remain overrated for quite a while—at least until Adam Vinatieri retires.

Postscript: While attending Montana State University in the mid-1960s, Jan Stenerud was a member of the college's ski team. While running up and down the stadium steps one day for a workout, Stenerud saw the football team's kickers practicing. He asked if he could try, and he made several soccer-style kicks. Coach Jim Sweeney soon invited him to join the football team.

4. SHANE LECHLER

If the whole idea of punting was just to blast the ball as far as possible, and who cares what happens next, then Shane Lechler would be the best punter in NFL history. But it's not. And he's not.

Since 2002, when he reached the 250 punts necessary to qualify for the record book, Lechler has been the proud owner of the highest career-punting average in NFL history. The record has a little extra cachet because the guy he unseated, Sammy Baugh, was a charter member of the Hall of Fame.

The problem with Lechler is that even though his punts travel farther than anybody else's punts, they're not good punts. Take 2006, for example. Lechler averaged 47.5 yards per punt, the sixth-highest figure in NFL history and fourth-highest since 1942. This is Hall of Fame stuff, right? Wrong.

Lechler's average was gargantuan, and numbers like 47.5 yards per punt are certainly eye-popping. But Lechler's thunderous stats are deceiving. Although his average punt traveled 47.5 yards, his net average was a pedestrian 36.4.

Best in the league? No.

Second-best in the league? No.

Third-best? No.

Try 23rd-best.

Not only was Lechler's net average one of the worst in the league in 2006, he knocked an NFL-worst 19 punts into the end zone for touchbacks, the most by any punter in *nine years*—the most since Craig Hentrich had 21 in 1997. Lechler also became the first punter with as many touchbacks as punts inside the 20 in *10 years*—the most since Lee Johnson in 1996.

The average return against Lechler in 2006 went 12.5 yards, which would have ranked third in the NFL in punt-return average.

In his seven NFL seasons, he's finished first three times in gross punting average, second three times, and eighth once. But net average is the true measuring stick for punters, and after leading the league in net average as a rookie, Lechler finished a pedestrian 15th, 25th, 3rd, 10th, 8th, and 23rd the next six years.

Lechler's punts have been so returnable over the years that he has the worst return-yards-against average *ever* among the 50 punters in NFL history with a career net of 34.8 or better. His 242 punts that have been returned have come back that same average of 12.5 yards. Only two other punters on that list are even close: Hunter Smith at 12.1 and Leo Araguz at 11.5.

Clearly, the best punting average of all time is the most misleading stat of all time.

Postscript: Shane Lechler comes from an athletic family. His father played football and his mom played basketball at Baylor, and his wife was an All-American volleyball player at Texas A&M. None of them were overrated.

5. CHRIS BONIOL

Chris Boniol had just turned 25. He had it all. A Super Bowl ring. A fat new contract. A share of an NFL record with seven field goals in a game. Streaks of 27 and 28 consecutive field goals. A 26-for-27 season in 1995 that, at the time, was the second-most accurate in NFL history. And a reputation as the finest young kicker in the game.

In his three seasons with the Cowboys, Boniol not only reached the playoffs three times, he made two field goals in Super Bowl XXX and became one of the most accurate place-kickers in NFL history. He impressed the Eagles so much that after the 1996 season, they stole him away from their division rivals with a four-year, $2.45 million offer sheet that the Cowboys didn't match.

Late in the 1997 season, Boniol made official what everybody knew: nobody in the history of the game could kick field goals like he could. On November 30, he made all three of his attempts against the Bengals in a 44–42 Eagles win at Veterans Stadium. The second one, a 25-yarder early in the third quarter, gave him the 100 successful field goals required to qualify for the NFL record books.

At that moment, Boniol became the most accurate kicker in NFL history. He had made 100 of 120 career field-goal attempts, and his 83.3 percentage knocked Doug Pelfrey out of the top spot while Pelfrey watched from the Cincinnati sideline. At that moment, Pelfrey was a distant second at 80.6 percent.

Hopefully, Boniol enjoyed his stay atop the kicking world because it didn't last long. He made 14 of 21 field goal attempts in 1998 with the Eagles, his .667 percentage ranking 25th-best among the 27 NFL kickers who attempted 16 or more field goals (ahead of Greg Davis and Cary Blanchard).

Then things got worse. The Eagles released Boniol before the 1999 season began, and he signed with the Browns, who released him before he played in a game. He bounced to the Bears and made 11 of 18 field goals. His .611 percentage in 1999 was 29th-best out of 30 kickers who attempted 16 or more kicks (ahead of only Richie Cunningham). Boniol is one of only three kickers in the past decade to struggle through consecutive seasons at 67 percent or worse (along with Martin Grammatica and Neil Rackers).

On December 19, 1999, only 25 months after becoming the most accurate kicker ever, and 10 days after his 28th birthday, Boniol attempted a field goal for the final time in his life. Kicking against the Lions at Soldier Field, he lined up from 37 yards out.

He missed.

Since retiring, Boniol has dropped to 24th in NFL history in field-goal accuracy at 78.5 percent. He made 87 percent of his field goal attempts his first three seasons and 67 percent his last three.

Postscript: Chris Boniol now runs a series of kicking camps for kids.

The Most Underrated Specialist of All Time

MATT STOVER

You can't find it in any media guide. You can't look it up in the NFL record book. You won't have any luck scouring the Internet for it, no matter how long you try. Outdoor field-goal percentage. It's the fairest way to judge place-kickers, and it's not even a stat.

Kicking in a dome is hardly a true measure of a kicker's ability. No wind, no precipitation, no surprises. Just a steady 72 degrees and calm. Kicking outdoors, with unpredictable winds, constantly changing conditions, and sometimes rain or snow—now *that's* football.

Consider the case of Jason Hanson, one of the 10 most accurate kickers in NFL history. Hanson has spent his entire 15-year career with the Lions, and, naturally, he's been far more accurate indoors, where he's made 84 percent of his kicks. Outdoors, he's made 78 percent. Without the indoor kicks, he's average.

Then there are the hardcore outdoor kickers who don't have the luxury of kicking eight, nine, maybe 10 times per season in a dome.

David Akers of the Eagles has played 115 of his 125 games outdoors. According to the record book, he's only the seventh-most accurate kicker in history. But his 83.6 percent *outdoor* figure is third-best ever.

Adam Vinatieri, on the other hand, while certainly one of the toughest big-game kickers in history, is the fourth-most accurate kicker on the books largely because he's converted 47 of 49 *indoor* kicks—96.0 percent.

Matt Stover has quietly recorded the best outdoor field-goal percentage in NFL history.

Outdoors, he's an 80.3 percent kicker—12th-best in history on the outdoor-only list.

Which brings us to Matt Stover, the greatest kicker in history that nobody knows about.

After sitting out his rookie year with the Giants with injuries, Stover has spent the rest of his 16-year career kicking for the Browns and Ravens, who are really the same team, even though they're different franchises. So he's never played a home game in a dome or even in a warm-weather city.

Yet, through 2006 he had made 85.1 percent of his outdoor field goals, the highest percentage in NFL history. Stover has played only 15 indoor games in his life, but in 192 outdoor games he's converted 384 of 452 field-goal attempts.

All-Time NFL Outdoor Kicking Stats

Kicker	Field Goals–Attempts	Percentage
Matt Stover	384–451	.851
Mike Vanderjagt	101–119	.849
David Akers	163–196	.833
Al Del Greco	143–172	.831
Shayne Graham	112–135	.830
Phil Dawson	142–174	.8161
Jeff Wilkins	124–152	.8158
Nick Lowery	106–130	.815
Pete Stoyanovich	206–253	.814
Norm Johnson	147–181	.812

Overall, Stover is the third-most accurate kicker ever and the only kicker in NFL history to convert 84 percent or more of his field goals eight straight years. He's made two Pro Bowl teams in 16 years, which is okay, but that's why he's leading off this underrated list.

Remove the tainted indoor numbers, and he hops past Shayne Graham and Vanderjagt into the number-one spot in a category that is officially unrecognized.

Stover holds an NFL record that doesn't exist. You can't get more underrated than that.

Postscript: Matt Stover grew up in Dallas as a huge Cowboys fan and sold programs during Cowboys games at Texas Stadium as a youth.

The Rest of the Most Underrated

2. TOMMY DAVIS

People have been declaring that Ray Guy is the greatest punter in NFL history for so long now that it's accepted as fact.

Everybody says it. *Shrug.* Must be true.

The truth is, he's not even the best punter in the history of the Bay Area.

Guy's reputation is understandable. He had the luxury of punting for a team that went to the playoffs 10 times in his 14-year career. He won three Super Bowls in an eight-year span with the Raiders and led the NFL in punting three times. He was a good enough athlete to get drafted by three major league baseball teams, and he could even *throw* a football 75 yards. He remains the only punter ever drafted in the first round. He once hit the roof of the Superdome in the Pro Bowl.

Not bad.

Just not the best.

Unlike Guy, Tommy Davis toiled in obscurity his entire football career. He punted from 1959 through 1969 for 49ers teams that never won more than seven games, never won a division title, and never reached the playoffs. So it's no surprise his tremendous career has been largely forgotten.

But despite playing all his home games three miles from the Pacific Ocean at cold, blustery Kezar Stadium, Davis put up routinely astounding numbers that nobody in NFL history has approached in the nearly half a century since he retired. He also led the NFL with 19 field goals in 1960, at the time the third-most ever in a season.

"When I was living in San Francisco, I used to go to all those 49ers games at Kezar Stadium, and fortunately, I had my stopwatch with me," says legendary football writer and historian Paul Zimmerman—Dr. Z of *Sports Illustrated*. "Those teams weren't that good, but Davis would put up 4.8 hang times regularly, and the crowd would always just go crazy cheering for him. There wasn't much else to cheer for. We'd be out there in the rain and the wind and cold, and he'd be hanging them up there 4.8, 4.9 every time. I've never seen a punter cheered like that in my life. Everybody talks about Ray Guy. Give me a break. I know, he hit the gondola. Big deal. He was a straight-down-the-middle punter. He never went for the sidelines. Tommy Davis was the greatest punter ever."

Davis's 44.7 career average is third-highest behind the overrated tandem of Sammy Baugh and Shane Lechler, but his consistency is what set Davis apart from other punting giants. He averaged 45.4 yards or higher *six* times, twice more than Baugh. When he retired in 1969, he owned six of the top 40 single-season punting averages in history. He's the only player to average 45 yards or better *five consecutive years*. He only had two of his 511 punts blocked—the second-best ratio among the top 10 punters in history.

Throw in his place-kicking stats, and the legend grows. He's still the only player in 49ers history with two field goals of 53 yards or more. Davis made 53-yarders against the Bears in 1964 and the Rams in 1965. His 99.4 extra-point percentage was a record when he retired and is now third-best. He led the NFL in field-goal accuracy in 1960—two years before he led the league in punting.

Postscript: Tommy Davis began smoking in high school and never stopped. He died of lung cancer on April 4, 1987. He was only 52 years old.

3. GALE SAYERS

It's possible to make a fairly convincing argument that Gale Sayers is one of the most overrated running backs ever. He only had two 900-yard seasons, never led the league in rushing touchdowns, and played more than nine games only four times before retiring before his 29th birthday.

This is the wrong chapter for that.

This chapter is about the most underrated specialists in NFL history, and Sayers is the most underrated kick returner the game has ever seen. Long before Devin Hester, long before Brian Mitchell, long before Eric Metcalf, Sayers was the most dangerous kickoff returner in football. But because of his phenomenal talent as a runner, his record-breaking 22-touchdown rookie year, and the knee injuries that led to the premature end of his career, Sayers's remarkable work as a returner has been long forgotten.

In his first career preseason game, August 12, 1965, against the Redskins, Sayers returned a punt 77 yards and a kickoff 93 yards, and he didn't slow down until his knees gave out a few years later.

Today, 35 years after he retired, Sayers still holds the NFL record for highest career kickoff return average at 30.6. Nobody else in NFL history has averaged within a full yard of that figure. Nobody who has played since Sayers retired has come within *three* yards of that figure.

He was that good.

Sayers shares the NFL record of six career kick returns for touchdowns, and his average of 37.7 in 1967 is second-highest in NFL history. He's also one of only eight players in history to return a punt and a kickoff for touchdowns in the same game.

Only four returners in history averaged 30 yards or better more than once. Sayers did it three times.

Sayers was also a gifted punt returner, although he didn't do it very often. He finished with a career average of 14.5 yards per return, which would be another NFL record, but his 27 career attempts aren't enough to qualify for the record book. Still, two of those 27 attempts went for touchdowns.

Combining punts and kicks, Mitchell averaged one touchdown every 82 returns, Metcalf one every 53, Donte Hall one every 50. Sayers averaged a touchdown every 14.8 times he returned a punt or kick.

Sayers was the best ever. Just not at what everybody assumes.

Postscript: It's odd that the Bears would fill this category so prominently. Devin Hester has revolutionized the return game at a time when special teamers are much faster and better coached. Hester averages one touchdown every 13.4 returns, and there is nothing underrated or overrated about that.

4. DON COCKROFT

Replacing Lou Groza was enough of a daunting task. Don Cockroft soon learned that would be only half his job. Cockroft was only supposed to be a place-kicker when the Browns took him in the third round of the 1967 draft. Groza was 43 years old and entering his 21st and final season, and Cockroft was the heir apparent to the great Lou "the Toe."

Nobody said anything about punting.

The Browns had an established punter in Gary Collins, who was only 26 years old and talented enough to lead the NFL in punting average at 46.7 in 1965, at the time the 11th-highest average in history. But Collins was also an outstanding receiver, and in 1966 he had finished sixth in the NFL with 946 receiving yards and second with 12 touchdowns. Early the next fall, Collins figured it was time to concentrate solely on receiving. It didn't hurt that he saw in practice just how good a punter Cockroft was.

"Early in my rookie year, Gary ran one of those 30-yard out routes on third down and came back to the sideline and said, 'Cockroft, get your ass out there and punt the ball,'" Cockroft recalled in Tony Grossi's 2004 book, *Tales from the Browns Sideline.*

Thus, the NFL's final two-way kicker was born.

By the late-1960s, specialization was starting to find its way into the NFL kicking game. Most of the great old combination guys—kicker-punters like Tommy Davis, Danny Villanueva, and Don Chandler—were gradually fading away, and foreign soccer-style kickers like Pete Gogolak, Toni Fritsch, and Jan Stenerud were popping up everywhere just to boot field goals. But these precocious soccer-style kickers couldn't punt, so for the first time teams were forced to start carrying two kickers on their rosters. By the mid-1970s there was only one full-time two-way kicker remaining: Cockroft.

And he may have been the best of all of them.

Cockroft, who spent his entire 13-year career with the Browns, finally abandoned punting after the 1976 season. But for eight years—from 1968 through 1976—he was as successful as anybody in the league in two divergent disciplines whose only similarity is that they involve kicking a football.

In 1972 he had one of the greatest seasons any specialist has ever had, making 82 percent of his field goals—at the time the third-best single-season percentage in NFL history—and being voted to the All-Pro team as a punter. Over the 1974 and 1975 seasons, he set an NFL record by making 16 consecutive field goals. Cockroft led the NFL in field-goal percentage four times and led the AFC five times.

He's the only man in NFL history to punt a ball 75 or more yards and kick a field goal 57 or more yards. In 1978, two years before he retired, he was still the NFL record holder for highest career field-goal percentage, at 67 percent.

Cockroft is not regarded anywhere near as highly as he should be, and for two entirely different skills.

Postscript: Don Cockroft is writing a book about the Browns' 1980 playoff loss to the Raiders, a game played in four-degree temperatures in Cleveland. In the game's final seconds, with the Raiders ahead 14–12 but the Browns on their 9-yard line, the Browns coach Sam Rutigliano went for a touchdown instead of letting Cockroft try a short field goal in brutal conditions. The play Rutigliano called, red right 88, resulted in a Mike Davis interception of Brian Sipe in the end zone and a Raiders win. Cockroft's book will be called Red Right 88: From Destiny to Despair.

5. JIM BAKKEN

Stop for a moment and just imagine how immense an honor it is to be named to an All-Decade team.

The team of the 1960s reads like a Who's Who of NFL greats: Deacon Jones, Paul Hornung, Bart Starr, Johnny Unitas, Ray Nitschke—all-timers.

Same with the 1970s team: Roger Staubach, Walter Payton, Jack Ham, Alan Page, Dave Casper—legends.

Now just imagine how monumental somebody would have to be to be named to *both teams*. He'd have to be a football god.

Dick Butkus is on both teams. He's one of the greatest linebackers ever.

Merlin Olsen's also on the lists, and he's perhaps the finest defensive tackle to play the game.

Larry Wilson's on them. Who knows why? That's a question debated in chapter 15.

Oh, and, um, Jim Bakken. Jim *who?*

Bakken isn't a household name or a first-ballot Hall of Famer like Butkus. But Bakken was the NFL's best kicker in the 1960s and still awfully good in the first half of the 1970s.

He led the NFL in field-goal accuracy twice in the mid-1960s and held the league record for career accuracy as late as 1969. Only two kickers in history—Hall of Famer Lou Groza (21 years) and Pat Leahy of the Jets (18 years)—spent more time with the same team than Bakken did.

Because he spent his entire 17-year career with the Cardinals during their 50-year streak without a postseason victory, Bakken's accomplishments have been largely forgotten.

How about this? In its one acknowledgment of Bakken's greatness, the Hall of Fame actually does have a display commemorating the four kickers in NFL history who have made seven field goals in a game. On the official Hall of Fame website, Bakken is listed with an NFL-record seven field goals against the Steelers on September 26, 1967.

He actually did it two days earlier.

They got the date wrong. Now that's being underrated.

Postscript: Jim Bakken made at least one field goal in an NFL-record 19 consecutive games over the 1966 and 1967 seasons. He broke Lou Groza's record by seven.

The Most Overrated NFL Record

CONSECUTIVE GAMES PLAYED BY PUNTER JEFF FEAGLES

He's never completed a pass, although he's thrown eight. He has minus-three career rushing yards. He's never scored a point, intercepted a pass, or sacked a quarterback. He kicks footballs for a living, and Jeff Feagles does it better than almost anybody who's ever lived.

Feagles has punted 1,514 times for 62,928 yards with 483 punts inside the opposing 20-yard-line. All NFL records.

A remarkable career. What's most impressive is that Feagles ranks third in NFL history with a 44.5 postseason punting average. That's how Feagles should be remembered.

He should not be remembered for consecutive games played. On November 27, 2005, Feagles played in his 283rd consecutive game when he punted for the Giants against the Seahawks in Seattle. An NFL record—and obviously overrated.

By the end of 2006, Feagles had played in 304 straight games over a span of 19 seasons with the Patriots, Eagles, Cardinals, Seahawks, and Giants. That's a marvelous achievement. Playing in 304 consecutive games at any position is a tremendous accomplishment. That means every autumn Sunday for nearly two decades Feagles hasn't gotten the flu, hasn't pulled a hamstring, and hasn't sprained his ankle. Feagles started playing when he was 22 years old and has continued without missing a game beyond his 40th birthday, which is incredible.

Jeff Feagles takes a hit of oxygen after a play in an exhibition game against the Broncos at Denver in August 2002.

But it's also silly to compare what Feagles does to what defensive tackles and guards and linebackers do. Jim Marshall played in 282 straight games, the NFL record before Feagles took it over. Bill Romanowski played in 243 consecutive games. Vikings center Mick Tingelhoff played in 240 straight games. Feagles never had to tackle Walter Payton like Marshall did. He never had to block Dick Butkus like Tinglehoff did. He never had to get run over by Craig "Ironhead" Heyward two games a year like Romanowski did.

Feagles drops a football toward the ground and then he kicks it. But there he is, right in the NFL record book—most consecutive games played.

"All I know," Feagles said, "is they won't put an asterisk next to it."

Postscript: Cal Ripken Jr. holds the baseball record for consecutive games played with 2,632 straight games over 17 years. A.C. Green holds the NBA record at 1,192, and Doug Jarvis holds the NHL record with 964 consecutive games.

CHAPTER 10

Running Backs

The Most Overrated Running Back of All Time

LARRY CSONKA

Here's what everybody remembers about Larry Csonka. They remember his brutal running style and his determination to punish defenders, to make them rethink any notion of trying to tackle him in the future.

Csonka's approach to running with the football has always been synonymous with America's approach to advancing any national goal: if you decide not to get out of the way, it's understood that we will run over you or through you to get where we're going. What's the greatest American battle cry of them all? "Damn the torpedoes! Full steam ahead!" by David G. Farragut, the first admiral of the U.S. Navy, in 1864.

Csonka was the great admiral's natural heir. So, when he was carrying the football, Csonka truly embodied the American spirit. Perhaps this is why he was so popular and has retained such a potent and enduring image as a great NFL ball carrier.

But here's what people forget about him. They forget that he ran for only 8,081 yards in his career, well below the 10,000-yard benchmark usually required for serious Hall of Fame consideration. Yet Csonka was enshrined in Canton in 1987, in just his second year as a finalist.

He is listed as a fullback in the Hall of Fame's official guide. But so is Cleveland Browns great Jim Brown, who is considered the greatest ball carrier of all time. Now, we can clearly conclude Larry Csonka is *not* Jim Brown, and vice versa. And when considered next to Brown, Csonka is clearly overrated.

So for a fairer comparison to other ball carriers, consider that Corey Dillon, going into the 2007 season, had run for 11,241 yards, and Ricky Watters had 10,643 career rushing yards. And, like Csonka, both of them have Super Bowl rings. Like Csonka, both of them were big, bruising backs and the featured ball carriers of their respective original teams.

Yet, unlike Csonka, both will probably struggle to get the call to Canton. They will be considered running backs instead of fullbacks. In addition, neither is used in the same breath when great NFL running backs are discussed. Yet, Csonka is considered a legend. He shouldn't be.

In his 11-year career, he never led the NFL for a single season in rushing. (Even Edgerrin James has done that twice. James makes this overrated chapter a bit later on.) The most he had in a season was 1,117 yards—that doesn't even crack the top 50 in single-season performances. He never led the league in touchdowns scored in a single season, either.

So, if it wasn't about yards or touchdowns, what was Csonka's appeal? He did lead the NFL in rushing yards per carry in 1971 with 5.4 yards per carry. Pretty good for a fullback. But did Csonka change or define a running style? Nope. Ever heard of Bronko Nagurski? Born in Rainy River, Ontario (now, that's the hometown for a fullback), Nagurski played for the Chicago Bears' Monsters of the Midway and was a charter member of Canton. Nagurski—a bruising fullback before anybody really passed the football, so defenses loaded up on him—was Csonka way before Csonka was Csonka.

Nagurski only played one year with the Bears' great quarterback Sid Luckman, 1943. And Csonka had a Hall of Fame quarterback, Bob Griese, throwing to a Hall of Fame wide receiver, Paul Warfield. And that opened up the football field.

Now take this into consideration: Csonka was running behind one of the greatest offensive lines ever assembled. His center, Jim Langer, is in the Hall

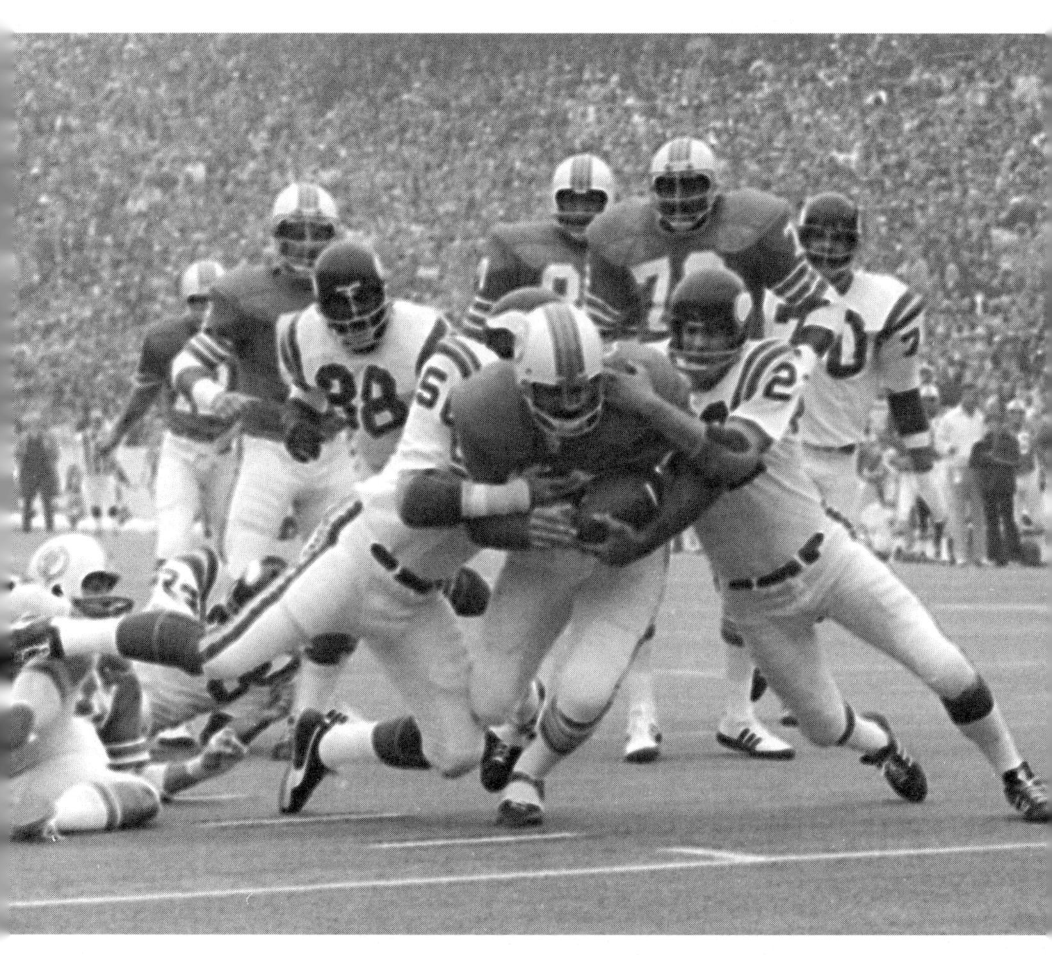

While fans might remember Larry Csonka for dragging tacklers for extra yards, as he does here against the Vikings in Super Bowl VIII, the big back's career total yards and touchdowns are surprisingly pedestrian.

of Fame. So is the great Dolphins guard Larry Little. And another guard, Bob Kuechenberg, should be in Canton and no doubt will get there soon. Which begs the question: why exactly did Larry Csonka have to run over all those tacklers in the first place?

Csonka's image as a great ball carrier was created, of course, by those slow-motion NFL Films scenes of his performances during the Miami Dolphins' undefeated season of 1972 and his back-to-back-to-back appearances in Super Bowls VI, VII, and VIII.

In Super Bowl VIII, he shredded the Minnesota Vikings for 145 yards and was named MVP. And the year before, in the undefeated season, he had 112 yards against the Redskins in Super Bowl VII. But in Super Bowl VI, the one the Dolphins lost to the Dallas Cowboys, Csonka was pedestrian—nine carries for 40 yards and a key fumble early in the game. A nonfactor.

And look at his contribution to the great Dolphins teams in comparison to a famous sidekick: Mercury Morris. In the perfect season, Csonka led the Dolphins with 1,117 yards. Morris wasn't far behind with an even 1,000 yards. But Morris scored 12 touchdowns, double Csonka's six touchdowns. Morris doesn't get nearly the credit.

Csonka had a reputation for being extremely sure-handed. He fumbled only 21 times in 1,891 carries. But his 11-year career had four very dark years—1975 through 1978. You cannot say that about very many Hall of Famers—nearly 40 percent of their career being unproductive.

And part of this was his own fault. He was determined to cash in on his fame, and he shocked the NFL by playing out his option in Miami to sign with the Memphis Southmen in the doomed World Football League. That nearly suicidal career move lasted just one year.

Csonka cashed a big check, but the WFL died midway through its second season. Csonka begged then–NFL commissioner Pete Rozelle to let him come back to Miami. But a pending lawsuit, Rozelle claimed, prevented it. Even his mentor, the legendary Dolphins head coach Don Shula, insisted he was powerless to do anything about it.

In 1976 Csonka was back in the NFL. He signed with the Giants and had three pedestrian seasons for three awful teams. New York finished last in the NFC East all three years.

Shula took him back in 1979, the last season of his career. He carried the ball 220 times—the most carries of his career—but he averaged just 3.8 yards per carry.

Postscript: The Dolphins won the AFC East in 1979 but were drubbed in the first round of the playoffs by the mighty Pittsburgh Steelers 34–14. Larry Csonka had his worst postseason performance: 10 carries for just 20 yards. He retired soon after.

The Rest of the Most Overrated

2. TIKI BARBER

When the nominees for the Hall of Fame class of 2007 were announced, 11 first-timers were on the list, including Ricky Watters, the iconoclastic running back who won a Super Bowl in San Francisco and then had six workhorse years in Philadelphia and Seattle.

Watters is not going to make it to Canton. His career is brought up here because he finished with 10,643 rushing yards, which is good enough for 16th on the all-time list. Believe it or not, that's one spot *ahead* of Tiki Barber, who retired after the 2006 season with 10,448 yards. How would you expect to know that? The celebration of Barber's career—and his impending retirement and move to full-time broadcasting—caused a near-total eclipse of the sports media sun. In the meantime, Watters has languished in near obscurity. (Partly because he was a majorly mysterious dude, but that's for another book in another galaxy.)

Back to Tiki. In short, his career has been habitually overhyped and overrated. Maybe it was that infectious smile. Maybe it was because he played in New York. Maybe because he fell in love with the camera and it fell in love with him.

But let's compare Barber to another former San Francisco 49ers running back, Roger Craig. Craig finished under the key 10,000-yard demarcation, at 8,189 yards, or 32nd on the all-time list. But he had to share a lot of carries with Wendell Tyler, Joe Cribbs, and Tom Rathman. And Craig's receiving yardage is almost identical to Barber's: 4,911 to 4,940. And Craig had 17 career catches for touchdowns while Barber only had 12.

Indeed, here's where Barber really falls short. As a runner, Barber scored only 55 times. Craig had 56 rushing touchdowns. Watters? An astounding 78 rushing touchdowns.

And both Watters and Craig won a championship. With the 'Niners, both of them were integral to the team's postseason success on offense. Craig has three Super Bowl rings. Watters has one. Barber, who has none, went to one Super Bowl with the Giants. And his performance in that game was ordinary—11 carries for 49 yards, no touchdowns (albeit against the historically good Baltimore Ravens defense).

In seven postseason appearances, Barber had just two memorable games. In a 2003 wild-card game in San Francisco, Barber had 26 carries for 115 yards and scored the only postseason touchdown of his career. And in the last game of his career, a wild-card contest in Philadelphia, Barber racked up 137 yards on 26 carries. The Giants lost both games. Indeed, Barber was a loser in his final four postseason appearances.

Barber is always called a big-numbers guy. But not when you compare him to another running back that had 10 years in the league—Barry Sanders of the Lions, who actually makes the all-time *overrated* Hall of Famers list in this book. Sanders finished with 4,821 yards more than Barber. He went to 10 Pro Bowls. Barber went to three. Of course, Sanders had many more carries, 3,062 to 2,216 for Barber, but Sanders also had 10 receiving touchdowns to Barber's 12, even though Sanders had many fewer receptions: 352 to Barber's 586. Overall, early in his career, Barber might have had more carries, but he just wasn't considered a workhorse back, and, frankly, his coaches didn't trust him with the football.

Indeed, that's the reason Barber made so few trips to Hawaii: the fumbles. Until head coach Tom Coughlin and his running backs coach Jerald Ingram showed up in New York, Barber gave the football away at alarming rate. From 2000 to 2003, the four seasons prior to Coughlin, Barber fumbled the ball 35 times, turning it over 17 times. Coughlin showed Barber how to hold the football "high and tight," and the turnaround was dramatic. From 2004 until he retired, Barber had just nine fumbles, losing just four. Sanders lost just 15 fumbles in his entire 10-year career!

That's why it was so perplexing that Barber went out of his way several times to criticize Coughlin and his coaching staff, specifically his insinuation that the reason he retired after just 10 seasons—at the height of his productivity—was because Coughlin overworked him.

"The grind took its toll on me and really forced me to start thinking about what I wanted to do next," Barber said. "And that's not a bad thing. That's a good thing, for me at least. Maybe not for the Giants because they lose one of their great players."

We'll see about that.

Postscript: Here's what longtime pro football writer Ira Miller, formerly of the San Francisco Chronicle, said to CBS SportsLine.com about Barber: "If he were playing in Cincinnati or Kansas City, would we be talking about him?"

3. HERSCHEL WALKER

The conventional wisdom says that Herschel Walker would be in the Hall of Fame if he had not come out of Georgia a year early and taken $5 million (then the richest contract in football history) from the New Jersey Generals to play in the doomed United States Football League.

The conventional wisdom is wrong.

Yes, Walker's first three years of pro ball were brilliant. Twice he was the MVP of the USFL. But that's like somebody saying they had a great high school football career—then finding out they never made it out of junior varsity.

The NFL doesn't recognize the more than 7,000 all-purpose yards Walker amassed in the USFL. And it didn't recognize the USFL, either. So the rival league filed a billion-dollar antitrust suit against Pete Rozelle and the big boys. After an 11-week trial, a federal court awarded the USFL $1. Rozelle's lead lawyer? Paul Tagliabue.

The real loser was Walker. He made his dough, but the years were gone. For his 13 years in the NFL, Walker has been credited for 18,168 all-purpose yards, which is still good enough for eighth place on the all-time list. But when examined on a year-by-year basis, that number is deceiving. Even in his Pro Bowl years, 1987 and 1988, Walker never led the NFL in any single season in any of the major rushing categories: rushes, rushing yards, or rushing touchdowns. As a result, he had little effect on his teams. In fact, it can be argued fairly convincingly that Walker had a negative impact.

Consider this: the Dallas Cowboys, Walker's first NFL team, were 31–17–1 in the three seasons before acquiring Walker. With Walker, the Cowboys went 17–35. Dallas traded him to the Minnesota Vikings for five players and seven draft picks, which resulted in, among others, the following players: Hall of Fame running back Emmitt Smith, defensive lineman Russell Maryland, and defensive back Darren Woodson. It was the largest player trade in NFL history. You know what happened next. Dallas went 67–29 over the next six seasons and won three Super Bowls.

Next stop: Minnesota. Same thing. In the three seasons BW (Before Walker), the Vikings went 28–19. With him, Minnesota finished at .500 (24–24) from 1989 through 1991. Once he was gone, the Vikings went 30–18 in the next three seasons, making the playoffs in each of those years.

It gets worse. In 1992 Walker was signed by the Philadelphia Eagles. In the four seasons before they acquired Walker, the Eagles went 41–23. With him, from 1992 to 1994, Philadelphia was 26–22. After he left, they got better, however, going 20–12 in the next two seasons (1995–1996).

He played one season with the New York Giants, 1995. In the two years BW, the Giants went 20–12. They were 5–11 with him. In the five years after he left, New York went a combined 43–36–1 and went to the playoffs twice and appeared in Super Bowl XXXV.

Postscript: Herschel Walker played in just four postseason games in the NFL. His combined totals were 28 carries for a paltry 132 yards. He never scored a touchdown in the playoffs.

4. SHAUN ALEXANDER

For years, behind his back, Shaun Alexander's teammates in Seattle have called him "Soft Shaun." For an NFL player, no nickname comes with more baggage. But considering that before he hurt his foot in 2007, Alexander never missed a snap in his first six seasons, the insinuation of the nickname would seem to be misguided.

What's more, he's a three-time Pro Bowler who won league MVP honors in 2005, when he set the record for touchdowns in a season with 27. So, why such a dishonorable moniker?

The reason: Alexander falls into that great middling category of running backs who have put up gaudy numbers that amounted to very little when it counted most.

The most convincing evidence of that came during the season he thought would convince his detractors that their criticism was way off base. In 2005 Alexander led the NFL with 370 rushes, 1,880 rushing yards, and 27 touchdowns. He was voted league MVP—perhaps making the greatest argument for waiting until after the postseason is finished before bestowing that honor.

Why? Because that postseason Alexander was pretty much a nonfactor. Again he put up big numbers in the NFC Championship game against the Carolina Panthers—34 carries for 132 yards—but the game was a blowout and would have been no matter what Alexander did.

Before that game, Alexander struggled mightily against the Washington Redskins' defense of Gregg Williams. The visiting Redskins lost a close game 20–10. Alexander's contribution? A meager six carries for nine yards.

Now look at Super Bowl XL. Alexander was mediocre, putting up a meaningless 20 carries for 95 yards. He did not get a sniff of the goal line. For a guy who took it to the house 27 times that season, that is coming up really, well, soft.

That Alexander makes the overrated list should come as no real surprise. A poll of NFL players taken before the 2005 season by *Sports Illustrated* named Alexander "the most overrated" running back in the NFL. Interestingly, the summer after his MVP season, the same magazine again took a poll of NFL players to determine which back they would build their team around. Alexander finished 10th. He got 1 percent of the vote.

Alexander is a product of one of the best offensive lines in football, namely left tackle Walter Jones and (for most of Alexander's career) guard Steve Hutchinson. Add right guard Chris Gray and center Robbie Tobeck. Those four blocked for Alexander for five straight years together. With those guys up front, most backs would have had the same success as Alexander.

Alexander, who runs flat-footed and often tentatively, has put no real stamp on the running back position other than being on the cover of *Madden NFL 2007*. He has no signature move, no breakaway speed. He inflicts no pain, no embarrassment—except the shame of big numbers that thus far have added up to very little.

Postscript: Here's what an NFC scout said about Shaun Alexander's running style: "Nobody fears him. If you decide you want to stop him, you can take him right out of the game. Make him a nonfactor."

5. EDGERRIN JAMES

Everyone thought Bill Polian should have had his head examined in 2005. What was the Indianapolis Colts general manager thinking, allowing Edgerrin James—one of the most prolific running backs in franchise history—to take a walk?

There's an old saying: "If you set out to make money, that's all you'll make. If you set out to make history, you'll make both."

James made his money, signing a four-year, $30 million, free-agent contract with the Arizona Cardinals prior to the 2006 season.

Without him, the Colts made history, winning Super Bowl XLI. Which, of course, leads to only one possible conclusion: Edgerrin James has been vastly overrated. He was a product of his multitalented Colts teammates—Peyton Manning, Marvin Harrison, Reggie Wayne, Dallas Clark, the list goes on—and his offensive coordinator, the unheralded and spectacularly underrated Tom Moore.

Want proof? In 2005, Edge's last year in Indy, the Colts finished the season with 1,703 yards rushing as a team. James accounted for 1,506 yards on the ground. In 2006, the championship season, with James in the desert, the Colts finished with 1,762 yards rushing as a team.

James's replacement? A rookie. Joseph Addai, the Colts' first-round pick, had 1,081 yards on 226 carries, or 4.8 yards per carry. In James's seven years with the Colts, he never got north of 4.6 yards per carry in a single season. His career average is a pedestrian 4.1.

Of course, Dominic Rhodes had 187 carries for 641 yards. So, Tom Moore's two-back system was far more effective—and, for Polian's sake, far less expensive. Here's a testimonial you don't often get: "These two backs are maybe a little more physical than James," said Baltimore Ravens head coach Brian Billick.

Last season, in Arizona, without that big Colts offensive line and a wildly productive quarterback, James averaged 3.4 yards a carry—a career low.

In Indianapolis, Addai was far more effective in another critical area: picking up the blitz. Let's just say, to paraphrase Manning, there weren't many "breakdowns in protection" in 2006. A staple on the *State Farm NFL Matchup Show* on ESPN is Merrill Hoge pointing out Addai decleating some blitzing linebacker with—as Hogey likes to say—"a rising blow, same foot, same shoulder."

That's the Chuck Noll way. Tom Moore once coached Hoge in Pittsburgh—for Noll. A young defensive back for Noll was, of course, Tony Dungy.

Postscript: It's sad that Edgerrin James and the Colts parted ways on the doorstep of a world championship. As his lost season in Arizona wore on, it wore him down. "It's getting old," he said.

But he was never bitter. During Super Bowl week, he hung out in Miami with his old Colts teammates, telling Sports Illustrated, *"These guys are my friends. Why wouldn't I want my friends to be happy? Isn't that what you're supposed to do—root for your friends?"*

Edge is a good dude but still overrated.

The Most Underrated Running Back of All Time

OTTIS ANDERSON

You probably don't remember much about Ottis Anderson. But how could you forget that forearm? Anderson swung that forearm from down below his thigh pads and propelled it high above his shoulder, anticipating the recipient of his blow with perfect timing.

With a huge pad from his wrist to his bulging bicep, Anderson's arm exploded precisely in the ribcage of the oncoming Buffalo Bills—one of the signature scenes of Super Bowl XXV. It was his personal axe handle, chopping through the Buffalo defense, striking linebackers Cornelius Bennett and Shane Conlan and defensive backs Nate Odomes and Leonard Smith like he was playing a game of mailbox baseball on a country road.

When he was finished, Anderson's team, the New York Giants, had discovered the only possible way to secure a stunning upset of the mighty Buffalo Bills to claim the Lombardi Trophy: let Anderson do it.

It was one of the most underrated Super Bowl performances by one of the most underrated running backs in league history.

Anderson finished with 102 yards on 21 carries and scored the game's final touchdown, a one-yard run that gave the Giants command of the game. More importantly, Anderson's dominant running performance was just what Giants head coach Bill Parcells wanted to beat the Bills—it was a game of keep-away.

The Bills' high-powered offense had control of the ball for a Super Bowl record–low 19 minutes and 27 seconds. Eventually, Bills place-kicker Scott Norwood would miss the potential game-winning field goal, and New York would win 20–19. Many Giants had outstanding performances in that game, but it was Anderson who was named MVP of Super Bowl XXV.

What made that performance all the more remarkable was that during the 1990 season, it was clear that Anderson's long career was beginning to run its course. He finished the year with just 784 yards on 225 carries, averaging just 3.5 yards a carry. This came after running for 1,023 yards in 1989—his sixth

After a long career, Ottis Anderson mustered up the strength to help pound the Buffalo Bills into submission in Super Bowl XXV. (Photo courtesy Getty Images)

career 1,000-yard season. And 1990 would be his final season of real productivity. Anderson would have just 53 carries in 1991 and handle the ball just 10 times in 1992, the last year of his career.

Still, by running for 1,023 yards in 1989, Anderson was one of only six running backs in NFL history to have more than 1,000 yards in a season in the second decade of his career. The others are Emmitt Smith, Walter Payton, Barry Sanders, Franco Harris, and John Riggins. And all of them are in the Hall of Fame.

Anderson has been left out of Canton. It's wrong. Let's examine the trend in Hall of Fame backs. When the Hall of Fame opened in 1963, it was pretty much understood that 5,000 career rushing yards would get you in. Then, in 1971 Jim Brown set the bar quite a bit higher, finishing his career with 12,312.

In just eight years' time, the threshold for consideration seemed to be 10,000 yards. Now that's not even good enough. Ricky Watters finished with 10,643 yards, and he played a pivotal role for the San Francisco 49ers' most recent championship. But Canton most likely is not Watters's future. Same for Eddie George (10,441) and Tiki Barber (10,448)—for different reasons.

Evidently, the Hall of Fame selectors are looking for some kind of special contribution to the history of the game. That's the only way you can justify Larry Csonka (8,081 yards) being inducted, although a strong case has been made that Bronko Nagurski redefined the fullback position three decades before Csonka.

So it looks like some unfortunate accident of timing is keeping Anderson out of Canton. But his singularly spectacular performance in Super Bowl XXV should be enough of a historical contribution to qualify. It was at least as significant—and good—as Csonka's MVP performance in Super Bowl VIII.

Csonka played 11 years. Anderson played 15 years—and don't forget, eight of those years he slaved away for the woeful St. Louis Cardinals, who drafted him in the first round in 1979.

When he became eligible for the Hall in 1998, Anderson's 10,273 career rushing yards put him ninth in that category among the list of running backs already in the Hall of Fame—right behind O.J. Simpson, who finished his career with 11,236 yards.

At the finish of the 2006 season, Anderson's rushing total put him 20th on the all-time list. His 2,562 rushing attempts? Sixteenth all time. You want scoring? Anderson is 17th all time with 81 rushing touchdowns—that's only nine fewer than Eric Dickerson, but seven more than Earl Campbell and 17 more than Csonka. All of them are in Canton.

Anderson's longevity and durability were remarkable. He was rookie of the year in 1979, then Comeback Player of the Year in 1989, and MVP of the Super Bowl in the 1990 season—the only running back in league history to achieve that trifecta that many years apart.

Postscript: Back to that Super Bowl performance and the Giants' opening drive of the third quarter, which lasted a Super Bowl–record 9 minutes, 29 seconds. The drive, which included a punishing 14 plays and went 75 yards, almost died on the Giants' 47-yard line.

It was third-and-one. Bill Parcells called on Ottis Anderson to find just enough room to keep the drive alive. Instead, Anderson ripped up Buffalo's gut for 24 yards, putting the Giants on the Bills' 29-yard line. It was the key play in the critical Giants' possession of the game, and it allowed New York to win its second Super Bowl in five years. It will probably send Parcells to Canton. Anderson should go with him.

The Rest of the Most Underrated

2. ROGER CRAIG

Marshall Faulk, Brian Westbrook, LaDainian Tomlinson, and Reggie Bush—those big stars owe a big debt of gratitude to the guy who made their careers possible, the player who morphed the running back position into a fantasy footballer's delight. That guy is Roger Craig. He was the first back to effectively run with the football and then explode out of the backfield to become a highly lethal receiver, with the shiftiness and guile to make linebackers look silly and cornerbacks overmatched.

It's no accident that Craig is the only running back in league history to go to the playoffs in all 11 years of his career. In 1985, with his signature high-stepping style (copied by Ricky Watters years later), Craig was the first running back in NFL history to amass more than 1,000 yards, both rushing and receiving.

Craig's hybrid contribution, which revolutionized the game, was really a creation of the genius of Bill Walsh, the San Francisco 49ers head coach who drafted Craig in the second round out of Nebraska in 1983.

Two seasons earlier the 'Niners had already won a championship (Super Bowl XVI), but Walsh knew he needed a running back who could really capture the essence of the West Coast offense, someone who could catch short passes that would turn into long gains.

Before there was the league-wide infatuation with YAC, or yards after the catch, there was just Craig. For his career, Craig averaged 8.7 yards per reception, just a shade under Marshall Faulk's nine yards per catch. And Faulk is a Hall of Fame lock.

"The thing about Roger was that he had the perfect set of skills for exactly what we wanted to do, and he changed the game as we knew it then and as we know it now," said Walsh. "He was the future of what the running back position would become."

And for that reason alone, Craig should be in the Hall of Fame. That's why he makes this list of underrated running backs—that and the fact that Craig seems to be falling off everybody's radar screen. Let's put a stop to that right now.

Call it the Tiki factor. With the hype machine in New York in full engagement, the combination of Tiki Barber's photogenic smile and a willing army of media enablers created the illusion that Barber reinvented the position. So now that he's retired, Barber has become the center of a debate—should he get into the Hall? Well, before Barber gets consideration, Watters should be seriously considered. And before either of them go to Canton, Craig should get in first.

Since we're focusing on the hybrid aspect of Craig's game, let's look at catching the football. Barber had only 20 more catches—586 to 566—but Craig started his career as a fullback and had to share time and touches with Wendell Tyler and one of the best pass-catching fullbacks of all time, Tom Rathman. Barber averaged 8.8 yards per catch, a negligible difference with Craig's 8.7. But Craig had 17 touchdown receptions to Barber's 12. In other words, Craig scored every 33 times he caught the ball, and Barber scored once every 49 catches.

Craig was forgotten again during the discussion of the Hall of Fame class of 2007, when Buffalo Bills running back Thurman Thomas was inducted. Eric Allen, the former Eagles cornerback who should go to the Hall himself, praised Thomas but overdid it: "He was the first back to truly show NFL teams how dangerous a back could be consistently catching the ball out of the backfield."

Uh, no, E.A., that would have been Roger Craig. Here's further proof. Thomas is considered a better ball carrier than Craig because he had more yards (12,074 to 8,189) and more touchdowns (65 to 56). But when you compare point production to overall *touches*, Craig beats Thomas. Craig scored six points once every 35 times he touched the football. Thomas scored a touchdown every 38 touches. Not that much difference, you say. They both made five Pro Bowls. So, they're about the same.

Except one more thing—as in The Thing Is the Bling. Craig, who scored a record three touchdowns in Super Bowl XIX, has three championship rings. Thomas has none. Now that Thomas is in Canton, Craig should go, too.

Postscript: Roger Craig made the Pro Bowl as both a running back and as a fullback. In Hawaii in 1985 he was the starting fullback for the NFC Pro Bowl squad, blocking for Walter Payton.

3. DARYL JOHNSTON

In his 11-year career, Daryl Johnston never finished in the top 10 in any major running back category. He is not in the all-time top 50 in any major category. So it's impossible to sit here and rattle off a bunch of statistical comparisons about why he's been overlooked. But when you examine the totality of Johnston's career and what he meant to one of the best football teams ever assembled—the Dallas Cowboys of the 1990s—and how he supported the career of the most prolific running back of all time—Emmitt Smith—then you can see why he makes this list.

It's a difficult argument to make. After all, as the second broadcast team for FOX-TV on Sunday afternoons, Johnston gets plenty of national face time. But you know what TV does—with a surreal ease, it emphasizes the moment in a way that almost erases the past. So people forget. They hear Johnston lucidly explain the nuances of the game, but they have no clue just how good a player he was, where he fits into the mosaic of the modern game. That's why he makes this underrated list.

First off, let's get something straight. Johnston should not be going to Canton. As fullbacks go, he's not Larry Csonka. He's not even Mike Alstott.

Johnston's career totals are 753 rushing yards on 232 attempts and just eight touchdowns. His numbers are far better as a receiver: 294 catches, 2,227 yards, and an average of 7.6 yards per catch (just higher than Alstott at 7.5). Johnston finished with 14 touchdown catches. As of 2006, his 11th year, Alstott had 13. Partly due to his superior rushing numbers and partly because Chris Berman created "the Good Hands with Alstott" nickname, Alstott went to the Pro Bowl for six straight years (1997–2002).

Alstott played in the Pro Bowl as a fullback, even though technically he was a ball carrier, and he really never has been a blocking fullback, per se. Johnston—known simply as "Moose"—was clearly one of the greatest blocking fullbacks of the modern era. Take Johnston out of the Cowboys lineup. Insert Alstott. And Emmitt Smith doesn't even sniff the Hall of Fame.

Johnston played in 16 postseason games—a record for a fullback. And for his first eight seasons, he did not miss a snap, despite the ungodly abuse his body took as Smith's lead blocker and picking up the blitz for Troy Aikman. And during those eight seasons, the Cowboys won three Super Bowls. During that time, Smith led the NFL in rushing four times. Johnston was an integral part of a blocking unit that included some of the best offensive linemen of their era, including Nate Newton, Erik Williams, Mark Stepnoski, and Mark Tuinei.

But it was Johnston who often got Smith free, got him past the second level of defenders. That's where Smith's big runs and big numbers came from—Johnston clearing out linebackers, allowing Smith to toy with defensive backs ill-prepared to bring him down.

The signature play of Smith's career was the Cowboys' famous lead draw from the I formation, with Johnston leading the way.

"He probably had half his career yards off that play," longtime Cowboys scout Gil Brandt wrote when Smith retired.

Smith retired as the NFL's leading rusher. So give Johnston at least half the credit for that.

Postscript: If you're ever at an NFL game when Daryl Johnston is the analyst for FOX, keep your eye on the field before kickoff. Like Troy Aikman, Johnston always walks the field before the game, not only to talk to players and visit with other broadcasters but to remind himself of the feel of the game.

That feel left him with a neck injury that robbed him of the final three seasons of his career. Another reason why he's overlooked and underrated.

4. COREY DILLON

Let's get something straight right away. Corey Dillon is not a nice guy. He's a tough guy, and he's a tough runner. He's a nasty, overpowering runner. On rare occasions, he can be crafty and sometimes nifty. But there is nothing nice about him. The way Dillon has approached his job as an NFL running back, nice is a four-letter word.

Here's a five-letter word to describe Corey Dillon's underrated career: great. You never hear Dillon's name mentioned among the NFL's all-time greatest backs. You should. His productivity and longevity make a very compelling case, yet he is continually overlooked—probably because he never tried to win a popularity contest, especially with the media.

It's tough to be Mr. Congeniality when you're slaving away for the woeful Cincinnati Bengals. Even though he was named to three Pro Bowls wearing a Bengals uniform, nobody really paid much attention to what he accomplished until 2000, when Dillon rushed for 278 yards in a game against Denver. Dillon broke Walter Payton's 23-year-old record of 275 yards. Three years later, Jamal Lewis broke it again with a 295-yard game. But take this into consideration: Lewis had 30 carries when he broke the record. Payton had 40 carries when he set the record in 1977. Dillon had only 22. Of the top nine rushing performances in league history, Dillon had the fewest carries by far.

Nice.

And for his career, Dillon's got some awfully nice numbers. After the 2006 season, his 10th in the league, Dillon had 11,241 rushing yards, which was good enough for 14th-best all time. That's O.J. territory, as in Simpson, as in the guy who may no longer own his Heisman Trophy but who still happens to be in the Pro Football Hall of Fame. Simpson finished his career with 11,236 rushing yards. Good for 15th-best all time. Dillon passed him on the all-time list in 2006. Dillon is just below Thurman Thomas on the all-time rushing list, and Thomas—also mentioned as a great NFL back—was in the Canton class of 2007.

And Dillon has a Super Bowl ring. In fact, what Dillon did in his championship season of 2004 with the New England Patriots is nothing short of extraordinary. Traded by the Cincinnati Bengals, Dillon revived his career and took the pressure off Tom Brady and the Patriots' passing game in a way that allowed Bill Belichick to get that coveted third Super Bowl title in four years—an NFL first. In 2004, at the ripe running back age of 30 years old, Dillon carried the football a career-high 345 times for a career-high 1,635 yards.

In the postseason that year, Dillon carried the football a whopping 65 times in three games. He gained 292 yards and scored two touchdowns, including one to beat the Eagles in Super Bowl XXXIX.

Just in case you were wondering, Simpson never gained more than 1,000 yards after he turned 30 years old. What Dillon did puts him in John Riggins territory. Riggo did something very similar at age 34 in 1983. In Washington, Riggins had fewer yards (1,347) but more carries (375) and more touchdowns (24). The Redskins lost to the Los Angeles Raiders that year in the Super Bowl.

Riggins, who got his ring a year earlier, finished his career with 11,352 rushing yards—13th on the all-time list. He was elected to the Hall of Fame in only his second year as a finalist. That should be Corey Dillon territory.

Postscript: Here's what the venerable Sports Illustrated *writer Peter King told the Cincinnati Bengals website about whether Corey Dillon's personality would be a factor in the discussion among Hall of Fame selectors: "There are two questions that I've never heard in that meeting room," said King, "a), was the guy a good interview, and b), what kind of guy he is."*

5. LORENZO NEAL

What, *another* fullback? A journeyman fullback makes this list? Yep, another fullback. There's a good reason why Lorenzo Neal has made a grand tour of the NFL. He's good—superbly underrated good. General managers know what Neal has done to make marginal running backs good and good running backs great.

Let's start in San Diego, most likely the last stop in Neal's career, which dates back to 1993, a long time for the brutal pounding absorbed by one of the league's all-time great blocking backs. The Chargers brought in Neal for one specific reason: they knew LaDainian Tomlinson was on the launching pad to greatness, and they needed somebody to help push the button. That somebody was Lorenzo Neal, a little Mack truck at 5′11″, 255 pounds.

Neal was already 32 years old when he arrived in San Diego in 2003. Nevertheless, his impact is easy to measure. With Neal in town, Tomlinson's touchdown total shot up from 13 in 2003, 17 in 2004, 18 in 2005, to a record 28 in 2006. In those four years, Neal did not miss a single game. In short order, Tomlinson has cracked the top 25 of all time in rushing yards.

Neal's first NFL stop was New Orleans. He blocked for running back Mario Bates, who enjoyed his best years when Neal wore a Saints uniform. In 1996, Neal's final year in New Orleans, Bates gained 584 yards. The following year Bates dropped to 440 yards and was soon gone from the league.

Neal had quick one-year stints with the Jets and Buccaneers, but he never got a head of steam. In Tennessee in 1999 and 2000, however, Neal helped Eddie George become a runaway train. George had back-to-back 1,000-yard seasons. When Neal left, however, George dropped to 939 yards in 2001, and his yards-per-carry average plummeted to 3.0, the lowest of his career.

Next stop: Cincinnati. Neal blocked for Corey Dillon for two years. At that point in his career, Dillon was young and on a tear. Neal helped sustain Dillon's high level of productivity—again assisting toward back-to-back 1,000-yard seasons. When Neal departed for the West Coast in 2003, Dillon had a major falloff—just 541 yards rushing.

In all, Neal cleared the way for an NFL-record 10 straight 1,000-yard rushers. Tomlinson, George, and Dillon—all of them deserve Hall of Fame consideration. And they ought to give a large part of the credit to the guy they call "Lo" Neal.

Postscript: In his first 14 years in the league, Lorenzo Neal averaged just 14.4 carries per season—fewer than LaDainian Tomlinson averages per game. But in 2006 Neal was asked to carry the ball on third down eight times. He was eight-for-eight on third-down conversions. Tomlinson was only five-for-six.

The Most Underrated NFL Record

PAUL HORNUNG'S 176 POINTS IN A SEASON

It took almost half a century for somebody to finally accomplish in 16 games what Packers halfback Paul Hornung did in 12. In 1960 Hornung scored 176 points, an NFL record that stood until LaDainian Tomlinson of the Chargers scored 186 in 2006. But Hornung averaged 14.7 points per game in his record-setting season, over a field goal per game more than Tomlinson's 11.6 average in 2006.

Think what 176 points in 12 games means.

Hornung shattered the NFL record of 138 points set in 1942 by another Packer, Don Hutson, breaking Hutson's mark by 38 points. He won the NFL scoring title by 71 points over Bobby Walston.

Hornung got off to a relatively slow start in 1960, scoring 29 points in the Packers' first three games before going on a scoring rampage that wasn't challenged for nearly half a century. Starting with the 49ers on October 23 at Lambeau and ending with the Bears on December 4 at Wrigley Field, Hornung scored 123 points in a seven-game span, more than 17.5 per game.

The craziest thing about Hornung's season is that although he scored at least one touchdown in 10 of 12 games, he never scored more than two in any game. But he made 41 extra points, kicked 15 field goals, and caught two touchdown passes.

Those Packers went 8–4, reached the NFL Championship game, and recorded plenty of blowouts. But Vince Lombardi didn't let Hornung pad his scoring title against overmatched teams. In a 41–14 blowout of the 49ers, Hornung scored two touchdowns. He scored once in a 41–7 win over the

Paul Hornung soars over the top for a touchdown against the 49ers during his record-breaking 1960 season.

Cowboys. He scored twice in a 41–13 rout of the Bears. That's what makes Hornung's record even more dazzling and underrated. If Lombardi had let him, he could have scored 200.

Postscript: Paul Hornung was called to serve in the army during the 1961 Berlin Crisis and wasn't available to play in the NFL Championship game against the Giants. But Packers coach Vince Lombardi called his friend, President John F. Kennedy, and asked him to release Hornung for the weekend. Kennedy obliged, and Hornung scored a then–championship game record 19 points in the Packers' 37–0 win.

CHAPTER 11

Linebackers

The Most Overrated Linebacker of All Time

SAM HUFF

A book like this would be zero fun and about as compelling as the Cleveland Browns offense if a few questions weren't raised about a pro football icon here or there and if the accepted views of how things go down in the NFL weren't challenged. It's either that, or right about now you're ready to cuddle up with your DVD box set of *The Sopranos*. So let's keep you interested a little bit longer by opening an old wound—whether Hall of Fame middle linebacker Sam Huff was all he was cracked up to be.

That's right, it's time to pick on Huff, who is mentioned in the same breath as Dick Butkus, Ray Nitschke, Mike Singletary, and Ray Lewis as the feared, game-changing monsters in the middle who redefined the position. Hey, Butkus may be considered the greatest defensive player of all time, but he was never on the cover of *Time* magazine.

That honor went to Huff in 1959. He was just 25 years old and in his fourth professional season for the New York Giants, which won the NFL championship during his rookie season, 1956. After Time Inc. made Huff its poster boy, CBS took it up a notch. CBS made Huff the first player to be miked up for a TV broadcast. In a groundbreaking feature foreshadowing the work of NFL Films and ESPN, Huff was the centerpiece of a 60-minute documentary called *The Violent World of Sam Huff,* which aired in October 1960.

The problem was that by that time, Huff's team, the Giants, had lost back-to-back NFL title games to Baltimore. Huff's team had already been unceremoniously dethroned by Johnny Unitas and the Colts. And Huff's defense was already being called, well, to be charitable about it, fraudulent.

And, perhaps partly because of jealousy and partly because the Giants did not win another title, the whispers about Huff began to grow louder and louder. There were whispers that a) his world wasn't that great, and b) he certainly was not as violent as a lot of other defensive stars emerging in the late 1950s and early 1960s, such as Nitschke, who would help to lead the Packers defense to five NFL titles. Or John Reger, a linebacker who made the Pro Bowl in 1959, 1960, and 1961 for the Steelers. If CBS was headquartered somewhere along the three rivers of Pittsburgh, maybe Reger would've been miked up.

In Jim Wexell's book *Pittsburgh Steelers: Men of Steel,* here's what Reger had to say about the attention heaped on his rival, Huff: "I think he's overrated," Reger said. "He was always piling on, and then they'd say, 'Tackle by Sam Huff,' over the loudspeakers, when all he did was jump on the pile. He was a good player, but they really blew it out of proportion....I remember when he went to the Pro Bowl. He was in the middle, and I played the right side and [Chuck] Bednarik played the left side. And it was the same thing. You'd always hear his name mentioned at the Coliseum in Los Angeles. And it'd be the same thing. He'd pile on and get credit for everything."

Huff had plenty of supporters. Here's what Vince Lombardi said: "It's uncanny the way Huff follows the ball. He seems to be all over the field at once." True enough, Huff finished his career with 30 interceptions—*double* Reger's total. But the often-overlooked Lee Roy Jordan, the Dallas Cowboys' great middle linebacker who played from 1963 to 1976, finished his career with 32, and he's not in the Hall of Fame and certainly not mentioned in the same breath as Butkus.

In 1961 Huff's Giants would lose another NFL Championship game—stomped by the Green Bay Packers 37–0. In 1962 they lost another title game: Packers 16–7 over the Giants. Huff would lose his fifth NFL title game

Putting popular perceptions aside, Sam Huff may not deserve to be placed among the greatest linebackers in history.

in 1963, when the Chicago Bears beat the Giants 14–10. New York head coach Allie Sherman had had enough. The scapegoat was Huff. He was traded to the Washington Redskins, and he was not happy about it.

In 1966, Huff's third season in Washington, the Redskins were crushing the New Giants 69–41. With seven seconds left on the clock, the Redskins' head coach, the legendary Otto Graham, told his players the game was over. It was a meaningless late November game. Both teams were going nowhere. But then somebody called timeout. Somebody wanted to run up the score on his old team.

In a *Sporting News* article in 1996, Huff took credit for being that somebody, for calling the timeout. "I certainly wanted to get even with the guy standing on the other sideline," said Huff, referring to Sherman.

But 10 years later the Redskins' website quoted former Washington guard and offensive captain Vince Promuto as saying that he called the timeout: "I've heard it 20,000 times that Sam Huff called that timeout. But being born in New York and playing in the 1960s when Giants quarterback Y.A. Tittle was playing and seeing him run up the score time after time when the Redskins were a lousy team, I thought, 'This is my opportunity.' I wanted to score one more time, just for kicks."

The Redskins kicked a field goal. The final score was 72–41. Washington broke the long-standing record for most points scored by one team in a game (70, set by the Los Angeles Rams in 1950).

This story illuminates a few things: the jealousies swirling around Huff came not only from his opponents but also from his own teammates.

And what about the Giants scoring 41 points on a Redskins defense that simply wasn't that good? The Giants had more yards in the game (389–341), more first downs (25–16), and their offense ran 29 more plays. That year, the Redskins finished 7–7. The Giants were 1–12–1. And Washington's defense gave up 25 points per game.

In his six years in Washington, Huff never led the Redskins defense to the postseason.

No doubt, Huff was a spectacular player. But should he be considered among the greatest all-time middle linebackers? As ferocious as Butkus? As accomplished as Nitschke? As fiery and respected a leader as Lewis?

To look further, let's go back to the start of the Huff story, back to the 1950s. When Paul Brown's innovative Cleveland Browns entered the NFL in 1950, the rest of the league had to find a way to stop them. Tom Landry, the Giants' defensive coordinator, devised the 4-3 defense, and Huff was the perfect specimen to play that position, mobile and tough. Cleveland won its last NFL title of the decade in 1955. Huff and the Giants prevailed over the Bears in the title game in 1956.

The following year the Browns drafted running back Jim Brown out of Syracuse University, beginning the great Huff-Brown battles of the next eight years. Against Huff's two teams, Brown's Browns finished 9–9–1. In those 19 games, Brown had 100 yards or more rushing nine times. In the prime of their careers, however, in the 14 regular-season games where Huff (with the Giants) played against Brown, the Browns' running back averaged a whopping five yards per carry. In 1964, Huff's first year in Washington, Cleveland won the Eastern Conference and the NFL title. Washington finished fourth in the conference, and Huff turned his attention toward revenge against the Giants.

This is not to say that Huff does not have a rightful spot in Canton. But he makes this list because he simply never measured up to some of the great middle linebackers in impact, postseason performance, and those hard-to-measure intangibles associated with that position.

Postscript: John Reger was also traded to the Redskins in 1964, the same year Sam Huff unhappily arrived in Washington.

The Rest of the Most Overrated

2. LaVAR ARRINGTON

If there were a chapter in this book titled "The Linebacker Who Just Refused to Reach His Enormous Potential," LaVar Arrington would have it all to himself. But there isn't, so he's stuck here. Overrated.

In 2000 Arrington was the second-overall pick in the draft, the first of two first-round picks of the Washington Redskins. With the next pick, the Redskins took offensive lineman Chris Samuels. Samuels then turned himself into a prototype pass-blocking left tackle, a franchise player. But after six up and mostly down seasons, Arrington acrimoniously left town.

He had the tools. He was 6′3″, 257 pounds. He had great speed and quickness. Coming out of Penn State, Arrington was supposed to be the next Lawrence Taylor, a quarterback marauder. He even wore L.T.'s number. And, like L.T., he thought he could be a freelancer, do what he wanted when he wanted. Bill Parcells tried to stop Taylor from doing that, but Taylor was so good he could get away with it. Arrington wasn't and couldn't.

He had one very good season, 2002, when he recorded a healthy 11 sacks, but that's all he was asked to do because that's all he could do: line up and blitz the quarterback. The following year, that didn't fool anybody, and he dropped off to just six sacks. The 2003 season was the last that Arrington forced a fumble or recovered a fumble. And he has just three career interceptions—all in 2001, his second year in the league.

In Washington he blew through two highly touted defensive coordinators, feuding with both Marvin Lewis and Gregg Williams, who finally benched Arrington in 2005. Believe it or not, in 2006 then–Giants general manager Ernie Accorsi, a Penn State guy who has a soft spot for Penn State guys, signed Arrington to a $49 million contract, which included nearly $9 million guaranteed in the first year.

Again Arrington underperformed. In six games, he had one sack. Unfortunately, he blew out his Achilles, which may prevent him from ever proving that he could live up to the hype. The Giants released him, and he's still looking to make his mark.

Postscript: At least the Giants didn't take L.T.'s jersey out of retirement. Arrington wore No. 55 for one year in New York.

3. TED HENDRICKS

You have to love a guy who once rode into practice on a horse, jousting with a traffic cone. There's a reason Curt Gowdy called Ted Hendricks the Mad Stork. He looked like a gangly bird, and he played out of his mind, enough to collect four Super Bowl rings.

But should Hendricks be in the Hall of Fame? And should he be in before Robert Brazile, the Houston Oilers linebacker who was just as much a madman on the football field? While Hendricks disappeared from the Pro Bowl during the lean years of his career in the mid-1970s, Brazile dominated the outside linebacker position, going to seven straight Pro Bowls—then a record for an outside linebacker.

And Brazile, whose impressive career has dropped off the radar for some odd reason, made the Pro Bowl when the Oilers were 5–9 in 1976, 11–5 in 1979, and 1–8 in 1982. Good or bad, he showed up. In fact, if Brazile had played his career in New York, he would have been R.B. before there was an L.T. By the way, Brazile's nickname? Dr. Doom. Most guys would take that over Mad Stork any day.

And when Hendricks played in Baltimore and Oakland, racking up four championships, he was on a team loaded with Pro Bowlers on offense and defense. Not Brazile. Hendricks's unusual frame, at 6′7″, 220 pounds, made him a natural pass rusher. But Brazile had more recorded career sacks—11, just nine for Hendricks. (Of course, for most of their careers, sacks were not kept as a statistic, so that's hard to measure. Suffice it to say that Brazile was as good a pass rusher as Hendricks was.)

Hendricks had unusually long arms, allowing him to block field goals and point-after attempts and to bird-dog interceptions—he had 26 interceptions—if he was in the right place at the right time. But that interception total, by the way, doesn't even put him in the top 10 of all time for linebackers.

Hendricks just never had the flat-out foot speed to be as versatile as Brazile was. He didn't cover as much field, although Brazile did have half the interceptions (13). This can be the only explanation for why Brazile has never been a part of the serious Hall of Fame discussion, and Hendricks is a classic sports TV favorite.

Then there is another contemporary of Hendricks's, Pittsburgh Steelers outside linebacker Andy Russell, who has two Super Bowl rings and made the Pro Bowl seven times. Russell, who had a very respectable 18 picks, is not in the Hall of Fame, probably because the two Jacks—Lambert and Ham—are in, and the selectors didn't want to overload Canton with Steel Curtain linebackers.

For the Raiders, Hendricks was considered the star. He was flamboyant and funny. But in Super Bowl XV, it was Raiders outside linebacker Rod Martin who tortured Ron Jaworski for three interceptions, a Super Bowl record—not Hendricks.

So, yes, Hendricks had a standout career, but as *Sports Illustrated*'s Peter King likes to say, "It's the Hall of Fame, not the Hall of Very Good."

And when Hendricks is placed in the context of those who played around him and during his era, his accomplishments are vastly overrated.

Postscript: Said Raiders quarterback Ken Stabler, "Most Raiders loved to party, but Ted Hendricks was a party all by himself."

4. JONATHAN VILMA

A first-round pick by the New York Jets—the 12th overall choice in the draft—middle linebacker Jonathan Vilma saw his productivity drop off considerably in 2006 after new head coach Eric Mangini made the switch from a predominantly 4-3 defense to a 3-4 defense.

Mangini thought he had another Tedy Bruschi on his hands. When Mangini was the defensive coordinator in New England, he often asked Bruschi to make the switch from middle backer to inside backer on the fly—with seamless results. Perhaps it was because of Vilma's lack of experience with the 3-4 defense and his general inexperience in the league, but Mangini's switch proved unusually difficult for Vilma to master in 2006. Offensive linemen routinely found Vilma and made him less troublesome in run defense.

Vilma had 68 tackles in 2006, nearly half his 2005 total of 128. That's a serious drop off—even for a guy playing in a new defense for the first time. As a first-round pick, Vilma should have been able to make a better adjustment. In the sack department, Vilma was shut out. Vilma's last full sack came in his Rookie of the Year performance in 2004. And he's had just two interceptions since he had three as a rookie.

Postscript: Even when Jonathan Vilma led the league in 2005 with 169 combined tackles, the Jets finished 29th in the league in rush defense. Said one AFC offensive coordinator, "In the last two years, we have spent zero time wondering where he is on the field. Right now, in his career, he's not what we call a difference-maker."

The Most Underrated Linebacker of All Time

BILL BERGEY

Nitschke and Singletary. Buoniconti and Butkus. When you talk about middle linebackers, these are the legends, their names synonymous with the position. Here's a name that should be part of that conversation: Bill Bergey. And here are a few facts to consider.

In the 1960s Dick Butkus was a star on a Chicago Bears team that never made it to the postseason. In the following decade, Bergey was traded from the Cincinnati Bengals to the Philadelphia Eagles for two first-round draft picks and a second-round pick. He then proceeded to steadily improve Philly's defense until he led it to the Super Bowl in 1980, even after missing most of the 1979 season with a devastating knee injury.

Like Butkus, Bergey was relentless and brutal, a vicious tackler who missed only two games in his first 10 NFL seasons.

Of course, in this group, Ray Nitschke of the Green Bay Packers has the most postseason experience and success, winning five NFL championships in Titletown. But Nitschke had an awful lot of help, a veritable Hall of Fame All-Star team on defense, including defensive tackle Henry Jordan, who kept a lot of blockers off Nitschke; defensive end Willie Davis, who pursued the quarterback in a way that changed the notion of a pass rusher; and Herb Adderley, arguably one of the top five cornerbacks of all time.

No way in the world would the beloved and highly productive Nitschke get on the overrated list. But Bergey never had that kind of phenomenal cast around him, and he was far better going sideline to sideline than Nitschke was. Perhaps Bergey was not as strong as Big Ray was, but he was certainly just as nasty. And, until Dick Vermeil arrived in 1976, Bergey's first head coach in Philadelphia was Mike McCormack. The name of Nitschke's head coach is carved on the side of the Super Bowl trophy.

As for Nick Buoniconti, *somebody* from the Miami Dolphins' undefeated No-Name defense had to go to the Hall of Fame. Buoniconti was a fabulous middle linebacker. But he played his first seven seasons in the AFL for the Boston Patriots. He missed playing against some of the greatest teams and offensive superstars in NFL history. Bergey was bigger, just as quick, and clearly just as formidable a tackler and quarterback of the defense as Buoniconti was. And twice a year in Philly, he faced a Cowboys team that was packed with great offensive talent.

A fullback from Arkansas State, Bergey could really run. His pass-coverage ability, while not Urlacher-like, really helped to launch middle linebacker as a position to be taken seriously deep between the hash marks. Unfortunately, he played for poor teams both in Cincinnati and early in his career in Philadelphia.

Though not mentioned among the legends of his position, Bill Bergey of the 1970s Philadelphia Eagles was as tough, mean, and good as any of them. This photo was taken at Ron Jaworski's annual charity golf tournament. Jeremiah Trotter (left) and Bill Bergey. (Photo courtesy Thomas E. Briglia/PhotoGraphics)

When Vermeil arrived and then Ron Jaworski came in at quarterback, the Eagles jelled, finally challenging the Dallas Cowboys for hegemony in the NFC East. Bergey not only went to the Pro Bowl four times for the Eagles, he successfully made the switch to a 3-4 inside linebacker in 1977.

But two years later, Bergey was hit with bad luck again. He suffered a knee injury in the third game of the 1979 season. Many thought his career was done. Not Bergey. Miraculously, Bergey returned for the Eagles' run to the Super Bowl in 1980, though he simply was not as quick.

Consider what might have been had Bergey played with better talent and not gotten hurt.

Postscript: Super Bowl XV was Bill Bergey's last game. If you want to get an idea how Bill Bergey played football, watch his son, Jake, play indoor lacrosse. You pray for the opposition—that they come out alive.

The Rest of the Most Underrated

2. JEREMIAH TROTTER

I know what you're thinking: the author of this book has worked at *The Philadelphia Inquirer* and has covered the Philadelphia Eagles. There can't be any other sane explanation for Bill Bergey and Jeremiah Trotter to be back-to-back, leading off this section of underrated linebackers. Paolantonio's got to be throwing a bouquet to Philly.

Nope. Trotter legitimately makes this list. So go ahead, be a longtime listener, first-time caller. Make your case. While you're on terminal hold with your sports talk radio station's producer, consider this.

Throughout his career, Trotter has been the victim of an orchestrated campaign to denigrate his skills. The biggest culprits? Eagles management. The Philly front office started a back-channel whisper campaign, claiming that Trotter wasn't worth the money he demanded in free-agent negotiations. That he was often out of position, often over-pursued in run defense. That he wasn't fast enough to play pass coverage. That his knees were shot.

That was in the spring of 2002.

After four highly productive years in a north-south defense that perfectly suited his skills, Trotter, who had already been to the Pro Bowl twice, bolted for the Washington Redskins. Once he got to the nation's capital, Trotter was miscast. And under Steve Spurrier, the Redskins were a train wreck. Then Trotter again hurt his knee.

So he begged Andy Reid for a return to Philadelphia in 2004. It was a triumphant return. But first Reid wanted to test Trotter's loyalty. The head coach made Trotter play special teams, an absurd notion only devised to prove who was boss.

Midway through the season, it was obvious that only Trotter deserved to be the starting middle linebacker. And *voila!* There was a vast improvement in the Eagles' run defense—from giving up 172 yards per game to 84 yards per game. And perhaps to spite Eagles management, even though he played only half the season at his natural position, Trotter was voted back to the Pro Bowl by his peers. In 2005 he had his best season ever, going back to the Pro Bowl and leading the defense as the Eagles made their first Super Bowl appearance in 24 years.

Some say Trotter has been the product of the system designed by longtime Eagles defensive coordinator Jim Johnson. Well, you can't have it both ways. You can't say he's no good and you've got to get rid of him, then claim he's only great because of what he's asked to do. Most linebackers perform at a high level when they do what they're asked to do. Indeed, that can be said of most good defensive players. It's the freelancers who don't make it. Trotter is not Brian Urlacher. He's not Ray Lewis. But Trotter has never been given the credit for what he has done. And the Eagles defense has never gotten enough credit for its contribution to the success of the Andy Reid era. Without that defense, Reid would not have a lucrative contract running through 2011.

Since 2000 the Eagles have earned six playoff appearances, tying with the Colts for the most in the league. The Eagles have won eight playoff games—only the Patriots have won more. And they have won an NFC-best five division titles during that span.

And while quarterback Donovan McNabb has often held the Eagles back in big games (for example, throwing up in Super Bowl XXXIX), the defense has been a rock. Here's how the Eagles defense has ranked since 2000: second in third-down efficiency (33.8 percent), second in red-zone efficiency (44.1 percent), third in sacks (305), and third in fewest points allowed per game (17.4). Here's the best indicator of a defense with great leadership: since 2001 the Eagles have allowed the fewest points (349) after their offense has turned the ball over.

You're saying, Yeah, but Trotter missed two years in the middle of that run, including the 2002 season when the Eagles went back to the NFC Championship game without him. Well, in that game they sure could have used him. With one of Trotter's replacements, Barry Gardner, on the field, the Tampa Bay Buccaneers connected on a touchdown pass on a crossing route to Joe Jurevicius. It was a backbreaking touchdown that almost certainly never would have occurred with Trotter patrolling the middle. In that game the Eagles really missed Trotter's presence. And that was the team's best year to win a Super Bowl, by beating a warm-weather team in the last game in Veterans Stadium, then taking on an inferior Oakland Raiders team in the Super Bowl. Saving a few bucks on Trotter in 2001 probably deprived the franchise of a Lombardi Trophy in 2002.

No player is revered more by his teammates. While safety Brian Dawkins has always been the spokesman for one of the league's most successful defenses over a five year span—and its spiritual leader—Trotter is the enforcer, both on and off the field.

Postscript: Wouldn't you fear a guy who wields an imaginary axe after every big tackle or sack? Why the axe? Growing up in the Texas hill country, Jeremiah Trotter chopped wood for his late father, Myra, in the family business.

3. MIKE STRATTON

So, you've never heard of Mike Stratton? Well, that's why you're reading this book, right? Way back in 1962, when the old American Football League was playing night games on fields where you needed to line up about 1,500 pickup trucks and turn on their lights to find the 50-yard line, Mike Stratton was drafted in the 13th round by the Buffalo Bills. Thirteenth round! Imagine if the NFL draft still had 13 rounds—Mel Kiper Jr.'s hair gel would have to be designed by NASA.

Stratton was 6′3″, 230 pounds—big for that era and strong as a gunny sergeant. Indeed, he served six years in the Marine Corps, which shouldn't be a shock. Stratton was born in Vonore, Tennessee, the Volunteer State. And when you see his young John Wayne–looking face with a chin that might've been carved in granite, you'd think this guy is straight out of the Battle of the Bulge or one of Teddy's Roosevelt's Rough Riders, charging up San Juan Hill.

Instead, Stratton attended the University of Tennessee, married a woman named Jane, had four children (somebody cue John Mellencamp), and just basically lived the American dream, which included having the honor and privilege of hammering ball carriers for a living on Sunday afternoons. Which he did with a nasty ferocity.

His biggest hit came in 1964, when the Buffalo Bills were finally able to crash a wall of mediocrity and emerge as AFL champs. The Bills had plenty of talent, including quarterback Jack Kemp and running back Cookie Gilchrist. They were even sound, as they say, in the kicking game with place-kicker Pete Gogolak and punter Paul Maguire.

But, until Stratton showed up, the Bills had no knockout punch on defense, nobody to fear. In the 1964 AFL title game, the Bills faced the haughty San Diego Chargers, who had beaten the Boston Patriots 51–10 in the title game a year earlier.

The Chargers went up early 7–0, and then the fog rolled into old War Memorial Stadium in Buffalo. It looked bleak. The catalyst for San Diego's offense, which was designed by the great Sid Gillman, was a young running back named Keith Lincoln, who ran for 38 yards on the first play from scrimmage. With 8:19 left in the first quarter, Lincoln broke into the left flat to catch a pass from Chargers quarterback Tobin Rote.

The pass was a bit high. Lincoln raised both arms to reach it. Just as the ball arrived, so did Mike Stratton, planting his right shoulder in Lincoln's right ribcage. Lincoln fell to the fog-shrouded, muddy field in a heap of near-death pain. One of his ribs was busted in two. Lincoln was helped off the field and never returned. The Chargers did not score another point. And the Bills won their first AFL title, 20–7.

That tackle would become known as the Hit Heard around the World, and it was fitting that it would have a military theme, given Stratton's background.

The Bills would win back-to-back AFL championships, enough to keep a franchise financially feasible in small-market Buffalo for decades to come. So give Stratton some credit for that. Kemp would, of course, go on to Congress and run for the Republican presidential nomination. So, depending on your politics, you can blame Stratton for that, too.

The head coach of that team was Lou Saban, and that tackle and those title wins helped launch his longtime career, as well.

That's why Stratton makes this list. He came from nowhere, helped define a style of play at a critical position, and did it with very little fanfare, making him one of the most underrated linebackers in league history.

Postscript: Mike Stratton has been overlooked in Buffalo, too. On the morning after the game, on the front page of the Buffalo Courier News, *there is a photo of Lou Saban with three players, Jack Kemp, Pete Gogolak, and running back Wray Carlton. Not pictured: Mike Stratton.*

In 1994 the Bills finally recognized Stratton's contribution, putting him on the Wall of Fame—30 years after the Hit Heard around the World.

4. DAVE ROBINSON

Just think. It might have been called the Landry Trophy.

It was the 1966 NFL Championship game, Green Bay Packers (coached by Vince Lombardi) at the Dallas Cowboys (coached by Tom Landry). It was fourth-and-goal, late in the fourth quarter, and Cowboys quarterback Don Meredith was setting up on the Packers' 2-yard line to score the tying touchdown that would have sent the game into sudden-death overtime.

Landry called for a rollout option right. Lombardi called for a blitz. Meredith took the snap, rolled to his right, and found Packers linebacker Dave Robinson right in his face. Robinson leveled Meredith as the ball was released and then intercepted it in the end zone. Game. Set. Match. The Green Bay Packers went to the first Super Bowl.

If Robinson hadn't gotten there, if Meredith had completed the easy touchdown pass, if the Cowboys had won, and if the Cowboys had won the Super Bowl—then maybe Vince Lombardi's name would not be on that beautiful, Tiffany-designed, silver championship trophy. Maybe Tom Landry would have the honor instead.

How's that for having a direct impact on NFL history? That's why Robinson makes this list.

He's one of the forgotten greats of the Packers' dynasty of the 1960s. Robinson was named to the NFL's All-Decade team, but he's not in the Hall of Fame—perhaps because there are already five players from that Packers defense in Canton. Without Robinson, the Packers might not have won a record three-straight NFL titles. Lombardi himself acknowledged that.

Robinson had more career interceptions (27) than his more famous running mate, middle linebacker Ray Nitschke (25), who is in the Hall. Not only did Robinson make the big play that sent the Packers to their first Super Bowl, he made the critical turnaround play in that Super Bowl—even before it was called such.

People forget that Kansas City came out of the gate on fire in Super Bowl I. The Chiefs were all over the bullies from the Bay. Until another Robinson blitz helped to turn the tide, that is. Down only 14–10, Chiefs quarterback Len Dawson took the snap at midfield, looking to get some momentum. Lombardi called another blitz. Both outside linebackers, Robinson and Lee Roy Caffey, came after Dawson. Robinson got there first and tipped the pass, which landed harmlessly in the arms of Packers free safety Willie Wood, who returned the ball to the Chiefs' 5-yard line. (By the way, Wood's in the Hall of Fame.)

The Chiefs never came close to midfield again. The Packers won the game going away, 35–10. The following year, it was Robinson who played a pivotal role in bottling up the Oakland Raiders' running game in Super Bowl II. Without Robinson, the Packers might never have reached the status of pro football immortality.

Postscript: Dave Robinson graduated from Penn State with a degree in civil engineering. After football, he moved to Ohio. He's a businessman and a chess champion.

The Most Misunderstood Sideline Moment in NFL History

THE GATORADE BATH

If the Sunday ritual of the NFL is a religious experience, then there must be holy water. That, of course, would be Gatorade.

After any momentous victory, dousing the head coach with Gatorade provides the final blessing, the unmistakable affirmation that this man with the headset and the look of blissful astonishment has just accomplished something big. And his players are rewarding him for it.

But that's *not* how it started. Among the great time-honored traditions in professional sports, perhaps none is more misunderstood than the dumping of Gatorade on the head of the head coach. For a game like pro football, which is often soaked in its own self-importance, the Gatorade bath is a bit of comedy, a moment of burlesque. But it could have just as easily been a bust.

The year was 1985. And the grating and sarcastic methods of New York Giants head coach Bill Parcells were wearing very thin—not on the media, but on his own players. It was the third year of the Parcells reign, and everybody was beginning to wonder whether the results would ever match his résumé. That skepticism started in his locker room.

On October 20, the seventh week of the season, the Giants were 3–3, a .500 team and playing like it. Coming to Giants Stadium were the powerhouse Washington Redskins, a team that had already won one Super Bowl under Joe Gibbs in the 1980s and was gunning for another.

So Parcells went looking for a whipping boy and found one in the person of nose tackle Jim Burt, himself a bit of an irascible character. (Behind closed doors, Burt referred to Parcells as "a big hemorrhoid"—and he was only half kidding.)

Parcells made Burt lift extra weights, including a few sessions in front of the entire team, reminding Burt day in and day out that Redskins offensive lineman Jeff Bostic was going to dominate him come Sunday.

Well, come Sunday, Bostic looked ordinary. And Burt had a big day—five tackles, one assist. The Giants blew out the Redskins 17–3, and, as the waning moments of a game that was firmly in hand wound down, Parcells put his arm around Burt on the sideline. "I really got you ready, didn't I?" Parcells said. For Burt, that was the last straw.

He went back behind the bench, fetched the orange bucket of Gatorade, and gave Parcells a cold bath. This was not a gesture of respect, but retribution.

Now, here's where it could have all fallen apart, where a tradition may have been still-born. Parcells, not then known for his soft-heartedness, could have easily turned to Burt and shot him one of those looks—you know the one: Gandolfini doing DeNiro doing Brando. Instead, the Big Tuna laid out a nationally televised grin.

The following year, the Giants turned the Gatorade bath into a national rite of passage.

In 1986 the Giants were on the road to their first Super Bowl victory, and linebacker Harry Carson gave new meaning to Burt's bath. After an opening day loss at Dallas, the Giants beat the San Diego Chargers 20–7. It really wasn't much of an accomplishment. The Chargers were on their way to 4–12, which put them last in the AFC West.

But Carson decided this was a good time to get Parcells again. And again Parcells embraced the moment. After each of the next 13 regular-season wins, Parcells got the same treatment, including the final week, when the team again wanted revenge on their coach for another demeaning outburst.

On December 20, the Giants had already wrapped up the division, and the Green Bay Packers were in town. The Giants got off to a terrific start, 24–0, but then they allowed the Pack—another team that would finish 4–12 that season—to climb back into the game. The halftime score was 24–17.

Here's what the players said at the time about the atmosphere in the Giants' halftime locker room.

"There was no panic," said quarterback Phil Simms.

"We had control of the game," said center Bart Oates.

And *The New York Times* reported that there was "no oratory, no panic in the locker room at halftime."

Not really. Parcells was furious. He started dumping out the trash cans—right on the heads of his players. The Gatorade blessing in reverse! "He went around the room and told players they were playing like trash," said one player, who asked not to be identified.

The Giants stormed out of the locker room and never looked back. They whipped the Packers 55–24 for their 14th victory of the year—the most in the team's 62-year history.

So, after the game, the players were in a mood for a little payback. Parcells got a good Gatorade soaking—but so did offensive coordinator Ron Erhardt.

The Gatorade bath, shown here being administered to its original recipient Bill Parcells while he coached for the New York Giants, was originally intended as a sign of retribution, not respect. (Photo courtesy Bettmann/CORBIS)

And a month later, after the Giants beat Denver in Super Bowl XXI, 39–20, the CBS broadcast team of Pat Summerall and John Madden began another tradition—Telestrating the Gatorade bath.

And in that one nationally televised moment, on the biggest broadcast night on the planet, the transformation was complete. The Gatorade bath became an official piece of Americana, a cultural happening that would be burnished in the minds of millions of football fans and passed down from the pros to college to high school.

More importantly, what began as one player's act of personal defiance turned into a national symbol of public respect.

No meaningful victory—no matter what its significance—is complete without that blessing of a thirst quencher, water and ice. Always plenty of ice. No matter how much a coach thinks he has it coming—or knows it's coming—it's the ice that provides, as Harry Carson said, the "shock to the system."

Postscript I: A month later, the Super Bowl–champion New York Giants visited the White House. Presidential aide Michael K. Deaver, the ad man and political consultant who choreographed Ronald Reagan's elections and his presidency, had a Gatorade bucket filled with popcorn waiting in the wings. When the Giants were assembled, President Reagan snuck behind the team and dumped it—not on Parcells, but on Harry Carson. The symbolism was obvious: the nation's authority figure was getting a measure of revenge for the Giants' authority figure.

Postscript II: Of course, this has made the folks who make Gatorade very happy and very rich. In 1987 the company, perhaps feeling a bit guilty about the windfall, sent Parcells and Carson each a $1,000 gift certificate to Brooks Brothers. Later in 1987 both of them signed personal endorsement contracts with Gatorade.

CHAPTER 12

Tight Ends

The Most Overrated Tight End of All Time

CHARLIE SANDERS

His supporters kept hammering home the 14.3 average. Higher than Mike Ditka's, they crowed. Higher than Kellen Winslow's, they boasted. Higher than Ozzie Newsome's, they bellowed. His career receiving average was higher, the Hall of Fame voters were told by Charlie Sanders's supporters, than *four of the six tight ends already enshrined in Canton.*

So Sanders must be a Hall of Famer, too, the argument went. And into the Hall Sanders went, Class of 2007.

It made sense, at least at first glance. Sanders did average 14.3 yards per catch during his 10-year career with the Lions, and it's true that only two Hall of Fame tight ends averaged more.

But what the voters weren't told is that during his era, 14.3 yards per catch wasn't anything special.

What the voters weren't told is that only once out of those 10 years did Sanders even lead the league's tight ends in yards per catch.

What the voters weren't told is that a whole mess of tight ends who never got close to the Hall of Fame and were contemporaries of Sanders had *higher* or similar career receiving averages.

Take a look:

Player	Receiving Average
Dave Parks	15.6
Milt Morin	15.5
Bob Trumpy	15.4
Henry Childs	15.3
Ted Kwalick	15.3
Jerome Barkum	14.7
Walter White	14.7
Jean Fugett	14.6
Reuben Gant	14.6
Riley Odoms	14.5
Charlie Sanders	14.3
Jim Mitchell	14.3

Tight ends back in the 1970s commonly averaged more than 14 yards per catch during their careers. Yet Sanders—who in none of his 10 seasons even ranked among the top three tight ends in the NFL in receptions—still became one of only seven modern tight ends admitted into the Hall of Fame.

Sanders was a capable receiver with outstanding downfield ability. But there was nothing extraordinary about his career.

Among his contemporaries *not* in the Hall of Fame—but who caught more passes—are Jerry Smith (421 catches), Charle Young (418), Riley Odoms (396), Russ Francis (393), Raymond Chester (364), and David Hill (358).

Smith, Francis, Odoms, Chester, and Young all had more receiving yards.

Smith, Chester, Francis, Barkum, Young, Odoms, Smith, and Trumpy all scored more touchdowns.

Notice a pattern?

A Hall of Famer should be one of the best to ever play his position.

Sanders never ranked among the top three tight ends in catches. Here are his year-by-year rankings among all NFL (and premerger AFL) tight ends: fifth, fourth, seventh, eighth, 12th, 12th, fourth, eighth, sixth, and 28th.

While he had a solid career as a tight end for the Detroit Lions, Charlie Sanders's stats are not significantly better than many players at his position who have never even been considered for the Hall of Fame.

Sanders never ranked among the top two tight ends in receiving yards. Here are his year-by-year receiving rankings among tight ends: fourth, third, sixth, seventh, 10th, eighth, fourth, sixth, fourth, and 25th.

Odoms, Smith, Francis and Chester all had more catches, more yards, and more touchdowns than Sanders, yet none of them has even reached the Hall of Fame's round-of-15 finalists.

Sanders never caught more than 42 passes in a season and never had a 700-yard season. But non–Hall of Famers Young, Ted Kwalik, Walter White, Milt Morin, Bob Tucker, Smith, Barkum, Odoms, and Chester all did both at least once.

The Lions reached the playoffs once while Sanders was in Detroit. In 1970, in their first postseason game in 13 years, they were shut out by the Cowboys.

Sanders didn't catch a pass.

Postscript: Charlie Sanders has worked in the Lions scouting department since 1998, after working as a coach from 1989 through 1996. In his 27 years with the franchise as a player, coach, and front-office executive, the Lions are 1–7 in postseason games.

The Rest of the Most Overrated

2. MARK CHMURA

Mark Chmura was a three-time Pro Bowl tight end with the Packers during their Super Bowl run of the 1990s. Because of the Pro Bowls, the Super Bowls, a close friendship with Brett Favre, and a healthy dose of old-time Packers grit, Chmura quickly developed into a fan favorite and one of the most popular tight ends in the league.

He had great size at 6′5″, 250 pounds, ran precise patterns, and was a decent enough blocker. He was also not even remotely the player everybody thinks he was.

Chmura spent his entire career—only seven years—with the Packers and averaged just 27 catches, 322 yards, and 2.5 touchdowns per season. Despite playing in a West Coast offense that relied heavily on the tight end, Chmura had just one 50-catch season and only one other season with more than 38 receptions.

During Chmura's seven seasons, nine NFL tight ends had more touchdowns, 10 had more catches, and 12 had more receiving yards.

Chmura topped out at 54 receptions in 1995. During his career, 17 other tight ends had at least 55 in a season, including two different guys named Mitchell: Johnny and Pete.

In four of his seven seasons, Chmura didn't even score a touchdown. He finished with just 17, or as many as Patriots tight end Ben Coates scored in 1996 and 1997 alone.

Brent Jones of the 49ers retired two years before Chmura but still had 51 more receptions while their careers overlapped. Steve Jordan of the Vikings retired five years before Chmura and still had more 55-catch seasons while their careers overlapped.

Remember Jamie Asher? Didn't think so. Over the 1996 through 1998 seasons, the Redskins tight end had more receptions and yards than Chmura. And he couldn't even get a job in 1999.

Jamie Asher?

Not once in his career did Chmura record a reception longer than 33 yards. While he was in the league, 67 tight ends had at least one reception longer than Chmura's longest. Among them were such legends as Alfred Pupunu, Michael Ricks, Keith Cash, Irv Smith, Scott Slutzker, and Deems May.

As mediocre as Chmura was during the regular season, he was worse in the playoffs. He managed more than 20 yards in only two of 11 career postseason games. Brett Favre passed for 246 yards when the Packers beat the Patriots in the Super Bowl. Chmura had 13 of them.

In the interest of fairness, it's important to point out that Chmura did have two career 100-yard receiving games—101 yards against the Vikings and 109 yards against the Bengals, both in 1995.

The Vikings and Bengals ranked 30th and 31st in the NFL in pass defense in 1995.

Postscript: In 1997 Mark Chmura refused to accompany the Packers to the White House, where President Clinton was hosting the Super Bowl champions. "It doesn't really say much for society...the morals he sets forth for our children," Chmura explained.

Three years later Chmura was arrested for luring his 17-year-old babysitter into a bathroom and sexually assaulting her. Although he was acquitted, he did "apologize for this mess."

3. JEREMY SHOCKEY

Jeremy Shockey was going to revolutionize the tight end position. The question wasn't whether he'd be the best tight end in football, just how long it would take.

"I honestly believe he has a chance to be the best that ever played that position," Giants tight end Dan Campbell said during Shockey's first training camp, the summer of 2002.

That's how hyped Shockey was coming out of Miami.

Shockey possessed that ideal combination of strength and athleticism that NFL scouts love, and he had the looks and personality made for Movado. He was a superstar before he played a down, a celebrity before he caught a pass.

Giants fans loved him because he brawled with teammates, hung out with shock jock Howard Stern, and challenged authority just for the heck of it. The media loved him because he had a lovable volatility, the playful look of the biker dude who lives next door—just cute enough to date your daughter, just dangerous enough that you wouldn't let him near her.

And his coaches? They didn't love him, but they tolerated him. He played like a maniac, played with the kind of enthusiastic brutality the Giants so sorely missed during a desultory 7–9 season in 2001 that followed a Super Bowl appearance in 2000. Shockey was the guy who was going to will the Giants back to the Super Bowl.

They're still waiting.

Shockey has been good and sometimes very good in his first five NFL seasons. But he hasn't become the best to ever play the game, and he hasn't even become the best to play the game *in his own division.*

Shockey's best year was his first, with 74 catches for 894 yards. His production flattened out after that, but it didn't matter. He was already on the Pro Bowl fast track. Once you go, you keep going. Shockey made four Pro Bowl teams from 2002 through 2006, despite only sporadically resembling the superhero he was built up to be.

In 2005 Shockey was third among tight ends in his own division with 65 catches. He had just two receptions longer than 20 yards in 2006. Some 31 tight ends had more, including Joe Klopfenstein—who Campbell never predicted would be the best to play the position. Shockey's 9.4 average in 2006 was 17th-best among all tight ends.

During his first five pro seasons, Shockey ranked only fifth among NFL tight ends in catches. Among those with more was Jason Witten of the Cowboys, from the NFC East, the Giants' own division.

And five years into his career, Shockey still hasn't experienced a postseason victory. The Giants were 0–3 in the playoffs through 2006 with Shockey in uniform, and his numbers—13 catches for 143 yards and a touchdown—were nothing special.

Shockey has had a nice career, and if he ever decides to make off-season conditioning with his friend and quarterback Eli Manning a priority and if he finds a way to stay healthy, he may one day live up to the hype. But for a guy who came into the league with such a cosmic buzz, for somebody who was going to redefine what the tight end position meant, he's just another decent player. And way overrated.

Postscript: Jeremy Shockey's first position coach was Mike Pope, who coached Mark Bavaro during an earlier tenure with the Giants. When the Giants drafted Shockey, Pope prepared a video for him showing each of Bavaro's 66 catches from 1986, when Bavaro surpassed 1,000 yards and the Giants won the Super Bowl.

The Most Underrated Tight End of All Time

MIKE DITKA

In the huddle during his professional debut with the Bears—a preseason game against the Montreal Alouettes of the Canadian Football League in the summer of 1961—Mike Ditka was instructed by quarterback Billy Wade to fake a buttonhook route and then streak down the sideline if the safety played him tight. Moments later, Ditka was in the end zone with a 70-yard touchdown catch.

Ditka had arrived, and the tight end position would never be the same.

"That play gave me confidence to be a pro," Ditka said years later. "I knew it wasn't impossible for me to outrun those guys."

Until the early 1960s, NFL tight ends were essentially extra offensive linemen, big, tough, slow blockers who occasionally caught passes on third-and-one or maybe for a few yards across the middle.

Perhaps known now more for his fiery and colorful personality as a TV analyst, Mike Ditka was a tough, athletic phenom at tight end for the Bears in the 1960s. (Photo courtesy Getty Images)

That all changed when the Bears drafted Ditka out of the University of Pittsburgh in 1961. He was steelworker tough and rugged enough that many NFL teams actually wanted to draft him as a linebacker, yet athletic enough to make plays down the field. Big plays that tight ends had never made before.

Although his career was curtailed by knee injuries, Ditka, in his first several seasons, altered the way NFL coaches and scouts viewed the tight end position, and he paved the way for modern-day athletic receiving tight ends like Tony Gonzalez, Antonio Gates, and Todd Heap.

Because of his success as a head coach with the Bears, his failed return to coaching with the Saints, and his recent career in broadcasting, Ditka's initial career as a groundbreaking tight end has been largely forgotten. Which is why he's the most underrated tight end in NFL history.

Ditka caught 12 touchdown passes in 14 games in 1961, which stood as an NFL record for tight ends for 43 years, until Gates caught 13 in 15 games in 2004. Ditka remains the only tight end in NFL history with 1,000 yards as a rookie.

In Ditka's first four seasons, he produced numbers that, a generation later, hold up among the best in history. No tight end in NFL history has ever had more yards (3,671) or touchdown catches (30) in his first four seasons than Ditka had. Thanks to deteriorating knees and a series of lousy quarterbacks (Wade, Rudy Bukich, Jack Concannon, and Virgil Carter), Ditka never caught more than 40 balls in a season after those first four years, though he did finish with more than 400 catches, nearly 6,000 yards, and 43 touchdowns. He retired with the second-most catches ever by a tight end.

Even though Ditka today is remembered as the grim-faced Bears coach roaming the sideline alongside Mike Singletary, Jim McMahon, and Walter Payton, in another life he was one of the few players in NFL history who actually changed the way a position was played.

Postscript: In 2006 Mike Ditka started his own wine company in conjunction with Mendocino Wine Company of Northern California. Ditka's line of wines includes a cabernet sauvignon, a chardonnay, a merlot, and something called "kick-ass red." Makes sense.

The Rest of the Most Underrated

2. SHANNON SHARPE

From the start, he was Sterling's kid brother. Sterling was the hot-shot wide receiver out of an SEC powerhouse, the seventh pick in the draft, a Packer for life. Shannon arrived in the NFL with none of his brother's cachet. He was a lightly regarded prospect out of a tiny Division I-AA college and the 192nd pick in the 1990 draft.

Sterling Sharpe had a short but brilliant run, with two 100-catch seasons and 65 touchdowns before a neck injury ended his career before his 30th birthday. Sterling was the personality, the celebrity, the future TV star. All Shannon did was put up some of the most mind-boggling numbers ever by an NFL tight end.

Shannon Sharpe was never known for his blocking, although he didn't shy away from contact when asked. He was an absolute nightmare for opposing linebackers and safeties, a consistently dangerous down-field weapon whose numbers stack up well against even some of the greatest wide receivers in history.

More than 800 catches. More than 10,000 yards. Sixty-two touchdowns. NFL records among tight ends in each category. Despite all of it, Sharpe usually took a backseat to more famous teammates John Elway and Terrell Davis, the Broncos' Super Bowl MVPs.

But he's the only tight end in history with seven straight 50-catch seasons and one of only four players with 11 50-catch seasons. In 2002 he set an NFL single-game record for tight ends with 214 yards against the Chiefs.

And his teams won. After Broncos head coach Dan Reeves converted Sharpe from a rarely used wide out as a rookie into a big-play tight end the next year, the Broncos went 83–45 over the next eight seasons, reaching the postseason five times and winning two Super Bowls.

Sharpe left Denver after 1999 and spent two years with the Ravens, winning a third Super Bowl, before finishing his career back in Denver. Even in his final season, he was still as productive as ever, with more than 60 receptions, nearly 800 yards, and eight touchdowns.

As good as Sharpe was during the regular season, he was at his best in the playoffs. He caught 62 passes for 814 yards and four touchdowns in 18 postseason games, and his 96-yard catch and run with a short pass from Trent Dilfer against the Raiders in 2000 is the longest pass play in NFL playoff history. Sharpe's 13 catches in 1993 against Oakland tied the playoff record for catches in a game. His 156 yards in the same game are the second-most ever by a tight end in the postseason. And his streak of 18 consecutive playoff games with at least one catch is third-longest in postseason history, behind only streaks of 28 games by Jerry Rice and 22 by Drew Pearson—both of whom, of course, played wide receiver.

Sharpe entered the league with little fanfare and spent his career playing in the long shadow cast by his famous brother and teammates. He was the most underrated member of an underrated family.

Postscript: After a week of trash-talking before a critical Ravens-Steelers game in 2001, Shannon Sharpe tagged then-Steelers receiver Plaxico Burress with the nickname Plexiglass. Burress caught eight passes for 164 yards, and the Steelers clinched the AFC Central title with a 26–21 win. But the name stuck.

3. MIKE VRABEL

He's not even a tight end, and still Mike Vrabel is one of the most underrated tight ends in NFL history.

Vrabel has spent most of his NFL career as an outside linebacker, notably with the Patriots since 2001. He has 38.5 sacks, 10 interceptions, and more than 500 tackles in his first 10 seasons, and his three career Super Bowl sacks are tied for second-most in Super Bowl history, behind only Charles Haley.

Good player. Sound player. Respected player.

And then there's Vrabel's other life.

Now and then, Patriots coach Bill Belichick uses Vrabel on offense as a short-yardage tight end. But he's not just another big side of beef that Belichick likes to deploy as an extra blocker. It turns out that Vrabel can catch the football. Really well.

Vrabel has eight catches and eight touchdowns. Nobody in NFL history has caught that many passes and gotten in the end zone on every one. The Patriots are 8–0 when he catches a pass, two of those wins coming in the Super Bowl.

In 2004 Vrabel caught two touchdowns in the regular season, as many as starting NFL tight ends Freddie Jones, Jeb Putzier, and Eric Johnson, who combined for 136 catches.

In 2005 he ranked 14th among all NFL tight ends with three touchdown catches, more than Tony Gonzalez, Jermaine Wiggins, and Erron Kinney, who combined for 202 catches.

But Vrabel is no novelty act. He's actually one of the greatest tight ends in Super Bowl history. Even though he's not technically a tight end.

He's one of only three tight ends in NFL history with two Super Bowl touchdowns. Jay Novacek and Dan Ross also caught two career Super Bowl touchdowns, but Vrabel is the only one who caught touchdowns in consecutive Super Bowls that he played in.

In Super Bowl history, only five players have caught more touchdown passes than Vrabel, *a linebacker*. And there are some vaguely familiar names in that group. Jerry Rice ring a bell? John Stallworth and Lynn Swann? Cliff Branch and Antonio Freeman?

He's never been to a Pro Bowl, so he's awfully underrated as a linebacker. But he's so underrated as a tight end, nobody even considers him one.

Postscript: Mike Vrabel spent his first four seasons with the Steelers without starting a game. He was so disappointed with the progress of his career that he considered quitting football and attending law school. When Vrabel reached the free-agent market, the Patriots were the only team interested in him as a starter. Within four years, he had been a key part of three Super Bowl championships.

CHAPTER 13

Pass Rushers and Defensive Linemen

The Most Overrated Defensive Lineman of All Time

HOWIE LONG

During a five-year span in the prime of his Hall of Fame career, from 1987 through 1991, Raiders defensive end Howie Long registered 21 sacks. During the same period, two players recorded 21 sacks *in one season*. And one of them, Chris Doleman, has never even been a Hall of Fame *finalist*.

Long was a good defensive end with a great personality, Hollywood good looks, and an astronomically high public profile, thanks to his movie appearances, Radio Shack commercials, and role as an analyst on FOX-TV's football coverage.

But the sacks? They were few and far between for a player considered by many to be one of the great defensive ends in history. Sacks weren't an officially recognized NFL stat in 1981, Long's rookie year. But in seven of his 12 final seasons, he ranked 40th or worse in the NFL in sacks. His one notable season was 1983, when he ranked ninth in the league with 13 sacks. That was

Though Howie Long had his share of memorable tackles during his career with the Raiders, including this takedown of the Green Bay Packers' Randy Wright in a 1984 game, his career sack numbers are paltry.

the only time he was even among the top 15 sack producers in the NFL. Long had three double-digit sack seasons in his career, all before his 26th birthday.

Here are Long's annual rankings in sacks: 22nd, ninth, 16th, 24th, 40th, 47th, 42nd, 43rd, 45th, 27th, 43rd. During his career, 45 NFL players had at least one season with 13.5 or more sacks. Long was not among them.

Long was the prototype player who was picked to Pro Bowl after Pro Bowl based on reputation. He was selected to eight Pro Bowl teams despite averaging 7.9 sacks per Pro Bowl season. In 1987 he accepted an invitation to the all-star game despite recording just four sacks and crossing the strike picket line.

Incredibly, Long didn't even have the most sacks *on his own team* during his 13-year stay with the Raiders. Greg Townsend had 107.5 during their 11 overlapping seasons, 23 more than Long. During that period, Long had more sacks in a season than Townsend just three times.

Four times—after the 1986, 1987, 1989, and 1993 seasons—Townsend had more sacks than Long, yet Long made the Pro Bowl. Townsend did not. In those four years Townsend averaged roughly four sacks per season *more* than Long (9.5 to 5.6).

Townsend also had one of the Raiders' six sacks in Super Bowl XVIII over the Redskins.

Long had none.

Postscript: Howie Long has appeared in several action movies and starred in the 1998 disaster film Firestorm *as Jesse Graves, a firefighter who battles a massive forest fire set by prisoners during an escape attempt.*

The Rest of the Most Overrated

2. JEVON KEARSE

His reputation was chiseled out of an astonishing record-setting rookie season in 1999 and, five years later, the largest contract ever given to an NFL defensive end. No defensive player has ever blasted out of the blocks like Jevon "Freak" Kearse. With his unstoppable first step, devastating quickness, and chiseled body, Kearse was a human wrecking ball, swinging his arms like anvils at the blind side of unsuspecting quarterbacks. When he wasn't getting a sack, he was delivering high-speed body blows that left quarterbacks a quivering mess.

Kearse sacked Browns quarterback Tim Couch three times in the second game of both their careers. And he had an AFC-high 14.5 sacks by the time his rookie season was over, plus two more in the playoffs. He would have had 15.5 sacks, but an apparent late-season sack against Danny Kanell of the Falcons was later changed by league statisticians to a rushing play.

Kearse was named Defensive Rookie of the Year, became the first rookie defensive end to start in a Pro Bowl in 21 years, and played in the Super Bowl—all before his 24th birthday.

Jason Taylor didn't have 14.5 sacks until his fourth season. Chris Doleman didn't have that many until his fifth NFL season. Lawrence Taylor and Michael Strahan didn't until their sixth seasons.

Since then? A steady decline. Kearse dropped to 11.5 sacks in 2000, then 10, then 9.5 in his next full season, then 7.5 and 7.5 in his two healthy seasons in Philadelphia after the Eagles gave him an unprecedented eight-year, $62.6 million contract. He finished fourth in the NFL in sacks as a rookie and has since dropped to 12th, 16th, 16th, 31st, and 31st.

The Freak? More like the Meek.

Let's exclude those drafted since 2003 because there is not yet a full measure of their careers. Of those drafted before then, only three players in NFL history have recorded 11 or more sacks as a rookie and never surpassed their rookie total. Just three. One is Vernon Maxwell of the Colts in 1983, and the other two are Kearse and his current Eagles teammate Darren Howard, who had 11 as a rookie with the Saints in 2001 and has yet to top that. That the Eagles have two of the three is astonishing evidence of poor talent evaluation by Philadelphia's brain trust.

Kearse was off to a terrific start in 2006, with three sacks in two games before suffering a season-ending injury, his second in five years. Nonetheless, he has just 18 sacks in three years since becoming the highest-paid defensive end in history. That means that going into the 2007 season, Eagles president Joe Banner has written Kearse a check for an average of $1.32 million *per sack.*

Kearse is past his 30th birthday and is six years removed from his last Pro Bowl season—his reputation far exceeding his current level of performance for quite some time, making him highly overrated.

Postscript: Before he grew into a defensive lineman, Jevon Kearse was a tight end and safety at Fort Myers High School in Florida. He returned four kickoffs for touchdowns as a high school junior.

3. COURTNEY BROWN

It doesn't happen often, but once in a while a defensive end comes along who is so powerful, so dominating, so gifted that he becomes the first overall pick in the NFL draft.

In 1973 the Oilers selected John Matuszak out of Tampa, and he went on to win two Super Bowl rings with the Raiders before embarking on a successful acting career. A year later, the Cowboys drafted Ed "Too Tall" Jones with the first pick, and he won an MVP award and a Super Bowl during his 15-year career. In 1976 the Buccaneers made Lee Roy Selmon the first pick in the draft, and Selmon went to six straight Pro Bowls on his way to the Hall of Fame. And in 1985 the Bills picked Bruce Smith, who made the Team of the Decade for both the 1980s and 1990s, retired as the NFL all-time sack leader, and will be a certain first-ballot Hall of Famer when his name comes up in 2008.

Sure seems like defensive linemen picked number one overall in the draft can't miss.

Which is why everybody figured Courtney Brown was such a stud. In 2000 the Cleveland Browns drafted Brown first overall, assuming he would follow in the footsteps of Matuszak, Jones, Selmon, and Smith.

"He's a tall, muscular defensive end with very long arms and excellent athletic ability," *Ourlads Guide to the Draft* gushed after the Browns took Brown. "His overall package was simply too good [for the Browns] to ignore."

So how does Brown stack up to the other number-one picks? He doesn't. In Smith's best season, he had 19 sacks. Brown had 19 sacks as well—in his first seven seasons *combined*. The next five defensive linemen and linebackers taken after Brown in the 2000 draft each have at least 30 career sacks. One of them, John Abraham, has 57.5—*more than three times as many as Brown.*

The best Brown has done during his underachieving, injury-ravaged career is a tie for 36th in the NFL with six sacks in 2003. That was his good season.

Brown earned about $25.3 million for 17 sacks with the Browns. After the Browns finally gave up on him, he drifted to the Broncos, where he had two sacks in 15 games in 2005 before missing all of 2006.

Brown earned about $3.6 million in 2005 and 2006. That's $1.5 million per sack with the Browns and $1.8 million per sack with the Broncos. At least he's consistent.

Postscript: The Broncos released Courtney Brown in March 2007 after he failed a physical. He's not expected to play again.

The Most Underrated Pass Rusher of All Time

ANDRE TIPPETT

Patriots linebacker Andre Tippett had the misfortune of playing virtually his entire career in anonymity in Foxboro, Massachusetts, at the same time Lawrence Taylor was busy becoming the most famous football player in the world 200 miles to the southwest in East Rutherford, New Jersey.

Taylor is universally credited with pioneering the role of the modern pass-rushing linebacker, but Tippett was almost Taylor's equal as a pass rusher. During the 11-year period that they both started—1983 through 1993—Tippett recorded 100 sacks and Taylor had 115. That's a difference of 1.4 per season.

Yet Taylor was a first-ballot Hall of Famer, and Tippett only made his first appearance as a finalist in 2007. Taylor was a three-time *Sports Illustrated* cover boy, and Tippett couldn't even make "Faces in the Crowd."

Taylor did lead the NFL with 20.5 sacks in 1986, but that was his only season with at least 16 sacks. Tippett had two of the greatest seasons ever by a linebacker, recording 18.5 sacks in 1984 and 16.5 in 1985. He led the AFC in sacks twice, and Taylor led the NFC in sacks only once.

"Anything L.T. could do, Andre could do it just as well," long-time teammate Irving Fryar said. "He could rush the passer just as well, stop the run just as well, cover backs out of the backfield just as well. He just never got the notoriety of L.T. because we played up in New England. But it never bothered him. Not a little bit. He didn't care about anything but winning. He was a phenomenal player and an equally phenomenal teammate."

And Taylor drew so much attention to himself by what he did off the field that there was no way the quiet Tippett could compete. Taylor was always in the news, just as often because of trouble off the field as success on it.

Tippett's 35 sacks over the 1984 and 1985 seasons remain the most ever by a linebacker in a two-year period. His 100 sacks were third-most in NFL history by a linebacker when he retired and sixth-most overall heading into 2007.

Five of the six linebackers from the NFL's 1980s All-Decade team have already been enshrined in the Hall of Fame—Taylor, Mike Singletary, and Jack Lambert—in their first year of eligibility, and Ted Hendricks and Harry Carson after longer waits. But Tippett wasn't even a finalist until 14 years after he retired. He should be in the Hall of Fame.

Maybe Tippett should have drawn a little more attention to himself and gotten suspended for two positive cocaine tests, like Taylor did at the peak of his career. *Something* to get himself noticed. Because just being one of the finest outside linebackers in NFL history obviously wasn't enough.

Postscript: Andre Tippett, who was raised as a Baptist, converted to Judaism in 1997 after marrying Rhonda Kenney, who was raised Jewish. Tippett studied Judaism in great depth before converting.

Andre Tippett, shown here chasing down Seattle Seahawk Dave Krieg in a 1984 game, wasn't much less of a havoc-wreaking force than New York Giants' legend Lawrence Taylor.

The Rest of the Most Underrated

2. CLYDE SIMMONS

For his entire career, Clyde Simmons was the answer to a trivia question: who played opposite Reggie White on the great defensive lines of the Philadelphia Eagles in the late 1980s and early 1990s?

But Simmons was actually a dominating defensive end whose remarkable exploits went largely unnoticed simply because he was playing in the shadow of the greatest defensive end in history.

From 1989 through 1992, a period in which the Eagles went 42–22 and reached the playoffs three times largely on the might of their defense, White recorded 54 sacks, the second-most in the NFL during that four-year span. The only player in the league with more sacks during that period was Simmons, who had 55.

Simmons was overlooked year after year on a defense loaded with superstars at every position. He was second among NFC defensive ends with 15.5 sacks in 1989 but didn't make the Pro Bowl, and he was tied for second among NFC defensive ends with 13 sacks in 1991 but again was bypassed. Simmons didn't reach a Pro Bowl until his seventh season, and then it was impossible for the voters to ignore him—he led the NFL with 19 sacks that year, at the time the sixth-highest single-season total in history.

Simmons is one of eight players in NFL history with two seasons of 15.5 or more sacks. What makes all of Simmons's accomplishments so astounding is that he was selected in a round of the draft that doesn't even exist anymore. The Eagles took Simmons out of Western Carolina in the ninth round, making him the 233rd pick overall and the 27th defensive end taken.

Yet he remains the only player drafted after the fourth round to record 19 sacks in a season. When he retired after the 2000 season, he ranked 11th in NFL history in sacks (and eighth among ends) and, entering the 2007 season, he was still 12th, ahead of such hotshots as Charles Haley, Pat Swilling, Neil Smith, and Sean Jones.

Unlike so many of the NFL's top sack specialists, Simmons was also a very tough and physical run stopper. And those who dismiss Simmons's production as the by-product of the constant double teams White drew, conveniently forget that Simmons had 45.5 of his sacks *after* leaving the Eagles. And in 1995 Simmons ranked third among NFC East defensive ends with 11 sacks with the Arizona Cardinals.

Despite this magnificent body of work, Simmons has never been a Hall of Fame finalist and probably never will be. He's the greatest defensive end nobody ever noticed.

Postscript: When the Eagles received word in December 1992 that Clyde Simmons had finally been selected to his first Pro Bowl in his seventh season, teammate Jerome Brown was so overcome with emotion that he punched a hole in a wall in the team's locker room at Veterans Stadium.

3. LESLIE O'NEAL

It must be a typo. What else could Leslie O'Neal's name be doing right there in the middle of a list of all-time NFL sack leaders? Just above Derrick Thomas, just below Richard Dent, tied with Lawrence Taylor.

He wasn't that good. Was he?

He was.

O'Neal is one of the top pass rushers in history. While Thomas, Dent, and L.T. are seen as some of the most hallowed players in history, O'Neal is remembered merely as a capable defensive end. When he's remembered at all. Maybe it was the fact that he played in the NFL outpost of San Diego, on a Chargers team that struggled to find its way out of the AFC West cellar.

But, other than people named Bruce Smith, O'Neal has more sacks than any defensive end in AFC history.

O'Neal was one of the most complete pass-rushing ends in the game in the late 1980s and through the 1990s. Despite losing nearly two full seasons early in his career to a severe knee injury, O'Neal was the most dominating unknown player of his generation. He didn't look like much in street clothes or in the locker room or standing on the line of scrimmage between plays. He wasn't the most muscle-bound guy, and he wasn't the biggest guy. But when the ball was snapped, he figured out a route to the quarterback.

O'Neal racked up 132.5 sacks in just 13 seasons, and his career average of 10.19 sacks per year is the third-highest in history among all defensive ends with 100 or more sacks, behind only Reggie White's otherworldly 13.2 sacks per season and Bruce Smith's 10.5.

In seven of his first eight healthy NFL seasons, O'Neal recorded 12 or more sacks, and only White and Smith—who are number one and number two on the all-time sack list—have more seasons with at least 12 sacks. O'Neal led AFC defensive ends in sacks three times, including a career-high 17 in 1992. The only AFC defensive ends with more in a season are Mark Gastineau and Jason Taylor.

When O'Neal retired after the 1999 season, only four defensive ends had more sacks. At the start of the 2007 season, he still ranked seventh in career sacks.

Nope. Not a typo.

Postscript: Leslie O'Neal missed parts of three seasons in his prime with a horrific knee injury he suffered on November 30, 1986, during a Chargers-Colts game in Indianapolis. He missed the last three games in 1986, all of 1987, and the first six games of 1988 before returning on October 16, 1988.

The Most Overrated Defense

THE PURPLE PEOPLE EATERS

It may have the greatest nickname in football history, but it didn't help the Vikings stop the run.

The Purple People Eaters were the front four of the Minnesota Vikings during their glory years, from 1968, when they reached the playoffs for the first time in franchise history, through 1978, when Hall of Famers Carl Eller and Alan Page played their final games in purple and gold.

This was a glorious period for the Vikings, who started out as an expansion team in 1961 but enjoyed little success until 1969, when they played in the first of four Super Bowls in an eight-year span.

The heart of the Vikings was the People Eaters, which consisted of Eller at left end from 1964 through 1978, Page at right tackle from 1967 through 1978, vastly underrated Jim Marshall at right end from 1961 through 1979, and either Gary Larsen (1965–1973) or Doug Sutherland (1974–1980) at left defensive tackle.

The Purple People Eaters were a remarkable group. First of all, they were astoundingly durable. Eller missed one game in 15 years with the Vikings, Page played in all 160 games while he was in Minnesota, and Marshall held the NFL record for consecutive games played at 282 until Jeff Feagles punted his way past him in 2005. Sutherland went eight years without missing a game, and Larsen missed five in his 11-year career.

From 1968 through 1978, the Vikings didn't have a losing season, won nearly three quarters of their regular-season games (112–42–2), and reached the postseason 10 of 11 seasons. The Vikings ranked among the top six in the NFL in fewest points allowed in eight of those 11 seasons, including three straight

Despite their longevity, Jim Marshall and his teammates on the Minnesota Vikings' Purple People Eaters never did seem to do much devouring of the competition when championships were on the line. (Photo courtesy Bettmann/CORBIS)

number-one rankings, from 1969 through 1971. During that three-year period, the Vikings actually allowed fewer than 10 points per game—9.88 to be exact.

So how could this phenomenal group be overrated? Because they kept getting trampled in the Super Bowl. The Purple People Eaters were savage pass rushers, but when asked in big games to stop the run, they failed every time. The Vikings not only lost all four of their Super Bowl appearances, their hallowed Purple People Eater defense got hammered in each one.

The Chiefs ran for 151 yards against them in Super Bowl IV, and the Dolphins ran for a Super Bowl-record 196 yards. But that was nothing. The Steelers broke the Dolphins' record in 1974, rushing for 249 yards against the Vikings in Super Bowl IX. That record lasted just two years, until the Raiders ran for 266 against Minnesota in Super Bowl XI.

They have not been to another Super Bowl since.

In four Super Bowl appearances, the Vikings went 0–4, losing by an average of 15 points per game. The Purple People Eaters got eaten alive in each game, allowing an average of 216 yards in those four Super Bowls. Only three other teams in history have allowed that many rushing yards in *any* Super Bowl.

To this day, the Vikings rank third, fifth, eighth, and 18th in most rushing yards allowed in a Super Bowl.

Underrated nickname. Overrated run defense.

Postscript: The Vikings allowed only five rushing touchdowns during the 14-game 1973 regular season but gave up three to the Dolphins that year in Super Bowl VIII.

CHAPTER 14

Super Bowl MVPs

The Most Overrated Super Bowl MVP of All Time

ROGER STAUBACH, COWBOYS
Super Bowl VI, January 16, 1972, Tulane Stadium, New Orleans

The final MVP ballots were turned in following the Cowboys' 24–3 win over the Dolphins in Super Bowl VI, and the results were nearly unanimous.

Sullen Cowboys halfback Duane Thomas had been selected the game's Most Valuable Player.

And why not? Thomas had rushed 19 times for 95 yards against the Dolphins and their third-ranked defense, including a three-yard touchdown run that turned a 10–3 third-quarter lead into a 17–3 lead. Thomas also caught a team-high three passes on a day when the Cowboys had more than two-and-a-half times more rushing yards (a then–Super Bowl–record 252) than net passing yards (100).

The Cowboys were Super Bowl champions because of their power running game, because of Thomas. Everybody who saw the game knew it.

But 1971 was a stormy year for Thomas, a 24-year-old Dallas native who had led the NFL with 11 touchdowns in just his second season. Thomas spent the entire year embroiled in a vicious salary dispute with the Cowboys and even sat out some early season games in protest. The Cowboys tried to trade

While it wasn't his fault that he was voted MVP of Super Bowl VI, Roger Staubach wasn't the best player in the Cowboys' backfield that day.

him before the season, only to see the trade overturned by league officials. Thomas was so furious over the way he felt he was being treated that he spent the 1971 season silent, refusing to speak not only with the media but also his teammates and even legendary Cowboys coach Tom Landry.

Even when Landry gave Thomas the news that he had made his first Pro Bowl team, Thomas remained silent.

"He nodded," Landry told reporters Super Bowl week.

In the early 1970s the Super Bowl MVP award was sponsored by *Sport* magazine, which presented the winner with a new car at a ceremony the day after the game. But the *Sport* magazine people suspected Thomas wouldn't show up. Although Thomas had done his job on the field all year, he hadn't cooperated with anybody off it. The last thing *Sport* magazine wanted was a no-show or a sideshow at its MVP lunch.

So the Duane Thomas ballots were torn up, and quarterback Roger Staubach was given the MVP award instead.

Staubach did throw two touchdown passes against the Dolphins, but he passed for only 119 yards and completed just 12 passes. Staubach hit just three passes over 11 yards, including a meaningless 21-yarder to Mike Ditka in the game's final few minutes after they had taken a 24–3 lead.

The right person was voted MVP. It's not Roger Staubach's fault, but the wrong person took the bows.

Postscript: Duane Thomas never played another game for the Cowboys, spent two disappointing seasons with the Redskins, and was out of football before his 28th birthday. Said Cowboys Hall of Fame defensive tackle Bob Lilly on the NFL Network's Super Bowl Champions *series: "I cannot tell people enough how good he was and how much I hated to see a person waste a possible Hall of Fame career. Every time I see him, I say, 'I fully expected you to be the next Jim Brown.'"*

The Rest of the Most Overrated

2. DEXTER JACKSON
Super Bowl XXXVII, January 26, 2003, Qualcomm Stadium, San Diego

It's not that Buccaneers free safety Dexter Jackson had a bad game. He did intercept Rich Gannon twice in Tampa's 48–21 win over the Raiders in Super Bowl XXXVII. It's just that cornerback Dwight Smith also intercepted Gannon twice—and returned both interceptions for touchdowns.

Jackson's returns went 25 and nine yards. Neither went for touchdowns.

Smith's returns went 50 and 44 yards. Both went for touchdowns.

Only one player in NFL history has returned more interceptions for touchdowns in the postseason in his life than Smith had in one game, and that was Willie Brown of the Raiders, who brought back three. But he accomplished it in 17 playoff games. Smith did it in one.

In Super Bowl history, only 13 running backs and only 12 wide receivers have scored two touchdowns in a game. Normal offensive players don't score twice in a Super Bowl that often, which tells you how crazy it is for a defensive player to do it.

In the 40 other Super Bowls, only seven other interceptions have been returned for touchdowns. In fact, with two interception returns for touchdowns in a single Super Bowl, Smith accomplished something no other entire team has ever done. In the last 20 years, there have been just five Super Bowl interceptions that went for touchdown returns—two by Smith and three by everybody else.

The only other player in history to return two interceptions for touchdowns in any postseason game was Aeneas Williams of the Rams in a 2001 conference semifinal against the Packers. But neither of his returns was as long as either of Smith's.

Smith still owns two of the eight longest interception returns for touchdowns in Super Bowl history. He accomplished something so rare that only 22 players have done it during the regular season.

Dexter Jackson had at outstanding game in Super Bowl XXXVII. Dwight Smith was nothing less than spectacular. Smith should have been the MVP. Not Jackson.

Postscript: Dexter Jackson was one of the most highly recruited quarterbacks in the nation coming out of high school but moved to defense when he got to Florida State and saw how talented Danny Kanell was.

3. LARRY BROWN
Super Bowl XXX, January 28, 1996, Sun Devil Stadium, Tempe, Arizona

Larry Brown's day of work consisted of allowing two pointless Neil O'Donnell passes to plop into his hands. And it made him a famous and wealthy man.

Brown, a Cowboys cornerback of modest accomplishment, wasn't trying to become MVP of Super Bowl XXX against the Steelers. O'Donnell was just so bad that Brown had no choice.

Third down and nine, six minutes into the third quarter. O'Donnell drops back to pass, doesn't see a receiver, so he decides to throw the ball *right to a Cowboys cornerback without a Pittsburgh receiver within 10 yards*. Plop.

Interception Larry Brown!

Second down and 10, four minutes left in the game. O'Donnell looks left, looks right, *sees Brown again! Thinks he's Andre Hastings! Throws the ball right to him.*

Interception Larry Brown!

Two interceptions. And Brown wasn't even covering anybody on either one. He was just kind of standing there, and O'Donnell twice, inexplicably, threw the ball directly to him.

Both of Brown's interceptions set up Emmitt Smith's rushing touchdowns and helped the Cowboys to a 27–17 win over the Steelers and their fifth Super Bowl championship.

Aikman was typically efficient, completing 15 of 23 passes with a touchdown pass and no interceptions.

The MVP award not only earned Brown a new Cadillac but also a new contract. Brown just happened to be heading into free agency, and the Raiders—who apparently hadn't bothered to actually watch the Super Bowl—decided that Brown's ability to let errant passes doink their way into his midsection was worth a lot of money.

The Raiders' judgment was about as good as O'Donnell's. They gave Brown a $13 million contract with a $3.5 million signing bonus, but he ended up playing just 12 games over two seasons for Oakland before they quietly released him. He returned to Dallas, played a few games for the Cowboys in 1998, and was out of football before his 30th birthday.

After the Super Bowl, Brown had one interception the rest of his career.

But for the rest of his life, when he's introduced, he's Super Bowl MVP Larry Brown. For the rest of his life, he's vastly overrated thanks to one fluke afternoon that had far more to do with the mistakes of the opposing quarterback than with Brown himself.

Postscript: In 1998 Neil O'Donnell faced the Steelers while playing for the Bengals. Steelers safety Lethon Flowers, still furious about O'Donnell's wretched performance in the Super Bowl three years earlier, said in the days before the game that O'Donnell should apologize to his former Steelers teammates for his performance in Super Bowl XXX. Instead, O'Donnell completed 20 of 26 passes for 298 yards with three touchdowns and no interceptions, and the Bengals won 25–20.

4. JIM PLUNKETT
Super Bowl XV, January 25, 1981, Louisiana Superdome, New Orleans

One minute and 48 seconds into Super Bowl XV, Ron Jaworski threw his first pass of the game. Tight end John Spagnola was his target near midfield, and for a moment he was open. Jaworski fired.

The Raiders were 3.5-point underdogs in Super Bowl XV, but they believed if they could slow down Pro Bowl running back Wilbert Montgomery and force the smart and efficient Jaworski into some mistakes, they could win their second Super Bowl in five years.

It wouldn't be easy. Jaworski led NFC quarterbacks with a 91.0 passer rating in 1980 and averaged just one interception every 37.6 passes, third-best in the league behind only Brian Sipe of the Browns and Gary Danielson of the Lions.

To open the game, the Eagles gained 11 yards on two rushing plays. On first-and-10, Jaworski eyed Spagnola down the field.

But Raiders outside linebacker Rod Martin, who had intercepted just two passes in his four NFL seasons, sliced in front of Spagnola and intercepted Jaworski, returning the ball 17 yards down to the Philadelphia 30.

The game wasn't even two minutes old, and the Raiders defense had seized momentum from the high-flying Eagles and their sixth-ranked offense.

Seven plays later, Raiders quarterback Jim Plunkett tossed a two-yard touchdown pass to Cliff Branch, and just six minutes into Super Bowl XV, the rout was on.

In the third quarter, Martin again stepped in front of a Jaworski pass intended for Spagnola, this time picking off Jaworski in Raiders territory. His second interception led to a Raiders field goal and tied the Super Bowl record for interceptions in a game then shared by Randy Beverly of the Jets, Chuck Howley of the Cowboys, and Jake Scott of the Dolphins.

The record didn't last long.

Martin's third interception followed in the fourth quarter, when Jaworski was trying to connect with running back Billy Campfield.

"I was so prepared for that game," Martin said. "Everybody made a big deal about how much we partied in New Orleans—and we did have a good time. But nobody knew that when I went back to my hotel room, I had a film projector and a screen set up and spent the whole week studying them and learning their tendencies."

Jaworski threw 12 interceptions all year, just seven in his last 12 regular-season games. Martin picked him off three times in one game. In one Super Bowl.

"Look at our defense," Martin said. "On the left side, there's Ted Hendricks, John Matuszak, and Lester Hayes, on the right side is Dave Browning, Dwayne O'Steen, and myself. Which side would you attack? So we knew where the ball was going."

Martin also had five tackles in the Super Bowl, including one for a loss of a yard against Eagles running back Leroy Harris, but despite the record-shattering performance, he wasn't named MVP.

Plunkett got the honor instead. And Plunkett did play well, completing 13 of 21 passes for three touchdowns and 261 yards. Plunkett, who had thrown just 15 passes over the 1978 and 1979 seasons before reviving his career as a 33-year-old curiosity, was the emotional choice. But Martin's performance against Jaworski was the true key to the Raiders' 27–10 win. He thwarted three Eagles drives and in the game's first moments gave the Raiders momentum they never lost.

"All these years later, people still think I was MVP of the Super Bowl," Martin said. "They swear to me I was MVP. They argue with me—'Yes, you were, I'm sure of it.' I try to tell them, 'No, I wasn't.' But they insist. Okay, if you feel that way, so be it. I'm not going to argue with you. I guess I'm the Peoples' MVP."

Postscript: Rod Martin was not considered a legitimate NFL prospect coming out of USC in 1977. As the 12th and final round of the draft neared its conclusion, the Raiders had one more pick left. Coach John Madden phoned USC coach John

Robinson, his friend from childhood, and asked him if he had any decent players left who hadn't been drafted. Robinson suggested Martin, who Madden made the 317th player taken overall.

The Most Underrated Super Bowl MVP of All Time

PHIL SIMMS
Super Bowl XXI, January 25, 1987, Rose Bowl, Pasadena, California

On third-and-four from the Giants' 31-yard line in Super Bowl XXI, quarterback Phil Simms dropped back, scanned the field, and threw over the middle to tight end Mark Bavaro, who was unable to secure a pass that was slightly overthrown but catchable. It was Simms's last incomplete pass of the game, and it came with one-and-a-half minutes left *in the first half.*

Simms nearly pitched a perfect game in Super Bowl XXI. He completed all but three of his 25 passes in the Giants' 39–20 win over the Broncos and was a perfect 10-for-10 in the second half, when the Giants turned a 10–9 deficit into a 39–20 victory and their first NFL title since Mickey Mantle won the Triple Crown in the Bronx.

"That might be the best game a quarterback has ever played." That comment came from Bill Parcells, who'd rather eat cold rigatoni than offer unqualified praise like that to one of his players.

Simms didn't spend the afternoon dinkin' and dunkin', either. He passed for 268 yards in the game and 165 in the second half, including a 44-yard strike on a flea flicker to Phil McConkey down to the 1-yard line to set up one touchdown, and a 36-yarder to Stacy Robinson to set up another. Simms also had a 22-yard bootleg run down to the 2-yard line in the fourth quarter that led to another touchdown.

All three of Simms's incompletions were in the second quarter. After completing his first seven passes of the game, he misfired when McConkey slipped while running his route. Simms completed his next three passes, and then rushed a short pass to Robinson on the left sideline on a third-and-eight.

The understated Phil Simms's nearly flawless performance in Super Bowl XXI ranks as one of the greatest ever.

Simms completed his next two attempts before overthrowing Bavaro on his final attempt of the first half. And that was it.

Simms's astounding performance came out of nowhere. During the regular season, he threw more interceptions than touchdowns, and his 22 interceptions were fourth-most in the NFL.

He also completed just 55 percent of his attempts—only 16th-best of the 27 quarterbacks who threw at least 200 passes in 1986. In six previous postseason games he had completed only 53 percent of his passes. So everybody considered his Super Bowl performance an aberration, and it has often been overlooked.

It shouldn't be. By completing 88 percent of his passes against the Broncos, Simms set not only a Super Bowl accuracy record but an overall postseason record, breaking the mark of 84.2 percent set by David Woodley of the Dolphins against the Patriots in a 1982 first-round game. In the more than two decades since Simms lit up the Broncos, the closest anybody has come to surpassing his accuracy record is Joe Montana, who completed 75.9 percent of his passes in Super Bowl XXIV four years later, also against Denver.

Simms's early years in the NFL were nothing special. He got booed, he got benched, and he got hurt. And his later years weren't much, either. He played only three more postseason games after the Super Bowl and didn't throw a touchdown in any of them.

Athletes in all sports spend their lives chasing perfection, but few ever achieve it. Simms came as close as any quarterback ever has. On January 25, 1987, before more than one hundred thousand fans jammed into the Rose Bowl, Simms became one of the immortals.

Postscript: Phil Simms's performance technically wasn't even the most accurate passing performance against the Broncos by a New York quarterback in 1986. On October 20, 1986, Pat Ryan of the Jets completed nine of 10 passes in the Jets' 22–10 win at the Meadowlands on Monday Night Football.

The Rest of the Most Underrated

2. STEVE YOUNG

Super Bowl XXIX, January 29, 1995, Joe Robbie Stadium, Miami, Florida

The last five quarterbacks named Super Bowl MVP threw a total of eight touchdown passes. John Elway threw one, Kurt Warner two, Tom Brady threw four in two games, and Peyton Manning just one.

Eight in five games.

Steve Young threw six.

In one game.

Forget the Super Bowl. Forget the playoffs. Young's performance for the 49ers against the Chargers in Super Bowl XXIX was one of the most superb by a quarterback in *any* game.

Steve Young was rarely acknowledged as Joe Montana's equal, especially by Montana. But this Super Bowl performance proved that Young was as talented as anybody. Even his revered predecessor.

It took Young three plays to throw his first touchdown, 44 yards to Jerry Rice. It took just three-and-a-half more minutes for the next, 51 yards to Ricky Watters. Young had thrown three touchdowns after 17 minutes and four by halftime.

By the time the 49ers had finished off the Chargers 49–26 in the highest-scoring Super Bowl ever, Young had broken the Super Bowl record of five touchdowns set by Montana.

And he did it against a San Diego defense that had allowed only 20 passing touchdowns all year—or fifth-best in the AFC. Indeed, that Chargers defense ranked a very respectable ninth in the league in points allowed that season.

No other quarterback in Super Bowl history has ever passed for 300 yards and thrown more than three touchdowns without an interception. Young threw six without an interception.

Young also completed 67 percent of his passes, seventh-best ever in a Super Bowl, and he passed for 325 yards, at the time just 32 shy of Montana's Super Bowl record. Young was even the game's leading rusher with 49 yards—more than San Diego's Natrone Means, who ran for more than 1,300 yards that season.

Most amazing is that Young played only a little more than three quarters that evening at Joe Robbie Stadium. Early in the fourth quarter, soon after Young racked up his sixth touchdown pass, 49ers coach George Seifert pulled him from the game, letting backups Elvis Grbac and Bill Musgrave finish up. Young threw just one pass in the game's final 13.5 minutes, and the 49ers got the ball back twice more—once at the San Diego 38-yard-line. So it's no stretch to think he could have thrown seven touchdowns if he really wanted to.

Maybe eight.

Postscript: Steve Young is the only player in pro football history to pass for 300 yards and rush for 100 yards in the same game. He did it while playing for the Los Angeles Express of the USFL in a 49–29 loss to the Chicago Blitz at Soldier Field on April 20, 1984.

3. FRANCO HARRIS
Super Bowl IX, January 12, 1975, Tulane Stadium, New Orleans

It was time to try something else. It was time to hammer Franco Harris right into the heart of the Purple People Eaters.

In the first half of Super Bowl IX, the Steelers offense didn't score a point and managed just 36 net yards against the vaunted Vikings defense. The Steelers' only offensive punch in that tepid first half came courtesy of Harris, who ran 11 times for 58 yards. Their 2–0 lead came courtesy of Dwight White's tackle of Fran Tarkenton in the end zone for a safety.

Coach Chuck Noll realized at halftime that the only way to get the offense rolling was to abandon quarterback Terry Bradshaw and the passing attack and just start pounding Harris—right at Alan Page. Right at Carl Eller. Right at Jim Marshall.

On the second play of the third quarter, Harris ran off left tackle for 24 yards. Two plays later, he powered nine yards for a touchdown and a 9–0 lead. By the time the game was over and the Steelers had won their first NFL championship 16–6, Harris had set Super Bowl records with 34 carries and 158 rushing yards, including 23 mighty rushes for 100 yards after halftime.

In the second half the Steelers threw seven times and ran 35 on the way to a Super Bowl–record 57 total carries, a mark that still stands. Harris outgained the Vikings by 57 yards in the second half (100–43) and actually outgained them by 39 yards in the entire game (158–119). In Super Bowl history, only John Riggins has carried the football more in a game.

Always humble, Harris's reaction when told after the game that he amassed 158 yards, was, "You have to be kidding."

Even after Harris trampled them, the Vikings showed him little respect.

"Franco Harris is a good running back, but we have faced others who were just as good or better," said Page, a Hall of Famer and now a Minnesota Supreme Court Justice.

Harris wasn't flashy, he didn't dance around and look pretty, and he didn't have world-class speed, so his achievements were often overlooked. But he controlled a Super Bowl like very few players ever have.

Postscript: In 1990 Franco Harris founded Super Bakery Inc., a Pittsburgh-based company that markets healthy doughnuts sold in schools, hospitals, and corporate cafeterias. Harris earned his degree at Penn State in food service and administration.

4. KURT WARNER
Super Bowl XXXIV, January 30, 2000, Georgia Dome, Atlanta

Kurt Warner produced unprecedented passing stats so routinely from 1999 through 2001 that his numbers in the Rams' Super Bowl triumph are easily overlooked. Just another great game for Warner. *Yawn.*

When you've passed for 41 touchdowns and more than 4,300 yards during the regular season, what's another 400-yard game?

But what Warner did, not just in Super Bowl XXXIV but that whole 1999 season, simply defies belief.

A year before Warner was selected Super Bowl MVP, he was playing for the Amsterdam Admirals in the World Football League. A year before that, he was with the Iowa Barnstormers of the Arena Football League. None of that mattered on January 30, 2000, when Warner shattered a gaggle of Super Bowl passing records in the Rams' 23–16 win over the Titans.

Warner, despite getting pummeled repeatedly by the Titans' ferocious front seven, passed for 414 yards, breaking Joe Montana's Super Bowl record by some 61 yards. Warner threw 45 passes, the most ever by a Super Bowl quarterback, without an interception.

And those 414 yards are still the most without an interception in any postseason game. Daryle Lamonica's 401 yards against the Jets in 1968 is next best.

Warner, the only quarterback to win a Super Bowl wearing jersey No. 13, completed 24 of 45 passes against the Titans, including the game-winning 73-yarder to Isaac Bruce that broke a 16–16 tie with less than two minutes left. Warner stood tall in the pocket and was leveled by Jevon Kearse a fraction of a second after releasing the ball. At the time, the Warner-to-Bruce touchdown was the longest fourth-quarter touchdown pass in Super Bowl history.

Rams quarterback Kurt Warner was so magnificent during the 1999 regular season, it's easy to overlook his record-setting performance in Super Bowl XXXIV.

"He took a pounding," Titans coach Jeff Fisher said afterward. "He was getting hit, hit, hit, but he just hung in there and made the big plays to win the game."

Postscript: Kurt Warner passed for 365 or more yards in four postseason games. Only 17 quarterbacks in history have thrown for that many yards in a playoff game once.

The Most Underrated Performance in a Super Bowl Win

CLARENCE DAVIS
Super Bowl XI, January 9, 1977, Rose Bowl, Pasadena, California

Clarence Davis played his entire career in obscurity, and even when he starred in a Super Bowl, that didn't change.

Davis spent eight years with the Raiders as a reserve tailback, content to return some kickoffs and get a handful of carries each game backing up Marv Hubbard, Charlie Smith, Mark van Eeghen, or whomever the Raiders' starting tailback was that year. When Davis did manage to get himself noticed, it was usually for his work as a kick returner. He ranked second to Mercury Morris in the AFC with a 27.2 average in 1971, and his 27.1 career average is eighth-best in NFL history.

Davis, slowed much of his pro career by sore knees after an All-American career at USC, never even led his own team in rushing, and he averaged more than 10 carries per game just once.

He did have talent. Davis averaged 4.5 yards per carry in spot duty, one of the top 20 figures in NFL history when he retired after the 1978 season before his 30th birthday. There were glimpses of brilliance. Davis ran for 116 yards and caught four passes for 82 yards in a 1974 win over the Browns. He gained a career-high 120 yards against the 0–8 Browns in 1975. And he managed three 100-yard games in 1977.

But in the biggest game of his life, Davis responded with the biggest performance of his life.

Davis rushed for 137 yards on just 16 carries in the Raiders' 32–14 win over the Vikings in Super Bowl XI.

The Raiders battered the Vikings' ballyhooed defense to the tune of 266 rushing yards that day, then a Super Bowl record and still third-most ever.

Operating mainly behind the blocks of van Eeghen, tight end Dave Casper, and right tackle John Vella, Davis delivered runs of 13, 16, 18, 20, and 35 yards.

And he could have had more. With the Raiders up big, Davis got the ball just once in the game's final 14.5 minutes, so he didn't have a chance to pad his numbers. With just a few more carries, Davis probably would have broken the Super Bowl rushing record of 158 yards set two years earlier by Franco Harris. Even with just 16 carries and only five runs after halftime, Davis still finished with what remains the seventh-highest rushing total in Super Bowl history.

Davis ran for more yards in a Super Bowl than Emmitt Smith ever did, with a higher average than Terrell Davis ever had.

The spotlight was never quite able to focus on Davis, no matter how much he deserved it.

Postscript: Clarence Davis was on the receiving end of the famous Sea of Hands catch during a 1974 divisional playoff game against the Dolphins. With 25 seconds left and the Dolphins leading 26–21, Raiders quarterback Kenny Stabler, while falling to the ground in the grasp of Vern Den Herder, lobbed a prayer into the end zone. Davis, a notoriously poor receiver who caught only 11 passes during the regular season, somehow outmuscled three Dolphin defenders for the eight-yard, game-winning touchdown. "They won it on a miracle play," Dolphins linebacker Bob Matheson said.

CHAPTER 15

Hall of Famers

The Most Overrated Hall of Famer of All Time

MARV LEVY

Marv Levy had already lost an unprecedented three straight Super Bowls. A year earlier his Buffalo Bills lost by the second-most lopsided score in the game's history, a 52–17 pasting by Jimmy Johnson's Dallas Cowboys in Super Bowl XXVII in Pasadena, California, on January 31, 1993. So, two days before his fourth-straight appearance in the world's biggest football game, Levy was being peppered with questions by an auditorium filled with reporters in Atlanta, Georgia. They had one question on their minds: what did the Bills head coach plan to do differently this time to actually win a Super Bowl?

He talked about competing hard and playing a sound game of football. Then Levy stunned the audience with this pronouncement: "We're not here to win the Super Bowl."

Mission accomplished. Two days later, on January 30, 1994, the Cowboys—this time coached by Barry Switzer—again pasted the Bills, 30–13, in Super Bowl XXVIII. Different year, different Super Bowl, different head coach on the opposite sideline, same result.

Despite the ignominious record of losing four straight Super Bowls, Levy was inducted into the Pro Football Hall of Fame in 2001. Levy, who has a master's degree in English history from Harvard, pretty much got a free ride through the normally contentious nominating process. Indeed, he entered the Hall in only his third year as a finalist. Debate about his Canton qualifications was pretty much quashed. Let's reopen it.

Here's why his supporters say Levy was put in the Hall. From 1988 to 1997, Levy's Bills led the AFC in winning percentage and were second only to the San Francisco 49ers.

When he retired in 1997 as the Bills head coach, Levy had 154 wins, 10th on the all-time list for head coaches. (As of 2007, Levy's win total ranked him 15th.) He had 120 losses for a winning percentage of .562.

But, as of 2007, of the top 20 head coaches in wins, that winning percentage is higher than only Weeb Ewbank and Chuck Knox.

Remove Ewbank from the argument. He was the only head coach to win championships in both the NFL and the AFL. Knox is not in the Hall. He had 193 wins but never even went to a Super Bowl.

What about Bud Grant? If you're going to put Grant in the Hall of Fame, why not Levy? Well, Grant's win total (168) and winning percentage (.607) are considerably higher.

The fact is that putting Levy in the Hall of Fame would diminish that honor bestowed on other more accomplished head coaches, especially his contemporaries: Joe Gibbs, who has three Super Bowl rings, and Bill Parcells, who has two. (Gibbs is in. Parcells will be.) Both totally outcoached Levy in the Super Bowl. So did Johnson and, believe it or not, Switzer.

But let's focus on Super Bowl XXV, the so-called "wide right" game where Scott Norwood missed a last-second field goal and the Giants won 20–19.

The Giants had no business winning that game. The Bills had no business being in a position to have to kick a desperation field goal to win it, either.

On offense, Parcells ordered the Giants to control the football, and thus the clock, with a punishing ground game that kept Bills quarterback Jim Kelly and his high-powered offense off the field.

On defense, Parcells's defensive coordinator, Bill Belichick, ordered the Giants defense to allow Bills running back Thurman Thomas to have enough success running the ball to provide at least the illusion that Buffalo could shred New York on the ground all day. This rope-a-dope defense again kept the ball out of Kelly's hands. Levy should have figured out that deception and called for opening up the game, throwing the ball down the field. Instead of taking what Parcells and Belichick gave him, Levy should have dictated the terms of the game. He didn't. The Bills lost. And Norwood took the blame.

Is that second-guessing? You bet. But, you know what? It's the Super Bowl. You're supposed to win the thing. A few years ago, the venerable Jerry Izenberg, a sportswriter from Newark's *The Star-Ledger*, wrote an impassioned defense of putting Levy in the Hall of Fame. Here's what he wrote: "It's not the final destination that's paramount. It's the journey itself that matters."

But here's the title of the book Izenberg wrote with Bill Parcells: *No Medals for Trying.*

Not to win a Super Bowl in four straight tries is inexcusable. But to lose by a combined score of 139–73 is monumentally embarrassing. And Levy, who was never named NFL Coach of the Year by the Associated Press (the official honor in that category), worked with Hall of Fame talent. Levy had Kelly, one of the most prolific passers of his generation. And he had Smith, a game-changing pass rusher who retired as the all-time NFL leader with 200 sacks. Wide receiver Andre Reed is sure to follow. You can't win one Super Bowl with that group? C'mon.

Look what Parcells, Joe Gibbs, John Madden, Bill Walsh, George Seifert, and Chuck Noll did with that Hall of Fame talent. They won Super Bowls. No doubt they deserve to be in Canton.

Now, what are the Hall of Fame selectors going to do about Jon Gruden and Brian Billick? Both won the Super Bowl. They have struggled since. But do they get denied Canton? They piloted superior talent and coached their teams to truly dominant seasons, then hoisted the Lombardi Trophy after convincing title game victories—with Brad Johnson and Trent Dilfer at quarterback. Put in this perspective, Levy is the most overrated member of the Hall of Fame.

Postscript: In January 2006 Marv Levy came out of retirement at age 80 to become general manager of the Bills. In 2006 Buffalo finished 7–9, third in the AFC East.

The Rest of the Most Overrated

2. WARREN MOON

Warren Moon threw 291 touchdown passes, one more than Johnny Unitas. So Warren Moon should be in the Hall of Fame, right?

But Vinny Testaverde has thrown just 21 fewer touchdown passes than Moon, and Testaverde—one of the all-around great gentleman in the history of pro football—probably will go to Canton only if he drives there himself.

So why is Warren Moon in the Pro Football Hall of Fame?

Who doesn't love Boomer Esiason? Nobody has done more to promote the good-guy and charitable image of pro football than Esiason has. And he threw 247 touchdown passes, which puts him 14th on the all-time list at the end of the 2006 season—not that far off from Moon's total. Plus, Esiason took the Cincinnati Bengals to Super Bowl XXIII, took them to the doorstep of the Lombardi Trophy until Joe Montana engineered an improbable 92-yard touchdown drive and the San Francisco 49ers won 20–16. But let's be honest, Esiason is not going to be a Hall of Famer.

Moon never took any of his four teams to the Super Bowl. Never took any of his teams past the first round of the playoffs. His postseason record as a starter: 3–7, with 17 touchdowns and 14 interceptions.

So why is Warren Moon enshrined in Canton?

Is it because Moon is a member of the exclusive club of quarterbacks who has passed for more than 4,000 yards in a single season? Moon did it four times. As of the 2006 season, Kansas City Chiefs quarterback Trent Green has passed for more than 4,000 yards three times. Is Green headed for Canton? Nope. Well, not unless he goes to the Super Bowl and wins it. Then he has a shot.

So why was Moon inducted in 2006—*in his first year of eligibility?*

By the way, in Houston, Moon passed more than 4,000 yards in back-to-back seasons: 1990 and 1991. In 1991 the Oilers finished 11–5 and won the AFC Central Division. But Moon's team was one-and-done, ousted in the first round of the postseason by the Denver Broncos, who lost the AFC Championship game. In 1990 Houston finished just 9–7, qualifying for the final AFC wild-card spot. The Bengals crushed them in the first round of the playoffs, 41–14. The Bengals starting quarterback in that game? That would be Boomer Esiason.

And Esiason did not play on a team with a pass-happy offense like Houston's "run-and-shoot," a big-numbers system that proved to be an illusion, disappearing in the postseason. From 1984 to 1993 in Houston, Moon piled up big, big numbers that, in the end, amounted to a whole lot of nothing.

In Minnesota, same deal—back-to-back seasons with more than 4,000 yards passing in 1994 and 1995. The Vikings won the NFC Central in 1994 but managed to score just 18 points against the wild-card entry, the Chicago Bears, losing 35–18 in the first round of the playoffs.

The next year, it was worse. Moon threw for 4,228 yards. The Vikings scored 412 points, second-most in their division. But the team finished 8–8 and did not make the playoffs.

In the mid-1990s, Moon's numbers are comparable to quarterbacks who accomplished about the same in that era, such as Dave Krieg, Jim Everett, and Neil O'Donnell (who actually took the Pittsburgh Steelers to a Super Bowl). For instance, in his career, Krieg finished with 261 touchdown passes, just 30 fewer than Moon, over a comparable time period with just about the same result for his team, the Seattle Seahawks. Krieg will *not* be a Hall of Famer.

So why is Warren Moon?

Postscript: In chapter 1 the argument was made that a history of pro football cannot be written without prominently mentioning Bob Hayes, whose speed revolutionized pro football. Hayes is in Michael MacCambridge's indispensable history of the NFL called America's Game. *Moon is not.*

Yet Moon is in Canton. Hayes is not.

3. DAN FOUTS

Let's stay in the same category: big-number quarterbacks who are in the Hall of Fame but who never did much in the postseason. Next entry: Dan Fouts.

Now, Fouts has only 254 touchdown passes—16 fewer than Vinny Testaverde, seven fewer than Dave Krieg. Just 10 more than John Hadl, the godfather of San Diego quarterbacks who made a big name by putting up big numbers. Hadl is not in the Hall of Fame.

Fouts was enshrined in Canton in 1993 in his first year of eligibility. Like Warren Moon, the decision was rationalized by some pretty gaudy statistics. But as with Moon, the case to put Fouts in Canton, when compared to the accomplishments of his contemporaries, falls apart.

San Diego's third-round pick in 1973, Fouts, unlike Moon, was not a journeyman quarterback. He spent his entire 14-year career with the Chargers and was magnificently prolific. Fouts is in the exclusive 40,000-passing-yards club, throwing for 43,040 yards in his career. Unlike Moon, Fouts was a league MVP, in 1982.

But, also unlike Moon, Fouts threw nearly as many interceptions as touchdown passes. Fouts threw 242 picks, a total just 12 shy of his touchdown passes. This is where it's important to compare Fouts to a contemporary of his who is *not* in the Hall of Fame: retired Bengals quarterback Kenny Anderson, who piloted Cincinnati to Super Bowl XVI.

Fouts never reached a Super Bowl. He came the closest in 1981. That year, the Chargers lost the AFC Championship game. The winners: the Bengals. The quarterback: Anderson.

You want numbers? Here's how Anderson stacks up to Fouts. In the early 1970s Anderson was a big star. He had a few down years, then reemerged in 1980, three years after the passing rules were liberalized to allow more freedom for the wide receivers, the beginning of the so-called wide-receiver decade. Plus, the league added two more games in 1978 to make a 16-game schedule.

Fouts did not have his big year until 1979, two years after the rules changes. Fouts threw for more than 4,000 yards in the next three seasons, but he also threw a lot of interceptions. In 1979, for example, he had 24 touchdown passes and 24 picks. The 1981 season was by far his best statistically, with 4,802 passing yards, 33 touchdown passes, and only 17 interceptions.

That year the Chargers finished 10–6 and beat Miami in overtime in the playoffs. But it was Anderson who stopped Fouts from going to the Super Bowl. Fouts had more passing yards in the game—185 to Anderson's 161. But Anderson was far more efficient. He had two touchdown passes and no interceptions. Fouts threw a touchdown pass but had two picks. Anderson was just a better performer in crunch time. Yet Anderson awaits the call from the Hall that may never come.

Fouts was fearless, tough, a fiery competitor. He was put in the Hall based on his numbers and his guile, but he just made too many mistakes in critical situations. Others of his era, such Joe Montana, Ken Anderson, and Jim Plunkett, did not.

Postscript: In 2000 NFL Films made a Best Ever Quarterbacks *documentary. Dan Fouts did not make the final cut.*

4. BARRY SANDERS

Enough picking on big-name quarterbacks. Let's pick on a big-name running back.

Barry Sanders. None bigger than that. Except in big games, of course. Sanders, who was inducted into the Hall of Fame in 2004 (his first year of eligibility), scored one touchdown for every 35 touches in his 153 regular-season games but just one touchdown in 112 postseason touches in six playoff games.

Indeed, Sanders's only career playoff touchdown was a 47-yard run against the Dallas Cowboys in a 1991 divisional round playoff game in the Pontiac Silverdome, the Lions' domed home stadium. The Lions won that game 38–6. Sanders's touchdown came in the final minutes of the fourth quarter with Detroit already leading 31–6. The following week, the Lions went on the road to play the Washington Redskins at RFK Stadium. Sanders was not a factor. Detroit took a 41–10 beating.

In fact, between then and mysteriously walking away from the game in his prime just shy of Walter Payton's all-time rushing record, Sanders appeared with the Lions in four more playoff games. All were losses. Sanders did not score in any of them.

Barry Sanders's penchant for disappearing in big games is part of his legacy.

Sanders's postseason performance supports the notion that he was a product of the cozy, climate-controlled Silverdome. Nice carpet for easy, stop-on-a-dime maneuvering. Seventy-two degrees. Detroit faithful keeping the defensive line off balance with high-decibel support.

In four career *outdoor* postseason games, Sanders averaged a paltry 2.8 yards per carry. He never scored a touchdown. And he never ran for more 65 yards in a single game. With Sanders, the Lions went 0–4 in outdoor playoff games, losing by an average of 17 points.

Nobody is suggesting that a bust of Barry should *not* be in Canton. He's the third-leading rusher of all time with 15,269 yards. He holds the all-time

NFL record for consecutive 1,000-yard seasons with 10, from 1989 to 1998. Sanders was the first player to rush for 1,500 yards in a season five times. He was selected to 10 Pro Bowls. In 1997, when he rushed for 2,053 yards, he was NFL co-MVP, an honor he should have not had to share with Brett Favre that season. In 1988 Sanders won the Heisman Trophy at Oklahoma State.

But this picture of perfection has a nasty blemish. Once Sanders got to the playoffs and got out of Silverdome, he was a much less effective player.

Take the wild-card playoff game at Lambeau Field in 1994. That season Sanders averaged 5.7 yards per carry—the second-highest total of his career. In the first round of the playoffs against the Green Bay Packers, on the frozen tundra, Sanders set an NFL postseason record for rushing futility. He had 13 carries for minus-one yard. He had three catches that day—for four yards. Which means he had 16 touches for a total of three yards—2.7 yards fewer than he averaged per rush in the regular season.

Now, the spirited defense of putting him in the Hall of Fame on the first ballot always includes the theory that Sanders was the only thing the Lions had going for them in the Barry Sanders era. And that's exactly what it is—a theory, and a bad one at that.

Are those defenders forgetting about wide receivers Herman Moore and Brett Perriman? The Lions stretched the field for Sanders—especially in the Dome. This helped him be wildly successful—in the regular season. And in the years when the Lions went to the playoffs, their defense was not awful. It was middle-of-the-pack—ranked 11th in 1991, 15th in 1993, 19th in 1994, 14th in 1995, and 10th in 1997.

There is another black mark on Sanders's career. His Greta Garbo act on the way out the door.

After rushing for 1,491 yards in 1998, Sanders abruptly and mysteriously retired. At the time he was 1,457 yards shy of Payton's all-time rushing record. His defenders say Sanders—who played the game with dignity and class—did not owe anybody anything. As long as he was at peace with the decision, that was enough.

That's bunk.

Here was a man who benefited greatly from the support of his teammates, his organization, and his fans, and he just turned his back on them without a word of gratitude. He left his teammates and a franchise in a lurch, to the point where the Lions demanded he return $7.3 million of his signing bonus.

Years later, when it was time for him to become eligible for Canton, Sanders had to be coaxed into providing some kind of explanation for his untimely retirement.

It was too little, too late.

Postscript: Of the five leading rushers in NFL history, Barry Sanders is the only one never to reach a Super Bowl. The others—Emmitt Smith, Walter Payton, Curtis Martin, and Jerome Bettis—all reached at least one Super Bowl. And all but Martin won at least one NFL championship ring.

5. LARRY WILSON

Why bring Larry Wilson into this? Good question. At this point in the football cosmos, there is no earthly reason to question the credentials of a guy like Larry Wilson, who by every measure had an unblemished, productive NFL career.

Wilson is credited with inventing the safety blitz. Whether or not that is literally true, Wilson certainly perfected it, forced other defensive coordinators and safeties to put it in their repertoires, and made the whole idea of attacking anybody or anything from out of nowhere a concept America could embrace and adopt. *The safety blitz.* Pretty cool.

Truth be told, it will never be known just how productive Wilson was in blitzing the quarterback. Sacks weren't a stat back then. It's clear he was effective, and feared.

And tough. Wilson, who played from 1960 to 1972, sort of fell out of the football consciousness until Mike Ditka—who's tougher than Iron Mike?—started talking about (of all people) Terrell Owens. On *SportsCenter* on September 18, 2006, Ditka challenged T.O., who was planning on a two- to four–week absence for a broken finger. Ditka said, "I remember Larry Wilson intercepted a pass with casts on both his hands!" It was a comment that no doubt sent a lot of fantasy footballers scrambling for the history books.

Well, it's true. In 1966 Wilson intercepted a pass with casts on both hands. He had broken both his wrists. Now, that's tough.

But does that make him a first-ballot Hall of Famer? Wilson was inducted in 1978, his first year of eligibility. His biggest claim to fame appears to be that 1966 season. That year Wilson had 10 interceptions—his career high. But that's four picks short of the single-season record of 14 set by Dick "Night Train" Lane in 1952. Three others had 13 in a season. Nine others have had 12. By those standards, Wilson didn't come close to the single-season record.

When Wilson retired, he had 52 interceptions, including five returned for touchdowns. One of his contemporaries at the time, Mel Renfro (a cornerback and safety with the Dallas Cowboys from 1964 to 1977), retired with 52 interceptions. Renfro went to 10 Pro Bowls; Wilson, eight. Yet, Renfro had to wait 19 years after retirement to get inducted into the Hall of Fame.

And it was clear that the Hall of Fame selection committee had set the standard for Canton enshrinement for the safety position in 1967, when the great Emlen Tunnell was inducted. Tunnel retired in 1961 with the then–NFL all-time record of 79 interceptions—*27 more than Wilson.*

The great Willie Wood, who was an integral part of the Green Bay Packers' first two Super Bowl victories, had 48 career interceptions. But Wood, just as punishing a tackler as Wilson, had to wait until 1989 to be inducted in Canton—a full 18 years after his retirement.

As for Wilson's postseason performance, it will remain a mystery. The Cardinals, a rancid franchise for most of its history, never made the playoffs in Wilson's 13-year career. (That fact, of course, is another piece of the puzzle. If Wilson was first-ballot Hall of Famer good—which is about as good as it's supposed to get—why didn't he lead his team to the postseason?)

So Wilson was the second safety inducted into the Hall of Fame—and in his first year of eligibility. So what? Well, his career accomplishments have been inflated and overrated, especially when you consider the injustice suffered by perhaps the greatest safety in pro football history.

Which brings us to the next section of this chapter—the most *underrated* members of the Pro Football Hall of Fame. Read on.

The Most Underrated Hall of Famer of All Time

PAUL KRAUSE

No one noticed Paul Krause.

There was the *Monday Night Football* gang—Mike and Joe and Tony, Suzy and Michele, only first names needed here. And on the Metrodome field Tom Brady and the mighty New England Patriots warmed up for the game while the home team, the Minnesota Vikings, tried to show America that a franchise saddled with one scandal after another was ready for prime time. It was the last Monday in October 2006.

To celebrate the evening, some of the old Vikings were on hand, including Carl Eller and Alan Page and the other Purple People Eaters, the defense that dominated the NFC's middle earth in the 1970s.

But no one seemed to notice Krause. Wearing a leather jacket, Krause stood on the sideline, carefully surveying the scene, just like he did when he patrolled the secondary for the Vikings, collecting an NFL-record 81 interceptions—a record that still stands.

He lives in Florida now. His shaved head was bronze and bright, reflecting the competing lights of the game's premier event. It was, he said, the first NFL game he's attended in a long, long time.

"I don't watch football," he said. "I have better things to do on Sunday afternoons."

You can't blame Krause for being a touch bitter. He retired in 1979 with the NFL record for interceptions and then waited 19 years to get noticed, to get his due. It wasn't until 1998 that Krause was elected to the Pro Football Hall of Fame in Canton, Ohio.

Did Kareem Abdul-Jabbar have to wait 19 years after setting an NBA career scoring record to get into the Naismith Memorial Basketball Hall of Fame? Did Hank Aaron have to wait 19 years to get to Cooperstown after hitting his 715th home run? Did Susan Butcher have to wait 19 years to get into the Iditarod Hall of Fame after winning her fourth Iditarod? No, no, and of course not.

The unassuming Paul Krause starred in the defensive backfield for the Redskins and Vikings from 1964 through 1979 and was a master at reading plays and making interceptions.

Here's what 81 interceptions means. Kenny Houston got into the Hall of Fame the first year he was eligible and had 32 fewer interceptions than

Krause. Larry Wilson was inducted his first year, and he had 31 fewer picks. As a team, after five years in existence, the Houston Texans were still 17 short of Paul Krause.

Krause is easily the most underrated Hall of Famer in NFL history.

Krause defined the term "center fielder" in football but thought seriously about pursuing that position in major league baseball. At Iowa, where he nearly flunked out, Krause was an All-American outfielder in his sophomore year. But he tore up his arm. (He still threw one touchdown pass in his NFL career.) So he decided to go into the NFL draft. The Washington Redskins took him in the second round in 1964.

In his first game as a rookie, against the Cleveland Browns, Krause picked quarterback Frank Ryan twice, stepping right in front of wide receiver Paul Warfield both times. Warfield was inducted into the Hall of Fame in 1983, just six years after he retired. Later in 1964, Ryan would lead those same Browns to a dominant 10–3–1 season and an NFL title, beating the Baltimore Colts and the great Johnny Unitas 27–0 in the championship game.

Beating the Ryan-to-Warfield combo is not what Krause chooses to remember about playing against the Browns as a rookie. "It was great because I was actually sharing the same field with Jim Brown, who was the greatest running back of all time," he said. Typical Krause. That's the way he played, too. He rarely gave wide receivers the time of day, just a hard time.

He didn't have track-star speed. He wasn't an intimidator or imitator. He had a singular style of guile, guts, and smarts. Right place, right time—all the time. For 16 seasons. Now that's hard to do. Krause played in 223 of a possible 228 games from 1964 through 1979. "He personified the term 'free safety,'" said his longtime coach Bud Grant.

Krause played in four Super Bowls and was a part of 11 consecutive winning seasons. Longevity—and durability.

But not flashy. Maybe that's what hurt him. Maybe he simply didn't look like a Hall of Famer. He just played like one. There was also the perception that he hung around too long. Krause had just seven interceptions in his last four seasons and was 37 when he retired in 1979. Many believed Krause just played out the string to break the interception record of Emlen Tunnell, who was known as "offense on defense," and who had 79 picks with the Giants and Packers. (Tunnell retired in 1961. Six years later, four years after the Hall opened in 1963, Tunnell was the first African American inducted into the Hall, an honor he richly deserved.)

Krause got his 78th interception in 1977. He had none in 1978, the first time in his career he got shut out. Many thought he should have retired then. But, an iconoclast to the last, Krause had his own timetable and agenda.

In 1979, early in the season, he cut in front of Detroit Lions wide receiver Gene Washington and tied Tunnell's record with his 79th pick.

Fast forward to week 14 in Los Angeles—Krause still tied with Tunnell. The Rams were about to finish 9–7 to win the Western Division. Rams quarterback Vince Ferragamo was having a solid year, but on the last play of the first half, he threw the football right down the chute between the hash marks. Ferragamo overthrew tight end Charle Young.

The quarterback never noticed Paul Krause playing center field. And the pass landed right in Krause's breadbasket. Like Willie Mays, Krause offered the ball a soft place to land. And Tunnell's record was broken.

"It was sweet," said Krause.

He got one more interception—number 81—on the second-to-last play of regulation. (The Rams won in overtime 27–21 and later won an unlikely berth in Super Bowl XIV. The Vikings finished 7–9.)

Krause, who was an All-Pro four times and went to eight Pro Bowls, has set a record that may never be broken. Going into the 2007 season, there wasn't an active player with more than 50 interceptions. Only three had more than 40—and all were well over 30 years old.

Eighty-one picks? That's unthinkable. Even if it took the Hall of Fame voters nearly two decades to realize it—and recognize it.

Postscript: In 1995 Paul Krause's wife, Pam, was badly injured in a car accident in Florida. Krause said, "The doctor told me, 'If you believe in God, start praying.'"

Pam was in a coma for more than five months, but she survived. Three years later, she attended Krause's induction into the Hall of Fame.

The Rest of the Most Underrated

2. FRED BILETNIKOFF

A player doesn't have to be defined by jaw-dropping numbers. Take Oakland Raiders wide receiver Fred Biletnikoff. His career can be defined by three words. Consistency. Clutch. Class.

And, oh, by the way, no one ever remembers him dropping a pass. "Not a one," said John Madden.

Madden should know. He was the head coach of the Oakland Raiders who saw a 189-pound college kid with long golden hair—who looked like a surfer—and turned him into one of the most respected wide receivers in NFL history.

Biletnikoff, a second-round pick out of Florida State, was slow. But he was precise. His technique was flawless. And his hands were freakishly large and very soft. When the ball arrived in the vicinity of No. 25 in silver and black, it was swallowed up. Why? Look at film clips and photographs of Biletnikoff catching the football. He always had his thumbs pointed away from the ball to provide a natural basket. His thumbs were unusually long, too, which made that basket larger than it should have been for a man his size.

You need some numbers? Biletnikoff held the NFL record of 10 straight seasons with 40 or more receptions from 1967 to 1976, an era when defense dominated the league. That's consistency.

Don't forget, this was a time in pro football when defensive backs could clutch and grab, smack and hold—do anything short of decapitating a wide receiver to break up the timing and rhythm of the passing game.

Still, because he didn't have separation speed, Biletnikoff was able to use timing and precision to get open. Especially when it counted most. He caught 70 passes for 1,167 yards and 10 touchdowns in the postseason, ranking him second all time in the NFL when he retired in 1978. That's clutch.

His biggest clutch performance came in Super Bowl XI on January 9, 1977, at the Rose Bowl in Pasadena, California. On the field that day, the Oakland Raiders, winners of 12 straight games, had six players who would later be enshrined in Canton: tight end Dave Casper, cornerback Willie Brown, linebacker Ted Hendricks, guard Gene Upshaw, tackle Art Shell, and Biletnikoff.

Biletnikoff did not score a touchdown. But he made the biggest catch of the game, a catch that typified his ability and legacy.

Against a Minnesota Vikings team known for its fierce defense, the Raiders were cocky and confident going into the game. But Oakland got off to a slow start. First there was a 29-yard field-goal attempt that hit the upright. Then they died inside the red zone and were held to three points.

Another trip into the red zone was stalled on the Vikings' 6-yard line. So Ken Stabler called on his most reliable player. Stabler dropped straight back and watched Biletnikoff work his magic. Split right, Biletnikoff stuck his head inside, and Vikings corner Nate Wright, in a tight bump-and-run coverage, went for the fake. Biletnikoff broke toward the flag and caught a dart from Stabler. Wright pushed him out of bounds inches short of the goal line. Seconds later the Raiders were in the end zone and had a 10–0 lead. Oakland won Super Bowl XI 32–14. Biletnikoff had four clutch catches for 79 yards. He was named the MVP.

Biletnikoff was the essence of what Al Davis tried to build in Oakland—a misfit of sorts who knew how to use his God-given talent to find a way to win. You can't use the phrase "Just win, baby"—a phrase which has become part of the American lexicon—without conjuring the image of the blond, flowing hair and the perfect route-running of Biletnikoff.

And his impact on the game has lasted generations. While you must have a Bob Hayes to open up the field, you must have a sure-handed receiver like Biletnikoff to work that sideline and to fearlessly catch the ball in horrific traffic.

And, of course, hold onto it.

Postscript: Stickum. In the 1970s all wide receivers used it. Biletnikoff, too. Here's what Hall of Fame cornerback Lem Barney said about No. 25: "He was a deceptive receiver. Everybody said he was slow, but he always seemed to get behind people. He was very fluid. He used that stickum on his hands and stuck his way into the Hall of Fame."

3. MEL BLOUNT

The Associated Press started giving out the NFL's Defensive Player of the Year Award in 1971. Nobody envisioned that a cornerback would ever deserve that honor. For the longest time, an NFL cornerback was considered an interchangeable part, somebody you just stuck out there on the perimeter to do whatever it took to keep the wide receiver from his appointed route—and the football. In short, a cornerback was considered a bit of a street hustler, somebody you needed until somebody else at least as qualified came along.

Cornerbacks got no respect.

Until Mel Blount came along.

Oh, he was a hustler, all right. And a hitter, and an enforcer, and a leader. In one season Blount proved to the NFL cognoscenti that being a cornerback mattered—in a big, big way. If you had the right guy with the right skills, he was, in fact, not interchangeable—certainly not easily replaceable.

As a result, Blount was the first cornerback to win the Defensive Player of the Year Award. The year was 1975. Blount played for the Steel Curtain in Pittsburgh. In the 1970s the Steelers' notorious defense had already collected two Defensive Player of the Year Awards. Both were given to defensive tackle Joe Greene—because, well, he was "Mean Joe." And in 1976 linebacker Jack Lambert would get his, but it would irk him to no end that the year before, Blount—a *cornerback!*—would get the honor before he did.

But in 1975 Blount redefined the position. Not only would a cornerback cover, he would tackle. He led the NFL in interceptions with 11 in 1975. But he was so aggressive around the ball that the league began to understand that the cornerback was another defensive position on the field that had to be feared.

At 6′3″, 205 pounds, he was taller than most corners. He didn't have great speed, but he rarely exhibited wasted motion. He was smooth and relentless—Shaft and Batman all rolled into one.

"It was just unique at that time for a guy like me to be a corner," said Blount. With his size, Blount developed into the perfect bump-and-run corner. His approach was universally imitated to the point where the league recognized that offenses needed help. Without scoring, the league would slowly expire. The rules were changed to let the wide receivers run free—and the 1980s became known as the decade of the wide receivers. Blame Blount for that.

He recognized what he had done. "People want to see 70-yard bombs and points on the board," said Blount, who was selected as the starting cornerback on the NFL's All-Time team in 2000. "That's what the fans want, so the league is going to make sure that nothing gets in the way of it happening."

Blount was put in the Pro Football Hall of Fame in 1989, his first year of eligibility.

Eighteen years after Blount won Defensive Player of the Year, another cornerback was honored. In 1993 Rod Woodson, also of the Pittsburgh Steelers, won. The following year cornerback Deion Sanders, who helped Steve Young finally win a Super Bowl, won.

These days you hear so much about Sanders and Woodson—they're TV stars who are credited with changing the way cornerbacks are viewed and valued. Not so. Mel Blount did that.

Postscript: Mel Blount was one of 11 children who grew up on a dirt farm in Georgia. After he retired from the NFL, he established a home for lost children in Taylorstown, Pennsylvania. "You have to guide boys," he said, "lead them in the proper direction, teach them discipline, or they'll be wild their whole lives."

4. SID GILLMAN

In 1901 an upstart group of businessman formed the American League to challenge the National League, then the establishment in professional baseball. For 60 years it was the only rival sports league to survive—until the 1960s, when another upstart group calling themselves the "Foolish Club" established the American Football League.

Foolish, yes. Think of it now—starting a league to challenge the supremacy of the almighty NFL. But that's what happened. And the AFL survived and flourished and forced a merger with the NFL in 1970.

That wouldn't have happened if not for the innovation of Sid Gillman. Before Joe Namath arrived, before the Super Bowl was founded, football fans came to embrace the old AFL for one good, old-fashioned reason: it was good football. Fun to watch. Wide open. Up and down the field. While the NFL was still Bednarik and Butkus and the power sweep, the AFL of Sid Gillman's

San Diego Chargers threw the football down the field—actually, all over the field. (The AFL used a longer, slimmer Spalding football to enhance the passing game—at Gillman's insistence.)

Gillman, who was head coach of the Rams in Los Angeles from 1955 to 1959, won the AFL championship in January 1964, a 51–10 drubbing of the Patriots—*51 points!* That season the Bears beat the Giants 14–10 in the NFL Championship game.

Gillman's experiments and the resulting explosion of offense could not have come at a better time for the AFL. A month earlier, a federal appeals court had thrown out the AFL's antitrust suit against the NFL, and it looked liked the upstarts were not going to survive.

But the AFL proved that there was a market for the game it showcased. After crushing the Patriots, Gillman—perhaps realizing that it was time to draw a line in the sand that the national press could understand—announced, "We're champions of the world. If anyone wants to debate it, let them play us."

With those words, it sounds like Gillman created the concept later known to the world as the Super Bowl. That game was three years away, and the unthinkable—a merger—would happen in 1970. In the meantime, Gillman's rivals in both leagues began to take notice of his tactics.

To keep up with Gillman, Kansas City Chiefs head coach Hank Stram invented shifts and motions on offense and the triple-stack defense. In New York, the Jets signed Joe Namath to the largest pro contract at the time: $427,000, not including a Jet-green Lincoln Continental. The ride was nice, but you can't sell Namath on playing in the AFL without the promise of being given a green light to throw the football.

Of course, the Jets and the Chiefs would be the first two teams from the upstart league to win the Super Bowl.

Postscript: Sid Gillman remained with the Chargers until 1971, when poor health forced him to pretty much retire. The Chargers would not make an appearance in the Super Bowl until 1995. But two of Gillman's coaching protégés would dominate the game for the decade after his retirement—Al Davis with the Oakland Raiders and Chuck Noll with the Pittsburgh Steelers. That's right, Gillman mentored Noll.

5. RAYMOND BERRY

Johnny Unitas is on everybody's list as the best quarterback in NFL history. No argument there. But Unitas didn't do it alone. Somebody caught all those passes. That somebody was Raymond Emmett Berry.

Berry was the quintessential southern gentleman who, when he came out of Southern Methodist University in 1954, had that astronaut haircut and good looks. In Berry, Unitas found the perfect match. Unitas was gruff. Berry was courteous. But both were technically proficient and dedicated to their craft.

Like Peyton Manning and Marvin Harrison—the current battery mates wearing horseshoes on their helmets—Unitas and Berry spent hours and hours on the practice field perfecting their timing.

Berry claimed to have perfected 88 different moves. Unitas knew each one. But they had one simple favorite, what they called the Q pattern. It was based on a 10-yard square pattern. "I'd go down about 10 yards and make my break, like I was squaring inside," Berry told *Sporting News* much later. "Then, when the defensive back made his move and tried to go inside with me, I'd plant my inside foot and head to the corner."

Simple but deadly. Berry led the league in receptions three straight years, from 1958 to 1960, and he caught a then-record 631 passes for 9,275 yards and 68 touchdowns in a 13-year career.

Here's why he's underrated. Look at what happened to Unitas after Berry retired after the 1967 season. In 1967 Unitas threw 20 touchdown passes and had a quarterback rating of 83.6. Without Berry, Unitas played six more years and threw an average of six touchdown passes per season, including a high of 14 in 1970. His quarterback ratings in the non-Berry years plummeted, averaging 53.1 in those six years, including a high of 70.8 in 1972, when he threw only 157 passes.

Postscript: In the Greatest Game Ever Played, the game that put the NFL on the national stage, there is no Johnny U. comeback without Raymond Berry. In the game-tying drive in the fourth quarter, Unitas hit Berry three straight times to set up Steve Myhra's 20-yard field goal to send the game into overtime. In overtime, Berry had two more catches.

In all, he had a then–playoff record of 12 catches for 178 yards and a touchdown.

Acknowledgments

A book like this takes an extraordinary level of research. You can't do it alone. I didn't. So I have a lot of people to thank, beginning with Patrick Carney, who will be a fine working journalist very soon, and Luke Hadden, whose dedication to this project was relentless.

Along the way, I've received guidance and help from the NFL, particularly from the unique brotherhood of league public relations directors. Many deserve a personal thank-you: Scott Berchtold, Derek Boyko, Kevin Byrne, Vernon Cheek, Ted Crews, Charlie Dayton, Dan Edwards, Harvey Greene, Pat Hanlon, Peter John-Baptiste, Jeff Kamiss, Craig Kelley, Stacey James, Bob Lange, Dave Lockett, Casey O'Connell, Reggie Roberts, Avis Roper, and Rick Smith.

Thank you Greg Aiello and Joe Browne at the NFL office in New York; Joe Horrigan and Chris Schilling at the Pro Football Hall of Fame; and at NFL Films, Hal Lipman and Greg Cosell, who taught me the value of watching film. Thank you Dan Frane, Terry McCormick, and Len Pasquarelli for your contributions.

Thank you Reuben Frank for your remarkable attention to detail, sparkling research, and creative flair, and Tom Bast at Triumph Books for being the driving force from start to finish.

This project would never have taken flight without the blessing of many people at ESPN, including David Brofsky, Vince Doria, Mark Gross, and

Norby Williamson. Thank you to Chris Berman, Stephanie Druley, Ron Jaworski, Seth Markman, and Bob Rauscher for your extraordinary support. Over the years, the help of my colleagues in the field—Mike Cambareri, Tony Florkowski, Michele Froman, Charlie Moynihan, and Marc Weiner—helped the ideas in this book take shape.

Reuben Frank would like to thank Al Cornog for his tireless research assistance during the preparation of this book. Without his 'round-the-clock contributions, many facts and figures never would have been unearthed.

Paul Zimmerman of *Sports Illustrated* and Ray Didinger of NFL Films, two brilliant football journalists and historians, graciously provided numerous insights, opinions, and wonderful stories about players, games, coaches, and teams. Thanks also to Rich Burg and Ryan Nissan of the Eagles' public relations office for research help.

Jared Sherman has an uncanny knowledge about details of NFL games and players from before he was born, and his opinions were interesting and helpful. Thanks as well to Andy Schwartz, Glenn Macnow, and Phil Sheridan for their contributions; Wayne Richardson and the sports staff at *The Burlington County Times* for giving me time off to finish this project; and my brother, Alan Frank, who showed me how much fun numbers can be. Thanks also to Jayson Stark for the inspiration and Robert Pollard for the music.

My mom, Libby Frank, gave me my passion for sports, and my dad, Morton Frank, instilled in me an appreciation of scientific method. Those two passions found a perfect meeting place in these pages.

Most of all, thanks to my beautiful family—my wife, Cindy, and daughter, Stephanie. Without their support, this undertaking would not have been possible.